Distance Education:
Issues and Concerns

Distance Education: Issues and Concerns has been co-published simultaneously as *Computers in the Schools*, Volume 19, Numbers 3/4 2002.

The *Computers in the Schools* Monographic "Separates"

Below is a list of "separates," which in serials librarianship means a special issue simultaneously published as a special journal issue or double-issue *and* as a "separate" hardbound monograph. (This is a format which we also call a "DocuSerial.")

"Separates" are published because specialized libraries or professionals may wish to purchase a specific thematic issue by itself in a format which can be separately cataloged and shelved, as opposed to purchasing the journal on an on-going basis. Faculty members may also more easily consider a "separate" for classroom adoption.

"Separates" are carefully classified separately with the major book jobbers so that the journal tie-in can be noted on new book order slips to avoid duplicate purchasing.

You may wish to visit Haworth's website at . . .

http://www.HaworthPress.com

. . . to search our online catalog for complete tables of contents of these separates and related publications.

You may also call 1-800-HAWORTH (outside US/Canada: 607-722-5857), or Fax 1-800-895-0582 (outside US/Canada: 607-771-0012), or e-mail at:

getinfo@haworthpressinc.com

Distance Education: Issues and Concerns, edited by Cleborne D. Maddux, PhD, Jacque Ewing-Taylor, MS, and D. LaMont Johnson, PhD (Vol. 19, No. 3/4, 2002). *Provides practical, research-based advice on distance education course design.*

Evaluation and Assessment in Educational Information Technology, edited by Leping Liu, PhD, D. LaMont Johnson, PhD, Cleborne D. Maddux, PhD, and Norma J. Henderson, MS (Vol. 18, No. 2/3 and 4, 2001). *Explores current trends, issues, strategies, and methods of evaluation and assessment in educational information technology.*

The Web in Higher Education: Assessing the Impact and Fulfilling the Potential, edited by Cleborne D. Maddux, PhD, and D. LaMont Johnson, PhD (Vol. 17, No. 3/4 and Vol. 18, No. 1, 2001). *"I ENTHUSIASTICALLY RECOMMEND THIS BOOK to anyone new to Web-based program development. I am certain that my project has moved along more rapidly because of what I learned from this text. The chapter on designing online education courses helped to organize my programmatic thinking. Another chapter did an outstanding job of debunking the myths regarding Web learning." (Carol Swift, PhD, Associate Professor and Chair of the Department of Human Development and Child Studies, Oakland University, Rochester, Michigan)*

Using Information Technology in Mathematics Education, edited by D. James Tooke, PhD, and Norma Henderson, MS (Vol. 17, No. 1/2 2001). *"Provides thought-provoking material on several aspects and levels of mathematics education. The ideas presented will provide food for thought for the reader, suggest new methods for the classroom, and give new ideas for further research." (Charles E. Lamb, EdD, Professor, Mathematics Education, Department of Teaching, Learning, and Culture, College of Education, Texas A&M University, College Station)*

Integration of Technology into the Classroom: Case Studies, edited by D. LaMont Johnson, PhD, Cleborne D. Maddux, PhD, and Leping Liu, PhD (Vol. 16, No. 2/3/4, 2000). *Use these fascinating case studies to understand why bringing information technology into your classroom can make you a more effective teacher, and how to go about it!*

Information Technology in Educational Research and Statistics, edited by Leping Liu, PhD, D. LaMont Johnson, PhD, and Cleborne D. Maddux, PhD (Vol. 15, No. 3/4, and Vol. 16, No. 1, 1999). *This important book focuses on creating new ideas for using educational technologies such as the Internet, the World Wide Web and various software packages to further research and statistics. You will explore on-going debates relating to the theory of research, research methodology, and successful practices.* Information Technology in Educational Research and Statistics *also covers the debate on what statistical procedures are appropriate for what kinds of research designs.*

Educational Computing in the Schools: Technology, Communication, and Literacy, edited by Jay Blanchard, PhD (Vol. 15, No. 1, 1999). *Examines critical issues of technology, teaching, and learning in three areas: access, communication, and literacy. You will discover new ideas and practices for gaining access to and using technology in education from preschool through higher education.*

Logo: A Retrospective, edited by Cleborne D. Maddux, PhD, and D. LaMont Johnson, PhD (Vol. 14, No. 1/2, 1997). *"This book–honest and optimistic–is a must for those interested in any aspect of Logo: its history, the effects of its use, or its general role in education." (Dorothy M. Fitch, Logo consultant, writer, and editor, Derry, New Hampshire)*

Using Technology in the Classroom, edited by D. LaMont Johnson, PhD, Cleborne D. Maddux, PhD, and Leping Liu, MS (Vol. 13, No. 1/2, 1997). *"A guide to teaching with technology that emphasizes the advantages of transiting from teacher-directed learning to learner-centered learning–a shift that can draw in even 'at-risk' kids." (Book News, Inc.)*

Multimedia and Megachange: New Roles for Educational Computing, edited by W. Michael Reed, PhD, John K. Burton, PhD, and Min Liu, EdD (Vol. 10, No. 1/2/3/4, 1995). *"Describes and analyzes issues and trends that might set research and development agenda for educators in the near future." (Sci Tech Book News)*

Language Minority Students and Computers, edited by Christian J. Faltis, PhD, and Robert A. DeVillar, PhD (Vol. 7, No. 1/2, 1990). *"Professionals in the field of language minority education, including ESL and bilingual education, will cheer this collection of articles written by highly respected, research-writers, along with computer technologists, and classroom practitioners." (Journal of Computing in Teacher Education)*

Logo: Methods and Curriculum for Teachers, by Cleborne D. Maddux, PhD, and D. LaMont Johnson, PhD (Supp #3, 1989). *"An excellent introduction to this programming language for children." (Rena B. Lewis, Professor, College of Education, San Diego State University)*

Assessing the Impact of Computer-Based Instruction: A Review of Recent Research, by M. D. Roblyer, PhD, W. H. Castine, PhD, and F. J. King, PhD (Vol. 5, No. 3/4, 1988). *"A comprehensive and up-to-date review of the effects of computer applications on student achievement and attitudes." (Measurements & Control)*

Educational Computing and Problem Solving, edited by W. Michael Reed, PhD, and John K. Burton, PhD (Vol. 4, No. 3/4, 1988). *Here is everything that educators will need to know to use computers to improve higher level skills such as problem solving and critical thinking.*

The Computer in Reading and Language Arts, edited by Jay S. Blanchard, PhD, and George E. Mason, PhD (Vol. 4, No. 1, 1987). *"All of the [chapters] in this collection are useful, guiding the teacher unfamiliar with classroom computer use through a large number of available software options and classroom strategies." (Educational Technology)*

Computers in the Special Education Classroom, edited by D. LaMont Johnson, PhD, Cleborne D. Maddux, PhD, and Ann Candler, PhD (Vol. 3, No. 3/4, 1987). *"A good introduction to the use of computers in special education. . . . Excellent for those who need to become familiar with computer usage with special population students because they are contemplating it or because they have actually just begun to do it." (Science Books and Films)*

You Can Do It/Together, by Kathleen A. Smith, PhD, Cleborne D. Maddux, PhD, and D. LaMont Johnson, PhD (Supp #2, 1986). *A self-instructional textbook with an emphasis on the partnership system of learning that introduces the reader to four critical areas of computer technology.*

Computers and Teacher Training: A Practical Guide, by Dennis M. Adams, PhD (Supp #1, 1986). *"A very fine . . . introduction to computer applications in education." (International Reading Association)*

The Computer as an Educational Tool, edited by Henry F. Olds, Jr. (Vol. 3, No. 1, 1986). *"The category of tool uses for computers holds the greatest promise for learning, and this . . . book, compiled from the experiences of a good mix of practitioners and theorists, explains how and why." (Jack Turner, Technology Coordinator, Eugene School District 4-J, Oregon)*

Logo in the Schools, edited by Cleborne D. Maddux, PhD (Vol. 2, No. 2/3, 1985). *"An excellent blend of enthusiasm for the language of Logo mixed with empirical analysis of the language's effectiveness as a means of promoting educational goals. A much-needed book!" (Rena Lewis, PhD, Professor, College of Education, San Diego State University)*

Humanistic Perspectives on Computers in the Schools, edited by Steven Harlow, PhD (Vol. 1, No. 4, 1985). *"A wide spectrum of information." (Infochange)*

Distance Education:
Issues and Concerns

Cleborne D. Maddux, PhD
Jacque Ewing-Taylor, MS
D. LaMont Johnson, PhD
Editors

Distance Education: Issues and Concerns has been co-published simultaneously as *Computers in the Schools*, Volume 19, Numbers 3/4 2002.

The Haworth Press, Inc.
New York • London • Oxford

Distance Education: Issues and Concerns has been co-published simultaneously as *Computers in the Schools*™, Volume 19, Numbers 3/4 2002.

The development, preparation, and publication of this work has been undertaken with great care. However, the publisher, employees, editors, and agents of The Haworth Press and all imprints of The Haworth Press, Inc., including The Haworth Medical Press® and Pharmaceutical Products Press®, are not responsible for any errors contained herein or for consequences that may ensue from use of materials or information contained in this work. Opinions expressed by the author(s) are not necessarily those of The Haworth Press, Inc. With regard to case studies, identities and circumstances of individuals discussed herein have been changed to protect confidentiality. Any resemblance to actual persons, living or dead, is entirely coincidental.

Cover design by Marylouise E. Doyle

Library of Congress Cataloging-in-Publication Data

Distance education : issues and concerns / Cleborne D. Maddux, Jacque Ewing-Taylor, D. LaMont Johnson, editors.
    p. cm.
"Co-published simultaneously as Computers in the schools, volume 19, numbers 3/4, 2002."
Includes bibliographical references and index.
    ISBN 0-7890-2030-0 (hard : alk. paper) – ISBN 0-7890-2031-9 (pbk : alk. paper)
    1. Distance education–Computer-assisted instruction. 2. World Wide Web. I. Maddux, Cleborne D., 1942- II. Ewing-Taylor, Jacque. III. Johnson, D. LaMont (Dee LaMont), 1939- IV. Computers in the schools.
LC5803.C65 D55 2002
371.3'58–dc21
                                                2002152087

Indexing, Abstracting & Website/Internet Coverage

This section provides you with a list of major indexing & abstracting services. That is to say, each service began covering this periodical during the year noted in the right column. Most Websites which are listed below have indicated that they will either post, disseminate, compile, archive, cite or alert their own Website users with research-based content from this work. (This list is as current as the copyright date of this publication.)

Abstracting, Website/Indexing Coverage . . . . Year When Coverage Began

- *Academic Abstracts/CD-ROM* **1994**

- *ACM Guide to Computer Literature* **1991**

- *Australian Education Index <www.acer.edu.au>* **2000**

- *Child Development Abstracts & Bibliography <www.ukans.edu>* . . . **2000**

- *CNPIEC Reference Guide: Chinese National Directory*
  of Foreign Periodicals **1995**

- *Computer Literature Index* **1993**

- *Computing Reviews* **1992**

- *Current Index to Journals in Education* **1991**

- *Education Digest* **1991**

- *Education Index <www.hwwilson.com>* **1999**

- *Education Process Improvement Ctr, Inc. (EPICENTER)*
  <http://www.epicent.com> **2000**

(continued)

(continued)

Special Bibliographic Notes related to special journal issues
(separates) and indexing/abstracting:

- indexing/abstracting services in this list will also cover material in any "separate" that is co-published simultaneously with Haworth's special thematic journal issue or DocuSerial. Indexing/abstracting usually covers material at the article/chapter level.
- monographic co-editions are intended for either non-subscribers or libraries which intend to purchase a second copy for their circulating collections.
- monographic co-editions are reported to all jobbers/wholesalers/approval plans. The source journal is listed as the "series" to assist the prevention of duplicate purchasing in the same manner utilized for books-in-series.
- to facilitate user/access services all indexing/abstracting services are encouraged to utilize the co-indexing entry note indicated at the bottom of the first page of each article/chapter/contribution.
- this is intended to assist a library user of any reference tool (whether print, electronic, online, or CD-ROM) to locate the monographic version if the library has purchased this version but not a subscription to the source journal.
- individual articles/chapters in any Haworth publication are also available through the Haworth Document Delivery Service (HDDS).

ABOUT THE EDITORS

Cleborne D. Maddux, PhD, is Professor of Education in the Department of Counseling and Educational Psychology at the University of Nevada, Reno, where he teaches courses on statistics and on integrating technology into education. He trains elementary and high school teachers in the state of Nevada on how to make the Internet a regular feature of their classroom agendas. Senior author of *Educational Computing: Learning with Tomorrow's Technologies,* a textbook now in its third edition, Professor Maddux has authored or co-authored numerous professional articles and books on informational technology in education and educational technology.

Jacque Ewing-Taylor, MS, is Project Coordinator for the U.S. Department of Education PT3 grant, Project Learning Links, at the University of Nevada's College of Education. She is pursuing a doctorate in information technology in education, and taught communications and technology courses in the Donald W. Reynolds School of Journalism. Ms. Ewing-Taylor conducts professional development workshops for trainers and teachers in presentation technology, public speaking, and critical thinking.

D. LaMont Johnson, PhD, is Professor of Education in the Department of Counseling and Educational Psychology at the University of Nevada, Reno. He is also Program Coordinator of the Information Technology in Education program. He teaches courses on the application of technology in education and trains teachers across the state of Nevada in using the Internet in their classrooms. Co-author of the textbook *Educational Computing: Learning with Tomorrow's Technologies,* now in its third edition, Professor Johnson has authored or co-authored numerous books and articles on educational computing and information technology in education.

Distance Education:
Issues and Concerns

Contents

INTRODUCTION

Cleborne D. Maddux
Jacque Ewing-Taylor
D. LaMont Johnson

The Light and Dark Sides of Distance Education

It is with considerable ambivalence that we introduce the topic of distance education. The ambivalence is not because we doubt the potential of distance education to improve, or even to revolutionize education. It is certainly not because we fear that distance education is in danger of public rejection and eventual abandonment. Rather, we believe strongly that distance education, specifically Web-based distance education, is the single most promising educational innovation of our lifetime. Further, we feel sure it will continue its current spectacular growth in both

CLEBORNE D. MADDUX is Professor, Department of Counseling and Educational Psychology, University of Nevada, Reno, NV 89557 (E-mail: maddux@unr.edu).
JACQUE EWING-TAYLOR is a doctoral student, Department of Counseling and Educational Psychology, University of Nevada, Reno, NV 89557 (E-mail: jacque@unr.edu).
D. LAMONT JOHNSON is Professor, Department of Counseling and Educational Psychology, University of Nevada, Reno, NV 89557 (E-mail: ljohnson@unr.edu).

[Haworth co-indexing entry note]: "The Light and Dark Sides of Distance Education." Maddux, Cleborne D., Jacque Ewing-Taylor, and D. LaMont Johnson. Co-published simultaneously in *Computers in the Schools* (The Haworth Press, Inc.) Vol. 19, No. 3/4, 2002, pp. 1-7; and: *Distance Education: Issues and Concerns* (ed: Cleborne D. Maddux, Jacque Ewing-Taylor, and D. LaMont Johnson) The Haworth Press, Inc., 2002, pp. 1-7. Single or multiple copies of this article are available for a fee from The Haworth Document Delivery Service [1-800-HAWORTH, 9:00 a.m. - 5:00 p.m. (EST). E-mail address: getinfo@haworthpressinc.com].

1

popularity and availability, and that future growth will involve nearly every imaginable level and type of schooling.

Our ambivalence is because we think distance education, like every new technology, has both a light and a dark side.

The potential advantages of distance education are easy to appreciate. These include, among others, the ability to reach learners in geographically remote locations or those in circumstances that mitigate against attendance at regular and traditional hours; the potential to reach many types of nontraditional students; and most importantly, the opportunity for students to work and learn at a style and pace most consistent with their own mental and physical constitutions.

The disadvantages of distance education are not as readily apparent, although they are becoming much more evident as implementation spreads across the country and across the world. One of the most serious of these problems is a lack of attention to educational quality control issues.

This problem is so pervasive that a mushrooming system of shoddy, online diploma mills has sprung up, complete with individual courses, complete certification programs in various fields, and bachelor's, master's, and even doctoral degrees available totally online. Hardly a week goes by that we do not receive an array of glitzy, four-color brochures advertising such offerings and boasting that no physical attendance on any campus is required. Courses, certification programs, and degrees are being offered in nearly every imaginable field including, incredibly, the helping professions such as education and counseling.

It is ironic that this and many of the other serious problems involving distance education are not technological in nature, but can be traced to a critical lack of principled leadership on campuses across the country. This situation has come about slowly, but has accelerated in the last 20 years or so, and can itself be attributed to multiple and complex changes in society at large. These latter societal changes are beyond both the scope of the present article and the expertise of its authors. However, some of the more direct and obvious influences are declining fiscal support for education; increasing public distrust and hostility toward government and governmental activities, including education; and widespread erosion of moral and ethical values and attendant increases in materialism.

These and other influences set the stage for the current trend toward commercialization of education and have resulted in a tendency for boards of regents and other controlling bodies to recruit educational leaders who believe that the proper model for education is the business model, and who tend to view ethics and morals as nonessential luxuries that are always secondary to monetary considerations. The business orientation brings with it the tendency to view students as customers and education as a mere commodity. If students are customers and education a commodity, and if, as every businessperson knows, *the customer is always right*, then education should be designed merely with the goal of pleasing students. By this thinking, if students are willing to pay money for online courses that require little, if any, thought or study, and that are incapable of transferring the essential culture of a profession, much less provide the essential social aspects of learning, then such courses are legitimate from a business point of view.

This thinking has evolved from a simplistic conception of the proper goal of education, which is legitimized by commercial thinking. In business, the ultimate and proper goal is *profit*, without which, no business can survive. Those who would impose the business model on education ignore the fact that the concept of profit is not meaningful or appropriate in an educational context. Therefore, the *methods* of business, aimed solely at providing profit, also make little, if any sense in an educational context. Education is charged with a gate-keeping function that does not exist in business. Business bestows its product on whoever can pay the established price, and the entire idea of a customer "earning" a product is ludicrous.

However, learning is not merely a commodity, and many of us would maintain that to treat it as such is to change and cheapen it. The business model in education exists without its reason for being (profit), and all that is left as a goal for educators who make this mistake is crass materialism and the pursuit of money and power for its own sake. Then, too, the public expects educators to provide youth with exemplary models of moral and ethical behavior, a situation unlikely to exist in an environment where money and power are venerated above all else.

The establishment and proliferation of the online diploma mills are not in themselves startling. After all, such diploma mills have existed for years before the Internet and the Web. What is startling and disappointing is that many traditional and prestigious institutions have begun to offer low-quality, online programs of their own, in clear competition with the private, online diploma mills, and, incredibly, with their own high-quality, on-campus programs.

Also contributing to the commercialization of education, in general, and the establishment of low-quality, totally online programs and degrees, in particular, is the private sector's recent realization that education is a potential source of great profit. This can be clearly seen in popular business literature, which is currently touting distance education as the newest growth industry, with estimated future profits in the billions of dollars. Major players such as IBM, Microsoft, and many others are serious about such profits, and are moving aggressively to secure a share of what they see as an incredibly lucrative potential market.

Many, if not most, presidents in institutions of higher education are cooperating fully in every aspect of the privatization movement, and many are inking contracts with commercial entities to collaborate in the delivery and marketing of a host of online programs and degrees of highly questionable value. This entrepreneurial zeal has introduced a number of new problems for professors and teachers, only one of which involves questions about intellectual property rights. The traditional legal principle that *ownership follows authorship* is currently being challenged as institutions finalize contracts with the private sector with the intention of appropriating rights to online courseware produced on their campuses. Some legal experts suggest that, if this trend is not challenged in court, inaction will be interpreted as legal acceptance; and the battle for ownership of intellectual property will be lost without a fight.

Because we are ambivalent about totally online distance education, and cautious in our acceptance of it, does not imply that we perceive there are no problems in education. There is much that needs revising at all educational levels, and especially in higher education. Inflexibility and arrogance have ruled on college campuses, primarily because we enjoyed a captive audience with few, if any, choices. Thanks to distance education, those days are gone forever, and good riddance to the attitude that students can *like it or lump it.*

Neither do we oppose all forms of distance education. We maintain Web sites for each of our on-campus classes, and we continue to explore new and better ways to supplement and improve traditional instruction through the use of technology–especially Web-based technology. As we stated at the beginning of this article, we believe the Web's potential to supplement and improve education is nearly unlimited in power. We are not optimistic, however, about the potential of totally online programs and degrees to do anything except further undermine the quality of education. The idea of a totally online PhD is, we believe, ludicrous beyond words. The only thing more disappointing than the offering of such degrees is the fact that there are students willing to pay for them. (Those interested in further exploring the effects of commercialism on education in general and distance education in particular may be interested in a much more detailed discussion in *Educational Technology* [Maddux, in press].)

It was because of our ambivalence about distance education that we wanted to edit a volume on this topic. Perhaps we are too pessimistic. Many of the contributors to this collection would probably find us so. Their optimism is refreshing and contagious, and the process of reading and selecting articles for this volume has reenergized us. We have realized anew that we do not simply live in *interesting* times; we live in *fantastic* times. This may be the greatest time to be alive in the history of man for those of us who are fascinated by technology and enjoy observing the effects of technology on culture.

What will be the ultimate effect of Web-related technology on education? Each of the authors in this volume has his or her own vision to share.

The research presented in this publication covers a broad array of interests and approaches. In "Adapting to Distance Education: How an Ethnographic Look at Student Experiences Can Inform Instructional Design," the authors report the results of an ethnographic study suggesting that distance education classrooms affect students' attitudes and behaviors. They looked at differences in communication and participation in classrooms that were connected remotely to the onsite delivery classrooms and found that student needs are different in different physical locations. Communication and participation differed significantly, and the article suggests that instructors take these differences into account when structuring distance education courses.

Along similar lines, the authors of "An Investigation of Methods of Instruction and Student Learning Styles in Internet-Based Community College Courses" and "Usability of Alternative Web Course Structures" conclude with concrete recommendations for enhancing the distance education experience. "An Investigation of Methods of Instruction and Student Learning Styles in Internet-Based Community College Courses" reports on a study equating learning styles to enrollment and retention in Internet-based courses. The authors recommend pre-enrollment testing and advisement to help ensure student success. "Usability of Alternative Web Course Structures" suggests conducting small-scale usability studies for all instructional Web sites. This research shows that doing so will increase the effectiveness of the site, decrease faculty workload, and improve the educational experiences of the students.

Two articles focus on specific tools, one technological and one that's been used in traditional classrooms for years. The author of "Mobile Wireless Technologies for Field-Based Teacher Interns and Their Partnership Teachers" focuses on handheld computers and mobile phones in teacher education. The article reports that pre-service teachers adopted the technology much more quickly than their in-service counterparts. The author predicts that current limitations to the technology will soon go away and this will be the classroom technology of the future. "The Use of Collaborative Groups in Traditional and Online Courses" recommends group projects for online courses, and finds no difference between online and in-class attitudes. The online students did, however, score lower on the final exam than did the in-class students, prompting the authors to encourage further study in this area.

"Multimedia, It's How You Use It: Reflections on a Selected Computerized Teaching Technology" is seemingly the most skeptical of our articles. This study suggests that one need not add bells and whistles to lectures; one only need be an "experienced teacher." While multimedia lectures may hold students' interest more, good teaching is still the key.

The second half of our collection focuses more explicitly on quality control, and several authors make excellent suggestions for its assurance. "Striving for Quality Control in Distance Education" provides an overview of distance education drawbacks and benefits, then lays out a plan for controlling quality in distance education programs. The authors of "Quality Control for Online Graduate Course Delivery: A Case Study" present a study showing the steps taken by one graduate program to ensure continuing improvement of online courses. Quality control is addressed at several levels, and this article offers a number of ways to develop a comprehensive quality control system within the three domains of development, delivery, and evaluation.

Addressing a major institutional concern with distance education, "Cost-Income Equilibrium for Electronically Delivered Instruction" (EDI) presents a basic cost-income model for EDI, noting that unless EDI is cost-effective, it won't be around long. This article marks significant progress in helping us understand the economics of EDI and strategies for making it cost-effective.

"Distance Education as a Discursive Practice: Voice, Discourse, and Pedagogy" moves us into a more theoretical look at distance education. The authors discuss the effects that technology use in teaching and learning have on relationships between teachers and students and how the learning space and experiences are changed by technology. These changes are difficult to quantify but play a role in student learning and, hence, are worthy of future research. Also from a theoretical approach, "Quality Control in Online Courses: Using a Social Constructivist Framework" advocates a social constructivist framework for online learning in order to create and deliver quality online courses. The authors lay out how they successfully did this in a graduate course on leadership and conclude with a list of questions for future research.

"Distance Realities: Rural Wisdom" is an upbeat article that shares the successes of a distance education initiative in rural Nebraska, in which two main keys to success were effective handling of complex management issues, and faculty development incentives. The authors discuss the problems and bumps encountered along the way, as well as their strategies and successes.

"Remote Labs: The Next High-Tech Step Beyond Simulation for Distance Education" asserts that laboratory experience courses present a unique set of challenges to the distance education environment. The authors discuss the use of simulations and present remote labs as an alternative. They detail remote lab use in several engineering disciplines, effectively showing how this would work.

"Hybrid Online Coursework to Enhance Technology Competencies of School Principals" makes a case for using technology to prepare administrators. The authors describe a hybrid online graduate class for administrators, and report that those who completed the course indicated an increased willingness to use technology, to support their principals who use technology, and to encourage technological initiatives.

"The Contributing Student: A Pedagogy for Flexible Learning" rounds out our volume by providing the reader with a new way to look at the subject under consideration, from within a different context than many of us have used in our own ponderings about distance education, its effectiveness, and its future. The authors take a broad approach to the topic and discuss their concept of "flexible learning" and how it applies to distance education. They use the "contributing student" model and describe how one university in The Netherlands revolutionized its program. Changing their pedagogical model was the key to their success, and that success depended on the marriage of institutional vision and policy, technology, and pedagogy. "Extending the Good Instructor" was their motto, and a good note on which to send the reader to enjoy the full text of all these interesting articles.

REFERENCE

Maddux, C.D. (in press). Information technology in education: The critical lack of principled leadership. *Educational Technology*.

RESEARCH ARTICLES

Lorraine C. Schmertzing
Richard W. Schmertzing

Adapting to Distance Education: How an Ethnographic Look at Student Experiences Can Inform Instructional Design

SUMMARY. A recent ethnographic study of 13 graduate classes in an interactive televised (ITV) learning environment ($N = 278$) provided insight for instructional designers into the process of adaptation that learners go through as they attempt to relate a new technologically mediated classroom to their traditional ways of managing teaching and learning. Participant observations of students' comments and actions clearly indicated a connection between the complexities of working with the tech-

LORRAINE C. SCHMERTZING is Assistant Professor, Department of Curriculum and Instructional Technology, Education Center Room 157, Valdosta State University, 1500 N. Patterson, Valdosta, GA 31698 (E-mail: lschmert@valdosta.edu).
RICHARD W. SCHMERTZING is Qualitative Researcher, College of Education, Education Center Room 77, Valdosta State University, 1500 N. Patterson, Valdosta, GA 31698 (E-mail: rwschmer@valdosta.edu).

[Haworth co-indexing entry note]: "Adapting to Distance Education: How an Ethnographic Look at Student Experiences Can Inform Instructional Design." Schmertzing, Lorraine C., and Richard W. Schmertzing. Co-published simultaneously in *Computers in the Schools* (The Haworth Press, Inc.) Vol. 19, No. 3/4, 2002, pp. 9-22; and: *Distance Education: Issues and Concerns* (ed: Cleborne D. Maddux, Jacque Ewing-Taylor, and D. LaMont Johnson) The Haworth Press, Inc., 2002, pp. 9-22. Single or multiple copies of this article are available for a fee from The Haworth Document Delivery Service [1-800-HAWORTH, 9:00 a.m. - 5:00 p.m. (EST). E-mail address: getinfo@haworthpressinc.com].

9

nology (e.g., using microphones, watching television, appearing on screen) and their ability to participate in class. Cultural anthropology and symbolic interactionism theoretically framed this study that shows communication and participation in class were different in the ITV classroom from the traditional classroom. *[Article copies available for a fee from The Haworth Document Delivery Service: 1-800-HAWORTH. E-mail address: <getinfo@haworthpressinc.com> Website: <http://www.HaworthPress.com> © 2002 by The Haworth Press, Inc. All rights reserved.]*

KEYWORDS. Interactive television, ethnography, distance learning, graduate education, communication, classroom culture, qualitative research

Institutions of higher education have been significantly influenced by the infusion of instructional technology into the academic domain (Thompson, 1999). The growth of distance education programs alongside Internet growth is one area in which that influence is obvious. Kirkpatrick and Jakupec (1999) argue that providing these flexible learning environments meets the needs of adult learners and at the same time delivers education providers an effective means of survival in an increasingly competitive marketplace. Universities recruit new, often nontraditional, students, create new learning environments, and ask faculty to teach classes in front of computer screens and television cameras. The implementation of formalized instructional design procedures has been touted as an effective way to transition into distance education and maintain a high degree of success and satisfaction in the teaching and learning experiences (James & Gardner, 1995; Moore & Kearsley, 1996; Verduin & Clark, 1991). One of the initial steps to quality instructional design focuses on gaining an understanding of the learners (Dick & Carey, 1996; Smith & Ragan, 1993). According to Willis (1993), "Research suggests that distance education and traditionally delivered instruction can be equally effective if the distance educator puts adequate preparation into understanding the needs of the student and adapting the instruction accordingly" (p. 22). But how does one do that? How does one know the needs of the student in a substantially new learning environment? Can it be assumed that these new learning environments are essentially traditional classrooms with a few technological add-ons? If that were the case, students' needs would be similar to their needs in traditional classrooms, but what if new distance learning environments are substantially different in structure and classroom culture and therefore require complex, diverse adaptive strategies on the part of students and teachers?

Our research suggests the latter. In a recent ethnography of graduate education classes during the inaugural year of a two-way audio, two-way video interactive distance learning classroom at a regional university in the South, we found substantial differences between interactive televised (ITV) classes and traditional classrooms and subsequently uncovered a variety of ways that students handle the differences. The ethnography provided insight into many of the complexities students face as they adapt to a new technologically mediated learning environment, and thereby increased our understanding of students' needs in those environments.

Although the complexities can be seen across multiple domains of the learning environment, including student relations, instructor roles, technology integration, and classroom participation, this article focuses on students' patterns of adaptations that relate to the use of technology in the classroom and how that process of adapting has an impact on classroom communication and student interaction. A deeper awareness of what students experience as they adapt to ITV classes should increase instructor sensitivity to student needs in various forms of distance education (DE) and assist instructors in designing instruction to more effectively assist learners in their adaptation to technologically mediated learning environments.

THE STUDY

Cultural anthropology (Geertz, 1973) and symbolic interactionism (Prus, 1996) provided the theoretical framework for this study in which traditional ethnographic and qualitative research methods were used to gather and analyze data (Agar, 1996; Maxwell, 1996). The data were gathered during a one-year ethnographic study of students taking graduate education classes during the inaugural year of an interactive televised distance learning classroom, the Interactive Distance Learning Studio (IDLS) (Schmertzing, 2000).

There were two sites involved in the study, a host site, which was the instructor's classroom, and a remote site that had a facilitator and interacted with the instructor via technological media. Sites were located approximately 70 miles apart—one at the main university campus and the other at a branch campus. Of the 13 graduate classes included in the study the branch campus served as host for 2 courses. Courses included in the study varied significantly in course content, course objectives, teaching style, and student responses. There were 278 students involved in the ethnography. A database was constructed to house open-ended survey information that was completed by 140 students. The Ethnograph v.5.3 was used to analyze data that were gathered in more than 400 hours of participant observations in classrooms, formal interviews and informal conversations with students and faculty, weekly e-mail correspondence, focus group interviews, and transcripts of videotapes. Thematic coding, frequency counts, and frequent debriefings between ethnographers L. and R. Schmertzing contributed to interpretation and ongoing analysis of the data (Schmertzing & Schmertzing, 2001; Spradley & Mann, 1975).

The quotes incorporated into this paper are direct quotes from student participants that are thematically representative of statements made by significant numbers of students. They are provided to substantiate the complex effects of elements in the ITV classrooms on students, their learning, and their attitude toward class. This data set was selected to open a window of awareness for instructors that might enhance their understanding of both the complexities students encounter in classes similar to the IDLS and the adaptive spectrum of behaviors they develop in order to accept the strange new environment as a classroom in which they can focus on learning.

THE SETTING

To anchor the setting of the ethnography in the context of this article, we have included one student's description of what it is like to have class in the IDLS. Paul, one of the remote students, explained,

> What happens is, you can see what is going on in the other class via a television monitor. So, if the teacher is teaching in your class, you just look at them and if they are in the other class, you have to watch them on a TV, you know, for lack of a better term. There are cameras in there in both of the rooms. So when you speak, you have to push a button, the camera zooms in on you [the mic is turned on], and the teacher at the remote location can hear you. But you also have to push the button if the teacher is in your classroom [in order for the other students to hear you], which goes against your, you know, your normal way of doing it. Normally you sort of raise your hand and then just start speaking because the person,

you know, to whom you are speaking, is right in front of you. But you have to remember that there is another class somewhere else and so, I think it is more difficult to remember to hit your button so you can be recognized. (HFt F I v107: See Note for detailed explanation of the codes used to identify informants.)

The description offered by this student clearly identifies technological components of the classroom that must be dealt with in order for a student to actively participate in the learning experience. Consideration of various ways students adapt to the technology with their own class participation not only informs us about what is going on, but also provides insight into strategies that instructors can use to lessen the time and energy required by students to adapt to the environment and thereby enhance the learning experience. In the IDLS, the technology is the conduit through which interaction occurs. Therefore, adapting to the technology is a key component in student involvement.

DISCUSSION

Interaction has long been touted as a key to successful distance learning classes (Moore & Kearsley, 1996; Wagner, 1997; Willis, 1993), as well as the foundation to most formal educational experiences (Ozmon & Craver, 1999). Multi-faceted interaction is required in order to achieve quality participation. Students in the traditional classroom interact with other students, the instructor, and the content when they participate in content-related class discussions or activities (McDermott, 1977; Mehan, 1980). In order to accomplish the same task in the IDLS, students also needed to interact with the technology, a form of interaction that is key to most quality interaction that occurs in distance learning classrooms (Hillman, Willis, & Gunawardena, 1994).

When students entered the IDLS for their first class experience, they were not only unaware of the technology that would be used to mediate participation in their class but they were also unaware of the adjustments they would have to make to maintain the level of engagement in class to which they had grown accustomed in their traditional graduate classes. Moreover, they did not expect that, due to the technology, they would encounter pacing differences in classroom communication as well as a new and unnatural awareness of self. Most students felt the effects of these unexpected circumstances the first night of class. A student from the remote site expressed concerns that surfaced in an e-mail that she sent me: "I did feel that I would probably be a lot less likely to ask the instructor questions because I really don't want to talk over the television. That may change as the class progresses, but now I am still a little uncomfortable with the thought." The experience this student spoke of indicates the need for students to adapt to a new learning environment.

As students attempted to adjust to the technological aspects of the IDLS, they were faced with complex issues that affected each student differently. Some students were very calm about the adjustment. Carol was one of those; she said, "Last semester I was extremely aware of and intimidated by the large screen. With a little practice, I don't think about it anymore." For other students the adjustment was more stressful at the beginning, but ultimately they made the adjustment. An example of such a student was one who told me, "Getting used to the equipment is almost nervewracking at the beginning, but it is not bad once the initial shock of the television aspect wears off." The majority of students who had more than one course in the IDLS noticed a difference in their performance in subsequent courses as a result of their awareness of the technological aspects of the room. Halfway through Martin's second class in the IDLS he told me the following:

> This class is a lot different from the last class because I didn't know what to expect in the last class. I actually feel more comfortable this time around. I was hesitant on simple things like pressing the microphone button to speak during the first class. Now, I've pressed it at least three times during this class. Overall, I think the more you attend these types of classes the more comfortable you are.

Early in their time in the IDLS, students were "intimidated," "in shock," and "unsure" of how to handle the technological aspects of the classroom. Their feelings and attitudes kept them from engaging the technology that was necessary to participate appropriately in class. Those feelings and attitudes, however, changed over time. The more social interaction students had in the technologically mediated classroom, the more information they processed about how things worked, and the more they understood about their environment. These new understandings offered them more options of how to relate to and consequently how to act in the IDLS classroom. A remote student remarked, "I'm not as uncomfortable when [the teacher] is over in [the other site] as I was my first semester doing the distance education. It doesn't make me as uncomfortable. I understand how everything works. I know where to look; I know what pressing that button does." The confidence that accompanied this student's clearer understanding changed her perception of what she was capable of and in turn changed her attitude toward class, which actually improved her performance.

Although this experience paralleled the experiences of many students in the IDLS, there were students who continued to be uncomfortable with the technology even after several semesters of classes in the environment. Joyce shared this with me after three semesters of classes in the IDLS, "Working with the equipment can be challenging. I have to get over being camera shy." Her thought patterns as they related to the technology were rooted in her dislike for being on camera. She was still challenged in her actions as they related to the technology because she never changed her thoughts and attitudes about her tendency to be "camera shy."

Given the complexity of student responses, the unique and varied nature of the classes, and the way that individual perceptions result in different constructions of meanings (Charon, 1998; Cole & Scribner, 1974; Salomon, 1979), it is not surprising that students adapted differently to the technological aspects of the interactive televised classroom. To Althea, "It was initially 'horrible.' I had never been in this type of environment. I found I didn't want to say anything initially, but I view it as a good control tool now. It was painful initially, puzzling in the middle, routine at the end. I enjoyed the learning process and I am happy that I stuck with it." Althea was clear about the way her thoughts changed toward the technological aspects of the IDLS and summed up the process of adapting to the environment in a way that many students identified with. At the beginning the initial introduction to the new technologically mediated way of having class was "horrible." It required effort, effort to the point of being "painful"; yet the effort paid off in the end, and she was "happy" that she had worked through the process. The "puzzling" process that she went through in the middle involved learning, understanding, and using the technology until it became "routine." Over time Althea was able to put aside the hurdle that her perceptions and expectations initially put in front of her. She changed her way of thinking, and she accepted a new way of doing traditional classroom things.

Beverly reported a similar experience from a slightly different perspective: "I did feel uncomfortable at first with the cameras, but I adjusted quickly. It was a little disturbing talking to a TV monitor, but it's been a growth experience. It can be frustrating and challenging, but overall it works very well. It does feel a little surreal, though." Beverly cushioned her discomfort with the technology three times by using a phrase that began with "but" and reminded her of the positive side of the experience. She attempted to replace her thoughts of the "discomfort," "disturbance," and "frustration" with the ideas that she had "adjusted," "grown," and "benefited" from the experience. By reminding herself of the positive aspects of the situation at the same time that she mentioned the negative, Beverly mentally moved toward an increased acceptance of the technologically mediated classroom–a method that instructors can encourage to help students adjust more positively.

The different rates at which students adapted resulted from a host of factors, including motivation, past experiences, and perceptions of the technology (Seels, Berry, Fullerton, & Horn, 1996). Students who appeared less engaged in class discussion were often students who perceived that they had no reason to learn to use the technology. They did not anticipate using this type of technology in the future in traditional classrooms and believed that they could accomplish their academic goals without it. Thus, they did not feel a need to use the technology in the IDLS and did not. These students, few in number, were students who turned their back to the monitor, focused on the instructor, and never "pushed their button." Their adaptive pattern did include the recognition that others in the classroom needed to engage the technology–as long as others engaged they saw no need to do it themselves.

On the opposite end of the adaptive spectrum were the students who embraced the technology, thought of it as useful, and consequently functioned naturally with little thought about cameras, buttons, or televisions. Students like Annette and Althea over time actually worked through an adaptive process from initial "painful" discomfort to a point where the class became "routine."

The majority of the students who participated in this study moved toward the acceptance of and adaptation to the technological aspects of the IDLS. Students who reported maintaining strong feelings of dislike for the technology entertained enough of an understanding of it to use it on occasion. Specifically, when their opinions on a topic of discussion were stronger than their feelings of dislike for the technological methods required to speak, they engaged the technology despite their dislike of it. In adapting to the technological aspects of the new classroom, most students seemed to rise to the occasion to meet their academic goals. If the class or instructor required student engagement with the technology, students adapted more quickly. The adaptation was not painless, nor did they all do it without complaint; nevertheless, they did it. If, however, students were not required to use the buttons or engage the technology, they did not generally volunteer such behavior.

The value of this discussion on students' adaptation to the technological aspects of the IDLS does not result from the simple truth that most students learned the appropriate behaviors for engaging the technology. Rather, the value results from an appreciation of the amount of time and energy students spent on the process of adaptation and in the types of attitudes they developed while making that adaptation. As Simonson and Maushak (1996) noted, "While attitudes have not been convincingly linked to achievement, they have been long considered an important component of the most important outcome of education: learning" (p. 985). Just as students' attitudes are likely to affect their learning of content, our data suggest that students' attitudes are a factor in adapting to the technology of the IDLS and that the time required for and the nature of that adaptation affect their learning. For some students the energy expended to overcome their anxieties and change their attitudes toward the technological aspects of their new learning environment was energy that they perceived to be taken away from their learning experience. For others, the perception was that adapting to technology was simply another thing they had to do. Finally, there were some for whom the perception was that little energy was required for adapting to technology. Regardless of how students perceived it, this process of adapting to the technology often went hand in hand with students' participation in the class.

I asked one student what mental processes she went through as she made decisions about participating in class discussions.

> Belinda: So I ask, "Does what I have to say carry as much weight as what I am hearing from these other people? Or is it going to make that much of a difference? [Is it] going to make that much difference worth fighting to get in?"

> Interviewer: By fighting to get in, you mean pushing the button?

> Belinda: Uh huh.

> Interviewer: Then, once you have done it and you have gotten in, then what do you think?

> Belinda: How did I sound? Did anybody else think it was worthwhile? Did anybody else see my point in what I was trying to

make? Sometimes, I may have something that I want to say but I didn't say it because, uh, I'm thinking she wants to move on to something else. There are enough people that have spoken and, sort of, the non-verbal I get from her is, "Okay, that is enough discussion, I need to move on." And then, sometimes, I'll just push the button [off] and just go back and not say anything.

When Belinda began to talk, it sounded as if she could have been talking about the traditional classroom, but then she got to her real point, "[Is it] going to make that much difference worth fighting to get in?" This student, similar to students in McHenry and Bozik's (1995) study, let us know that in her thought processes she was weighing what she considered the significance of her comment against the difficulties she felt that she would face if she tried to share her ideas. The use of the word "fight" implies discomfort and uncertainty with the pacing of the discussions in class. Belinda did try to read the cues of other participants, but backed out of the discussion anyway. Although she was not quite willing to stay with the process long enough to make her comment heard, she was nonetheless attempting to adjust to the technological mediation so that she could participate in class discussion.

Other students were held back by a disturbing self-awareness brought on by the presence of the television monitors.

Cheri: But there were a lot of times when I really, really, really wanted to get more involved. But then, on the flipside of that, there were a lot of times when I was unsure about some things, and I didn't turn on the microphone button. Because, like everybody else, I didn't want to feel stupid. I would look around and I could read the expressions of everybody else, and then I'd feel like it was okay. Because I'm not the only one that's lost right now. I could tell it by their face. They weren't saying nothing, but they were just as lost as I was. They're just as scared as I am to tap that button.

Interviewer: Why is that?

Cheri: Because we don't want to look stupid. In this setting, as well as you're asking this question, you're up on this big monitor. Not only are you looking stupid, but everyone is looking at you, looking stupid, you know, and you might be thinking, "That is the dumbest question." And you don't want to feel stupid.

Interviewer: You sense that they're staring at you?

Cheri: Uh huh. And to be honest, since we're on that monitor, I hate that monitor. But then, I'm the type of person, I don't like to hear myself on tape either; I don't like to.

Cheri often wanted to participate in class but was inhibited by the way the technology made her feel. Her explanation for not participating ranged from feeling scared, to looking stupid, or judging herself in relation to the other students. These feelings could have occurred in a traditional classroom, but she went on to point out that, "in this setting you're up on this big monitor," and everyone is "looking at you looking stupid."

Cheri understood the technological procedures for class participation. She even looked at other students' expressions to read cues about what was acceptable for contribution, but she also considered ideas related to her own technologically amplified self-awareness and personal involvement that caused her to hesitate instead of participate.

When asked about class participation in the IDLS, Darby articulated her concerns about several of the issues that have been previously raised.

I find it is slower than a regular classroom. I find that it inhibits my own reactions and questions. I feel a little self-conscious, and I'm not particularly self-conscious about asking questions, but the very fact that I have to hit the button. Well, first [the instructor's] got to know I want to hit the button so she can switch her camera off, then I have to hit the button and the camera's going to zoom in on me. And if I have another question again in three minutes, it's like I just asked a question and I feel so much more on stage. This may be just a typically female thing of, well, I don't want to look like I'm just hogging the, um, you know being too pushy, too aggressive, or asking too many questions, but then I get irritated or frustrated because I have a question, or more so, a comment. I get frustrated, certainly in the beginning; it seemed like we wasted so much time.

Darby recognized that the pacing was "slower than a regular classroom," and that the procedures were changed. Furthermore, she indicated how her feelings toward self were impairing her willingness to participate. Darby felt "self-conscious" and that her own participation was inhibited because she had not been able to accept the procedural changes and work with them in a natural way. As long as Darby lacked the ability, or the willingness to gain the ability, to participate in class without struggling through her anxieties, she remained on the less engaged end of the adaptation continuum, unable to accept and adjust to what she realized were differences between the traditional classroom and having class in the IDLS.

For students in the IDLS, grasping the use of technology was only a fraction of the understanding and adjustment necessary to successfully participate in content-related class activities. Students also needed to gain a degree of comfort with the new pacing in the classroom, learn to recognize and read new cues for gaining entry onto the floor of conversation (McDermott & Roth, 1978; Shultz, Florio, & Erickson, 1982), and overcome their tendency to think of self-related issues. As in each of the other areas, some students adapted quickly, with little effort, while others still struggled with the same issues after multiple classes in the environment.

CONCLUSION

It is clear that technologically mediated classrooms, be they interactive, TV-based, or online, are different from traditional classrooms. Furthermore, it is equally clear that not all technologically mediated classrooms are the same. We recognize that distance education learning environments have differences in the form and structure of the technological mediation (e.g., not all ITV classrooms have push button microphones). What is clear, however, when we look at the culture of learning environments we are creating with distance technology, is that students (and teachers) are finding the old ways of "doing" class are no longer adequate. Even those who try to do things the traditional way find that they are forced to adapt to new structures and procedures. Our data suggest that, over time, students will make those adjustments but that the process will generate significant diversity of response among the students and that the final level of adaptation may range from grudging tolerance of new technology to an enthusiastic embracing of it. Most importantly, whatever the levels of variation in student adaptation, because teaching and learning is often a social process that involves all class members in the construction of knowledge (Blumer, 1969), those levels and processes of adaptation will affect learning. Our assumption then, is that, the more instructors know about students' efforts to adjust to new technologically mediated classrooms, the better able they are to successfully design instruction. Thus, efforts to understand these complex new learning environments and ways in which class members adapt to them are essential for the creation of distance classrooms that are also powerful and effective learning environments. We believe that such understandings are only possible through in-depth analysis of these new "classrooms" and the experiences of the people who inhabit them.

NOTE

(HFt F I v107) represents a code used by authors to identify source material from data and should be interpreted as follows: H–host student, Ft–location code, F–gender code, I–interview data code, v–transcription code, 107–location of statement within transcription.

REFERENCES

Agar, M. H. (1996). *The professional stranger* (2nd ed.). San Diego, CA: Academic Press.

Blumer, H. (1969). *Symbolic interactionism* (3rd ed.). Berkeley, CA: University of California Press.

Charon, J. M. (1998). *Symbolic interactionism: An introduction, an interpretation, an integration* (6th ed.). Upper Saddle River, NJ: Prentice-Hall.

Cole, M., & Scribner, S. (1974). *Culture and thought: A psychological introduction.* New York: Wiley.

Dick, W., & Carey, L. (1996). *The systematic design of instruction* (4th ed.). New York: Harper Collins.

Geertz, C. (1973). *The interpretation of cultures.* London: Perseus.

Hillman, D. C. A., Willis, D. J., & Gunawardena, C. N. (1994). Learner-interface interaction in distance education: An extension of contemporary models and strategies for practitioners. *The American Journal of Distance Education, 8*(2), 30-42.

James, W. B., & Gardner, D. L. (1995). Learning styles: Implications for distance learning. In M. H. Rossman & M. E. Rossman (Eds.), *Facilitating distance education* (pp. 19-32). San Francisco: Jossey-Bass.

Kirkpatrick, D., & Jakupec, V. (1999). Becoming flexible: What does it mean? In D. Keegan & A. Tait (Eds.), *The convergence of distance and conventional education: Patterns of flexibility for the individual learner* (pp. 57-70). New York: Routledge.

Maxwell, J. A. (1996). Qualitative research design: An interpretive approach. In L. Bickman & D. J. Rog (Eds.), *Applied social research methods series (41).* Thousand Oaks, CA: Sage Publications.

McDermott, R. P. (1977). Social relations as contexts for learning. *Harvard Educational Review, 47*(2), 198-213.

McDermott, R. P., & Roth, D. R. (1978). The social organization of behavior: Interactional approaches. *Annual Review of Anthropology, 7,* 321-345.

McHenry, L., & Bozik, M. (1995). Communicating at a distance: A study of interaction in a distance education classroom. *Communication Education*, *44*(4), 362-374.

Mehan, H. (1980). The competent student. *Anthropology and Education Quarterly*, *11*(3), 131-152.

Moore, M. G., & Kearsley, G. (1996). *Distance education: A systems view*. Albany, NY: Wadsworth.

Ozmon, H. A., & Craver, S. M. (1999). *Philosophical foundations of education* (6th ed.). Upper Saddle River, NJ: Merrill.

Prus, R. (1996). *Symbolic interaction and ethnographic research: Intersubjectivity and the study of human lived experience*. New York: State University of New York Press.

Salomon, G. (1979). *Interaction of media, cognition, and learning: An exploration of how symbolic forms cultivate mental skills and affect knowledge acquisition*. San Francisco, CA: Jossey-Bass.

Schmertzing, L. C. (2000). *Graduate student perspectives on an interactive distance learning studio: Culture and adaptation in technologically mediated classrooms*. Unpublished doctoral dissertation, University of West Florida, Pensacola, FL.

Schmertzing, R. W., & Schmertzing, L. C. (2001). Domains of adaptation in technologically mediated classrooms: An ethnographic report. In J. Price, D. Willis, N. Davis, & J. Willis (Eds.), *Information technology and teacher education annual* (pp. 2424-2430). Norfolk: Association for the Advancement of Computing in Education.

Seels, B., Berry, L. H., Fullerton, K., & Horn, L. J. (1996). Research on learning from television. In D. Jonassen (Ed.), *Handbook of research for educational communications and technology* (pp. 299-377). New York: Simon & Schuster Macmillan.

Shultz, J. J., Florio, S., & Erickson F. (1982). Where's the floor? Aspects of the cultural organization of social relationships in communication at home and in school. In P. Gilmore & A. A. Glatthorn (Eds.), *Children in and out of school: Ethnography and education* (pp. 88-123). Washington, DC: Center for Applied Linguistics.

Simonson, M., & Maushak, N. (1996). Instructional technology and attitude change. In D. Jonassen (Ed.), *Handbook of research for educational communications and technology* (pp. 384-1016). New York: Simon & Schuster Macmillan.

Smith, P. L., & Ragan, T. J. (1993). *Instructional design*. Columbus, OH: Merrill.

Spradley, J. P., & Mann, B. (1975). *The cocktail waitress: Woman's work in a man's world*. New York: Wylie.

Thompson, D. (1999). From marginal to mainstream: Critical issues in the adoption of information technologies for tertiary teaching and learning. In D. Keegan & A. Tait (Eds.), *The convergence of distance and conventional education: Patterns of flexibility for the individual learner* (pp. 150-160). New York: Routledge.

Verduin, J. R., Jr., & Clark, T. A. (1991). *Distance education: The foundations of effective practice*. San Francisco, CA: Jossey-Bass.

Wagner, E. D. (1997). Interactivity: From agents to outcomes. In R. J. Menges & M. D. Svinicki (Series Eds.) & T. E. Cyrs (Vol. Ed.), *New directions for teaching and learning: No. 71. Teaching and learning at a distance: What it takes to effectively design, deliver, and evaluate programs* (pp. 19-26). San Francisco: Jossey-Bass.

Willis, B. (1993). *Distance education: A practical guide*. Englewood Cliffs, NJ: Educational Technology Publications.

William A. Doherty
Cleborne D. Maddux

An Investigation of Methods of Instruction and Student Learning Styles in Internet-Based Community College Courses

SUMMARY. This study investigated learning styles and students' perceptions of the helpfulness of Internet-based methods of instruction among students enrolled in Internet-based courses at the four Nevada community colleges. The study found tentative evidence that reflective learners were more likely to enroll in the Internet-based course included in the study than active learners (chi-square = 6.37, $p = .012$). The results also supported the idea that global learners were less likely to complete these Internet-based community college courses than sequential learners (chi-square = 7.93, $p = .005$). An analysis of students' helpfulness ratings for 13 specific methods of Internet-based instruction found no significant correlations between learning styles and perceived effectiveness of instructional methods. *[Article copies available for a fee from The Haworth Document Delivery Service: 1-800-HAWORTH. E-mail address: <getinfo@haworthpressinc.com> Website: <http://www.HaworthPress.com> © 2002 by The Haworth Press, Inc. All rights reserved.]*

WILLIAM A. DOHERTY is Community College Professor, Department of Business and Computer Technology, Truckee Meadows Community College, Reno, NV 89512 (E-mail: bdoherty@tmcc.edu).
CLEBORNE D. MADDUX is Associate Editor for Research, *Computers in the Schools*, and Professor, University of Nevada, Reno, Department of Counseling and Educational Psychology, Reno, NV 89557 (E-mail: maddux@unr.edu).

[Haworth co-indexing entry note]: "An Investigation of Methods of Instruction and Student Learning Styles in Internet-Based Community College Courses." Doherty, William A., and Cleborne D. Maddux. Co-published simultaneously in *Computers in the Schools* (The Haworth Press, Inc.) Vol. 19, No. 3/4, 2002, pp. 23-32; and: *Distance Education: Issues and Concerns* (ed: Cleborne D. Maddux, Jacque Ewing-Taylor, and D. LaMont Johnson) The Haworth Press, Inc., 2002, pp. 23-32. Single or multiple copies of this article are available for a fee from The Haworth Document Delivery Service [1-800-HAWORTH, 9:00 a.m. - 5:00 p.m. (EST). E-mail address: getinfo@haworthpressinc.com].

23

KEYWORDS. Web-based instruction, distance education, learning styles

The International Data Corporation predicted that the Internet will be responsible for increasing the number of distance-education students from 710,000 in 1998 to 2.2 million by 2002. This group will represent 15% of all higher education students (Rochester, Boggs, & Lau, 1999), and literature suggests that they may experience higher dropout rates than students in traditional college courses.

While no national statistics have been reported for dropout rates in distance education courses, studies of individual institutions suggest that they are generally higher in distance-education courses than in their on-campus counterparts. Studies of the Dallas County Community College District have shown an 11% to 15% difference between course completion rates in the district's on-campus courses and those in its distance education courses (Carr, 2000). At Tyler Junior College in Texas, the course completion rate for 35 Internet-based courses was 58%; for traditional courses, the rate was 71% (Carr, 2000). The University of Central Florida reported that in fall 1998 the withdrawal rate was 9% from the university's Web-based courses, and 5% from on-campus courses in the same subjects (Carr, 2000).

One factor that can affect distance education dropout rates is student satisfaction (Swift, Wilson, & Wayland, 1997), and cognitive theory suggests that some elements of Internet-based courses may be differentially attractive to students depending upon their learning styles (Soloman & Felder, 1999). A universally accepted definition of learning styles has not been established. However, learning styles have been described as the characteristic cognitive, affective, and psychological behaviors that serve as relatively stable indicators of how learners perceive, interact with, and respond to the learning environment (DeBello, 1989). Kolb (1976) found that students' learning styles played a significant role in their preferences for areas of study. Kolb speculated that students favored courses and content areas that matched their preferred learning styles.

Very little quantitative research specific to learning styles and Internet-based methods of instruction has been published (Jung, 1999), and the results have been mixed. In a study investigating the relationship between student learning styles and the learning strategies they employed in an Internet-based course, no significant relationships were identified (Shih, Ingebritsen, Pleasants, Flickinger, & Brown, 1998). Federico's (2000) study of postgraduate students did find a relationship between students' general opinions of Internet-based instruction and learning styles measured by Kolb's Learning Styles Index. While this study did not focus on specific methods of instruction, it found that students with assimilating and accommodating learning styles demonstrated significantly more agreeable attitudes toward the design and use of network-based instruction than students with converging and diverging learning styles. Limbach, Weges, and Valcke (1997) found that 75% of the students in Internet-based courses at the Open University preferred a deductive learning mode that starts with a theory and moves toward practical examples and implementation of that theory. Limbach et al. did not test for specific learning style types, but this learning preference is typically associated with reflective learners, similar to the assimilating style that Federico (2000) found most agreeable to network-based instruction.

The conclusions reached in most of these studies indicate advances in this area of study require measurement of learning styles in a manner that has a theoretical correspondence to specific instructional strategies. The current study attempted to address this need by comparing student learning styles measured by the Index of Learning Styles (ILS) (Soloman & Felder, 1999) with methods of instruction that have a theoretical correspondence to each learning style.

STATEMENT OF THE PROBLEM

The purpose of this study was to gather empirical evidence on learning styles and preferred methods of instruction among students in Internet-based community college classes. The study investigated the following research questions:

1. Is there a difference in the distribution of learning styles as measured by the ILS between students in Internet-based community college classes and college students in general?
2. Is there a difference in the distribution of learning styles as measured by the ILS between students who start Internet-based community college classes and students who successfully complete those classes?
3. Is there a relationship between student learning styles and student preferences for specific methods of instruction in Internet-based community college courses?

METHODOLOGY

The study included volunteer students enrolled in Internet-based classes offered by the four Nevada community colleges. The investigation included a pilot study in the spring 2000 semester and a final study in the fall 2000 semester. The pilot study included 71 classes from 9 different academic areas; the final study included 76 classes from 15 different academic areas. The average enrollment in each class was 25 students.

Learning style data were collected using a Web-based version of Soloman and Felder's (1999) Index of Learning Styles (ILS) Questionnaire. The ILS is an instrument that measures adult learning preferences across four separate dimensions: active/reflective, sensing/intuitive, visual/verbal, and sequential/global. As with most other learning styles indicators, the dimensions are not mutually exclusive. Theory suggests that each learner uses both sides of each dimension in the course of learning. However, given the choice, each student has preferences for the modes he or she uses to learn. A Web-based questionnaire designed specifically for this study was used to gather data on student preferences for the 13 Internet-based methods of instruction shown in Table 1. A copy of the instrument can be obtained by writing the senior author.

For the first research question, a one-sample chi-square test was used to compare the learning style distributions from the final study to expected distributions established by prior research. Psychometric normative data have not been published for the ILS, but findings from previous studies using other instruments indicate theoretical distributions of college student learning style preferences as 62% active and 38% reflective (Kolb, 1976), and 60% sensing and 40% intuitive (Myers & McCaulley, 1985). Theoretical distributions are not available for the sequential/global and visual/verbal learning style dimensions. The Bonferroni correction for two concurrent tests was used to establish a procedure-wise alpha of .025 to maintain an experiment-wise alpha of .05.

For the second research question, a one-sample chi-square test was also used to compare the learning style distributions from the final study to expected distributions found during the pilot study. The two groups included in this study could not be compared as independent samples, because the final study group included students who also completed their classes. It should be noted that the one-sample method that was used in this study to compare the distribution of learning styles is a weak test in that regard. The Bonferroni correction for four concurrent tests

TABLE 1. Correlations Between Learning Styles and Perceived Helpfulness of Methods of Instruction

Method of Instruction	Active/Reflective Score	Sequential/Global Score	Sensing/Intuitive Score	Visual/Verbal Score
Schedule	−.002	.029[a]	−.106[a]	−.045
E-mail	−.112[a]	−.021	−.108[a]	−.157
Text Presentations	−.051	.056	−.192[a*]	−.052[a]
Threaded Discussion	−.022[a]	.023	.048	−.007
Course Map	−.128	.103[a]	.010	−.149
Links for Exploration	−.257[a**]	.158[a]	.051[a]	−.099
Chat	−.099[a]	.033	.095	−.140
Graphics, Animation	−.218	.128	−.158[a]	−.259[a*]
Interactive Activities	−.193[a]	−.017	.038	−.155
Video Presentations	-	-	-	-[a]
Instructor Control	-	-	-	-
Audio Presentations	-	-	-	-[a]
A/V Conferencing	-[a]	-	-	-[a]

[a]Theoretical relationship
* $p < .05$
**$p < .01$

was used to set the procedure-wise alpha at .01 to meet an experiment wise alpha of .05.

Data on the third research question regarding the relationship between learning styles and design elements were analyzed using a Spearman Rank Correlation Coefficient correlation matrix. An experiment-wise alpha of .05 was used, and the Bonferroni correction was used to establish a procedure-wise alpha of .001.

The primary limitation of this study is the bias introduced by voluntary participation. Voluntary participation was chosen because it allowed for responses from a more diverse set of courses. However, the results may not be representative of the entire population. This study was also limited to community college students in the University and Community College System of Nevada. Community college students are often part-time students, and may not be seeking a degree. There are also typically fewer restrictions to enrolling in community college courses. Therefore, the results may not apply to all levels of college instruction. Finally, the number of responses received was a relatively small percentage of the total students enrolled in Internet-based classes.

RESULTS

One hundred and fifty students responded to the questionnaire in the final study, representing a 21% response rate. In general, students indicated a preference for the sensing, sequential, and visual learning styles. This study found evidence that students enrolled in Internet-based community college classes in Nevada included a significantly larger number of reflective learners than college students in general. It also found evidence that global learners may be less likely to complete Internet-based community college classes than sequential learners. No significant differences in distributions were found for either the sensing/intuitive or visual/verbal learning style dimensions.

Figure 1 shows a majority of students from both the pilot study (68.4%) and the final study (58%) expressed a preference for the sequential learning style. Theoretical distributions of college students on this learning style have not been established; therefore, it was not possible to test the first research question on this learning style dimension. The results of the one-sample chi-square comparison of the pilot study and the final study were significant for the sequential/global learning style. Therefore, the null hypothesis that the distribution of learning styles of community college students who enroll in Internet-based classes is 69% sequential and 31% global as measured by the ILS was rejected. The results showed that the students enrolled in Internet-based classes included significantly more global learners (42%) than was predicted by the pilot study of students who had successfully completed their Internet-based classes. This provides tentative evidence that global learners may be less likely to complete Internet-based community college classes.

Student comments provided additional anecdotal support for this hypothesis. Responses from the pilot study of students completing an Internet-based class included four comments requesting a more structured class consistent with sequential learners' preferences and no comments reflecting a global learner's preference for less structure. By contrast, the study of students starting an Internet-based class included four comments requesting less structure, in addition to five comments that requested the additional structure preferred by sequential learners.

Figure 1 also shows that the majority of respondents to the pilot study (54.3%) preferred the reflective learning style, while the majority of respondents to the final study (52%) preferred the active learning style. There was no significant difference between the pilot and the final study. However, a one-sample chi-square test showed that the distribution of students in the final study was significantly different from the

FIGURE 1. Distribution of Sequential/Global and Active/Reflective Learning Style Scores

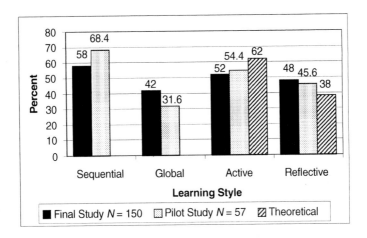

theoretical distribution of college students established by prior research (chi-square = 6.37, p = .012). As a result, the null hypothesis that the distribution of learning style preferences of students in Internet-based community college classes as measured by the ILS is 62% active and 38% reflective was rejected. The results showed that the students enrolled in Internet-based classes included significantly more reflective learners (48%) than was predicted by past research. This supports Limbach, Weges, and Valcke's (1997) findings for the Open University and Federico's (2000) study of postgraduate students.

Student helpfulness ratings shown in Table 2 were highest for e-mail and a detailed schedule. Student ratings were lowest for chat. Audio presentations, video presentations, and audio/video conferencing were not available to the students who responded to the survey. A review of these ratings indicated a possible response bias, as each student's helpfulness ratings tended to be consistent for all methods of instruction. No significant correlations were found between helpfulness ratings and student learning styles. However, trends identified between links and active learners, graphics and visual learners, and text presentations and sensing learners may be areas for future study.

DISCUSSION

This study did not investigate the reasons behind the skewed distribution of learning styles. However, based on Kolb's theory that students gravitate toward classes that emphasize learning styles they prefer, it would be reasonable to hypothesize that the Internet-based classes in this study emphasize methods of instruction that are more attractive to reflective and sequential learners. This provides tentative evidence that student learning styles play an important role in both student retention and student enrollment in Internet-based community college classes.

In dealing with student retention, colleges can approach the role of learning styles in Internet-based courses from two directions. The first is revising the curriculum to provide methods of instruction that are more attractive to global learners. Literature suggests that global learners prefer to follow an almost random sequence through material (Felder & Soloman, 1999). They are likely to benefit from exploratory links that provide practical examples of course material to help them make connections. They are also likely to benefit from creative activities that allow them to identify how the pieces of information fit together.

The hyperlink nature of Internet-based courses appears to provide the ideal environment for global learners, allowing them to explore a course in any sequence they want. What may be missing is unifying activities that allow them to make connections between the various topics and sources of information provided in the course. However, there is little quantitative research to guide the design of specific methods of instruction to meet the needs of global learners in Internet-based courses.

TABLE 2. Student Helpfulness Ratings for Methods of Instruction

	N	Min.	Max.	Mean	S.D.	Median
E-mail	148	2	8	7.08	1.28	8
Schedule	145	2	8	6.97	1.37	7
Interactive Activities	84	3	8	6.93	1.31	7
Course Map	116	3	8	6.75	1.25	7
Threaded Discussion	139	1	8	6.65	1.73	7
Text Presentations	106	1	8	6.39	1.42	7
Links	105	1	8	6.38	1.63	7
Pictures, Graphics, Animations	71	1	8	6.32	1.79	7
Instructor Control of Computer	3	4	7	5.67	1.53	6
Chat	102	1	8	5.49	2.27	6

As a result, a second alternative available to colleges is better advisement. Students expressing an interest in Internet-based classes should complete a learning styles assessment, and global learners should be provided with a clear understanding of the limitations of Internet-based classes in addressing their learning preferences. Ideally, these students should also be provided with strategies for dealing with these limitations if they do decide to pursue an Internet-based class. These strategies might include arranging meetings with other students to discuss the course material, or setting aside additional time for exploring supplementary course materials.

From the enrollment perspective, these results have two implications. The first is that Internet-based classes may be providing an attractive alternative to traditional classroom instruction for reflective learners. This idea is best illustrated by a comment from one respondent to this study: "I like having a class that I can just get the stuff done without all the extra fluff in lecture classes that's just a waste of time." This type of student may have motivational problems in traditional classes, or may avoid college classes all together. As a result, community colleges may want to specifically target this type of student with information about Internet-based classes and how they fit the reflective student's style of learning. The second implication of these results is that the methods currently used by many community colleges for Internet-based instruction may not be attractive to the majority of college students who prefer the active learning style. For these students, colleges have the same options discussed above, modification of the curriculum to better meet their needs, or better pre-enrollment advisement.

CONCLUSIONS AND RECOMMENDATIONS

This study has provided tentative evidence that learning styles play an important role in both enrollment and retention in Internet-based college courses, but additional research is needed in two areas. First, longitudinal studies that track the actual dropout rates of students by their learning style preference is required to confirm the evidence found in this study. Second, further experimental research is required to establish a relationship between specific methods of instruction used in Internet-based classes and student learning styles. If additional support for these hypotheses can be established in future studies, it may prove valuable in reducing the dropout rates and increasing student satisfaction in Internet-based college classes.

REFERENCES

Carr, S. (2000). As distance education comes of age, the challenge is keeping the students. *The Chronicle of Higher Education*. Retrieved May 23, 2001, from http://chronicle.merit.edu/free/v46/i23/23a00101.htm

DeBello, T. C. (1989). *Comparison of eleven major learning styles models: Variables; appropriate populations; validity of instrumentation; and research behind them.* Paper presented at the national conference of the Association for Supervision and Curriculum Development, Orlando, FL. (ERIC Document Reproduction Service No. ED312093)

Federico, P. (2000). Learning styles and student attitudes toward various aspects of network-based instruction. *Computers in Human Behavior, 16*, 359-379.

Felder, R. M., & Soloman, B. A., (1999). *Learning styles and strategies.* Retrieved March 23, 1999, from http://www2.ncsu.edu/unity/lockers/users/f/felder/public/ILSdir/styles.html

Jung, I. (1999). *Internet-based distance education bibliography.* Retrieved October 15, 2000, from http://www.ed.psu.edu/acsde/annbib/annbib.asp

Kolb, D.A. (1976). *Learning style inventory: Technical manual.* Englewood Cliffs, NJ: Prentice-Hall.

Limbach, R., Weges, H. G., & Valcke, M. M. A. (1997). Adapting the delivery of learning materials to student preferences: Two studies with a course model based on 'cases.' *Distance Education, 18*(1), 24-43.

Myers, I. B., & McCaulley, M. H. (1985). *Manual: A guide to the development and use of the Myers-Briggs Type Indicator.* Palo Alto, CA: Consulting Psychologist's Press.

Rochester, J., Boggs, R., & Lau, S. (1999). *Online distance learning in higher education, 1998-2002* (International Data Corp. Report no. W17827). Framingham, MA: International Data Corporation.

Shih, C., Ingebritsen, T., Pleasants, J., Flickinger, K., & Brown, G. (1998). *Learning strategies and other factors influencing achievement via Web courses.* Madison, WI: University of Wisconsin. (ERIC Document Reproduction Service No. ED 422 876)

Soloman, B. A., & Felder, R. M. (1999). *Index of learning styles questionnaire.* Retrieved February 15, 1999, from http://www2.ncsu.edu/unity/lockers/users/f/felder/public/ILSdir/ilsweb.html

Swift, C.O., Wilson, J.W., & Wayland, J.P. (1997). Interactive distance education in business: Is the new technology right for you? *Journal of Education for Business, 73*, 85-89.

Albert L. Ingram

Usability of Alternative Web Course Structures

SUMMARY. The usability of Web sites is coming to be a major concern for corporations and other organizations. Usability typically consists of five elements: learnability, efficiency, memorability, error rates, and satisfaction. Although the relative importance of these elements may differ between educational sites and commercial ones, usability is no less important for instructional Web sites. In this article we discuss what usability means for instructional Web sites and report on a small study comparing the usability of two different course structures. Some differences were found, which, if confirmed, could have implications for how we design instructional sites. Basic usability testing is recommended for all education and training sites, especially as part of formative evaluation. *[Article copies available for a fee from The Haworth Document Delivery Service: 1-800-HAWORTH. E-mail address: <getinfo@haworthpressinc.com> Website: <http://www.HaworthPress.com> © 2002 by The Haworth Press, Inc. All rights reserved.]*

KEYWORDS. Web-based instruction, usability, Web courses, instructional Web sites, course organization, course structure

As the World Wide Web proliferates, companies and Web developers are increasingly concerned with ensuring that visitors to specific

ALBERT L. INGRAM is Assistant Professor, Instructional Technology, College of Education, 405 White Hall, Kent State University, Kent, OH 44242 (E-mail: aingram@kent.edu).

[Haworth co-indexing entry note]: "Usability of Alternative Web Course Structures." Ingram, Albert L. Co-published simultaneously in *Computers in the Schools* (The Haworth Press, Inc.) Vol. 19, No. 3/4, 2002, pp. 33-47; and: *Distance Education: Issues and Concerns* (ed: Cleborne D. Maddux, Jacque Ewing-Taylor, and D. LaMont Johnson) The Haworth Press, Inc., 2002, pp. 33-47. Single or multiple copies of this article are available for a fee from The Haworth Document Delivery Service [1-800-HAWORTH, 9:00 a.m. - 5:00 p.m. (EST). E-mail address: getinfo@haworthpressinc.com].

Web sites can navigate the sites and find the information they need. In short, they are concerned with the *usability* of the sites. Fields such as human factors, ergonomics, and related disciplines have grown steadily for decades, but the Web reaches more and more technologically unsophisticated users. This fact alone has made it imperative for designers to consider how people use the Web as well as how to make such use easier. The field that addresses those questions is coming to be called usability engineering (Nielsen, 1993). If Web designers do not address usability questions, many users may not find the information and opportunities they need and will become frustrated. These negative feelings could undermine the growth of the Web in both its size and its usefulness to most people. For commercial sites, this translates directly into lost sales. For example, a recent report notes that large numbers of people view only a small part of the Web sites that they visit and leave because of their frustrations, and another study shows that a majority of people fail to complete an online sales process because it is too difficult (Roberts-Witt, 2001).

In his classic book on the subject, Jakob Nielsen (1993) defines usability of any technological system as consisting of five major characteristics: learnability, efficiency, memorability, error rates, and satisfaction. *Learnability* refers to the ease and speed with which novice users can learn the system; it applies primarily to early use of the system. *Efficiency* comes into play after the user has learned the system and refers to the ease and speed with which one can use the system after it has been learned. The *memorability* of a system is the ease with which one can return to the system after some period of time and still remember how to use it. *Error rates* are important for telling us not only how often one makes mistakes with the system but also how critical they are and how easily one can recover from them. Finally, there is the subjective criterion of *satisfaction*: Do the users like using the system and believe that they got something out of it?

It is probably not possible to design any complicated system, such as a Web site, so that it performs optimally in all areas. Any real-world design is likely to involve compromises among the five goals. In addition, on the Web, as Spool, Scanlon, Schroeder, Snyder, and DeAngelo (1999) point out, the usability of a site will depend on the user's purposes. Surfers need different things from buyers, who need something different from students, who need something different from researchers. Of course, a key element of all Web sites is the exchange of information of some kind between sites and visitors. This implies that there may be general usability principles that can be applied to all or most

Web sites. In this paper we are primarily concerned with the fact that the purposes of those who use an educational site are likely to be very different from those of casual surfers or commercial site visitors. How can we test the usability of site for those users? Can we begin to discern any empirically based usability principles for education?

A key tenet of usability engineering is that usability cannot be separated from testing systems with representative users. Through empirical studies as well as increasingly sophisticated theories, we may improve at predicting what will work and what will not. Even so, users, through their actual use of the system, are the final determiners of whether a system is usable. This does not necessarily mean that you survey or interview users to obtain their opinions of how the system should be (re)designed. It definitely does mean that you observe users performing representative tasks, record their error rates, and collect other data. This activity is commonly called *usability testing* (Rubin, 1994).

There are few studies to give us information about who performs good usability testing and who does not, but from using the Web regularly it seems clear that most sites are never tested for usability. Instead, we see sites in which locating the needed information is difficult and time-consuming, getting lost is easy, and frustration is the order of the day. Problems range from unclear directions for filling out a form through poorly identified buttons and links to confusing site structures where one can get "lost in hyperspace." Most of us have experienced problems like this as well as many more. One solution to them is to test the designs of sites and pages and to redesign the materials based on those tests.

Even before the widespread adoption of the Web, the problem of disorientation–getting lost in hypermedia materials was becoming clear (Kim & Hirtle, 1995). Hypertext and hypermedia have been touted as educationally important for some time; at the same time, it has been evident that many people have difficulty using such materials effectively. Unlike a linear book (which can, of course, be used nonlinearly), hypertext may provide few clues to help users keep track of where they have been, recognize what they have read and what they have not, know how much is left to absorb, and so forth. Perhaps learners will improve their skills in learning from hypermedia as it proliferates, or maybe only skilled learners will be able to make the best use of it. Either way, we need to find the means for assisting people in learning from this medium. In part, that means making instructional sites as usable as possible.

Most usability testing on the World Wide Web has focussed on commercial sites. Companies are increasingly finding that they have strong financial incentives to make their sites as usable as possible. Often these tests are done privately either by the company itself or by another firm hired to do it. It can be difficult for the rest of us to make use of such data, either because it remains proprietary or because it is too specific to a single site. Occasionally, however, there have been usability tests on a variety of sites whose results are made publicly available so that we can draw more general conclusions. One such test was performed by Nielsen (1994), and a more recent example can be found in Spool et al. (1999).

Among the findings of these general usability tests are that users have a very low tolerance for Web sites that do not work correctly, that are slow, or that are just unpleasant to use. Nielsen found that users wanted the ability to search a site easily, although they did not necessarily make good use of such capabilities. Therefore, good navigation, structure, and other elements are also necessary. Among his "top ten mistakes" in Web site design are (Nielsen, 1996; Nielsen, 1999):

1. using too advanced technologies that slow things down and are not supported by older browsers; this limits and frustrates the audience;
2. using scrolling text and animations to convey content; they are difficult to read and to distinguish from the numerous ads that now appear online;
3. lack of navigation support (standard buttons, location information, and so forth) which can cause users to become disoriented;
4. non-standard elements like link colors, which make the pages less predictable and more difficult to use; and
5. slow download times usually caused by large graphics and other media; this is very frustrating to folks with low bandwidth connections.

Spool and his colleagues (1999) tested a variety of sites for how easy it was for users to find specific information and found some surprising results. They concluded several things:

1. Graphic design has little to do with a site's usability.
2. Text links are central to the user's experience (because slow download speeds often make these navigational elements available first).
3. Navigation and content are inseparable.
4. Surfing and information retrieval are very different activities.

These findings probably have implications for educational and instructional Web sites as well. For example, many colleges and universities are using standard Web course templates and systems to make it easier for faculty to put courses online. Often the assumption is also that having a common course structure will enable students easily to find their way around each new course they take. However, if Spool et al. (1999) are correct in saying that navigation and content are inseparable, this may not be the best way to go. Different subject areas and even different courses within subjects may require different navigational structures to help students make the best use of the Web site.

The intolerance for slow downloads is also important, since it should lead us to be careful about how we present information and interactions. Technology for its own sake is less important than ensuring a high-quality browsing experience. The distinction between surfing and information retrieval is especially important for education, since instructional effectiveness demands that we discourage casual browsing and encourage deeper information retrieval, use, and retention. To a large extent these issues and their impact on educational sites should be settled empirically through usability testing, formative evaluation, and other techniques.

The current study provides an example of how this can work. Usability of an instructional Web site can be analyzed and tested in the same way as other systems. When we speak of the usability of a Web site, we are talking more about navigating the site itself than about learning how to use a specific browser. We may have little or no control over the specific software that our students use or how well they both learn and use it. For students or other users who are new to both Web use and a specific site, these two issues might overlap. This overlap may confuse the issue of evaluating the usability of an instructional Web site design with that of evaluating the browser. The latter is more the responsibility of Netscape and Microsoft and other companies currently producing Web browser software than of the specific site designer. For studies such as the current one, we may want to focus on students with some general Web experience who are allowed to pick their favorite browser.

Overall, a good instructional Web site should have characteristics similar to the general characteristics specified by usability engineering. It should be *easy to learn*: A newcomer to the course should be able to find her/his way around the site and figure out the structure of the site and the locations of various types of information readily. Second, it should be *efficient* for the increasingly experienced students. As the semester progresses, students should be able to quickly and easily find the information, activities, and tasks that they need to do well in the course.

They should not be unduly distracted by information that they needed at the beginning of the course but no longer require.

Web sites have the important property of being easily changed, reorganized, and updated. Therefore, we might explore the idea of changing a site and its structure as students become more experienced in it. Although this might conflict with other usability goals, we might find that the needs and habits of students change over time as they progress through the instruction. This is an empirical issue that might be resolved by repeated usability testing through a semester.

Memorability is a less important aspect of most instructional Web sites, except over very short time periods. We normally expect students to access our sites regularly during a course, thereby reducing the need for them to remember for long periods how to use them and where to find things. After the student completes the course, the memorability of the Web site becomes largely irrelevant, since the user will rarely need to return to it. In the author's experience, students often request continuing access to online course materials but rarely take advantage of it after the semester is over.

Web sites, however, present special challenges as far as *errors* go. We may have little control over which browsers students use or how stable they are, but we can make sure that our links, programs, and scripts work correctly. Even so, different browser versions often interact in unexpected ways with elements like JavaScript. Therefore, reducing these kinds of errors should be a key goal of our sites. In the normal course of events this information might be difficult to obtain. For example, Web server logs can only give us partial information about errors, since they cannot record what happens at the client end of the transaction. If a JavaScript runs incorrectly after the page is downloaded, the server may never record it. On the positive side, few such errors are likely to be fatal, and browsers and users can usually recover from them easily.

The other side of error reduction concerns the errors that students make in navigating a site, even when technically everything works correctly. For example, a student may explore several blind alleys while searching for a specific piece of information before either finding it or concluding that it does not exist on the site. Or they may enter ineffective search terms into a search engine for the site, thus failing to find what they need. A final example would be the student who diligently browses the site, but misses whole sections, large or small, because of navigation or memory (human, not computer) problems.

Student *satisfaction* with a site is, of course, a subjective phenomenon, but one that is important in keeping students returning to our sites. Without return visits, it is hard to see how students can learn from our sites. Satisfaction with a site could be measured in many different ways, familiar to instructional technologists and others everywhere: questionnaires, surveys, interviews, etc. In addition, Web server logs (Ingram, 1999-2002; Peled & Rashty, 1999) can sometimes provide data about repeat visitors. A key task is to identify what aspects of a site contribute to and detract from student satisfaction. That work has just begun.

A typical usability study for an instructional site follows a pattern (Rubin, 1994). Students from the target population of the course are brought into a testing lab where they are given a series of key or common tasks that any student might need to perform on the instructional site. The students would not yet be familiar with either the site or with the subject matter of the course, but would be representative of those who might take the course. As students perform those tasks, they are observed, perhaps even videotaped. Among the questions that might be asked in the study are:

1. Did the students perform the tasks successfully?
2. How efficiently did they perform the tasks (e.g., the number of links they had to follow to find specific information)?
3. How many errors did they make in performing the tasks? How significant were the errors? How readily did they recover from those errors?
4. How quickly did they learn the site, so that future tasks became easier?
5. How much did they enjoy using the site? How satisfying was it to successfully complete a task? How frustrating was it to fail?

The tasks that the students perform should be ones that any student in the course might have to do, either on assignment or from their own needs. For example, tasks could range from finding the details of a specific assignment to answering content questions about the course. In a usability study one is not necessarily testing the *educational* effectiveness of a site; instead one is trying to determine whether students can navigate through the site, find what they need efficiently, and otherwise use the site successfully. Thus, a usability study is different from a formative evaluation of an educational site, although it may be part of such an evaluation. See such texts as Dick, Carey, and Carey (2001) for information about formative evaluation.

USABILITY TESTING ON INSTRUCTIONAL WEB SITES WITH DIFFERENT STRUCTURES

Although usability testing is customarily applied to very specific sites, it is also used in an attempt to draw more general conclusions about how the Web should work. It is possible to compare two different sites, not merely to help us decide which one to make public, but also to test specific aspects of site structure or implementation. In designing and developing instructional Web sites, for example, it might be useful to examine whether there are ways of organizing course material that students generally prefer from a usability standpoint. We should not lose sight of the possible uniqueness of the interaction between such factors as course content, learners, and usability. But we should look for more general principles as well.

We might expect that the structure of a Web site will affect the site's usability. There are several basic patterns that we might use in designing instructional Web sites. A site could be linear, in which users are directed through a series of screens in order. It could be hierarchical, in which a branching tree structure is used. Finally, it could be a true Web, in which pages are linked to each other on an essentially ad hoc basis, according to the dictates of the information contained in them. Of course, most sites of any size are likely to have elements of two or three of these structures. Overall, however, we can often identify one key pattern in a site.

To be more specific, university-level course materials can be organized in any of several different ways as well. Two of those ways are (a) as a content hierarchy based on the structure of the subject matter, and (b) according to the major assignments and objectives of the course. Other organizational structures might include one based on the schedule of the course or idiosyncratic ones that follow the needs of the instructor and content. While we can obtain feedback about the subjective impressions of students toward these different organizations, we can also examine educational and usability issues more directly. Clearly, we should do formative evaluations of different courses with different site organizations as well as their effects on learning. In addition, we can examine different course organizations from a usability perspective.

The brief study reported here begins that second task. In it we compare two different course organizations for usability. The goal of the study is to determine whether the different Web course materials structures affect the learnability, efficiency, error proneness, and satisfaction associated with doing common tasks on the Web sites. Memorability is not part of the study, since it is a short-term study only. This characteristic really applies only over the long term, when users return repeatedly to a site and have to remember how to use it. Efficiency is also a relatively long-term phenomenon and will be only partly studied here.

Learnability, errors, and satisfaction are all key elements. They are assessed through the usability studies and user questionnaires. The overall objectives of the study are to determine if the two course organizations described (content organization versus assignment organization) lead to differences in the learnability, error rates, satisfaction, and, to some extent, efficiency of the sites. If they do, it will have implications for how we design instructional Web sites in the future.

METHOD

Subjects

The course materials tested were designed for graduate students in instructional technology, many of whom take a course entitled Instructional Applications of the Internet. The students who take the course commonly vary widely in their prior knowledge of instructional design, instructional technology, and the Internet. They typically include both men and women and range in age from the mid-twenties to the forties and fifties. In addition to instructional technology students there are also occasionally students from other departments such as business and communications. The test subjects were drawn from these populations. Ten subjects were tested with each course organization.

Procedures

Test subjects first responded to a short questionnaire on their prior knowledge and experience using the Internet and the Web and their knowledge of the subject matter of the course. Subsequently, they performed a series of 11 tasks in random order. The test monitor observed the tests and videotaped each one. After completing the 11 tasks, subjects completed a second questionnaire to assess their satisfaction with using the system.

Task List

In these usability tests, students were asked to perform the same tasks regardless of which Web site they were using. All information was available on each site; only the organization differed. The sites are available at the following addresses. They are the original sites, even though the materials for the ongoing course have changed since this study was conducted: *http://www.albertingram.com/netclass1/* and *http://www.albertingram.com/netclass2/*.

There were 11 tasks, all of which were typical of things that a student would be likely to have to do in the course itself. The tasks were:

1. Find the instructor's telephone number.
2. Supply the size, in pixels, of a standard Palace background picture.
3. Complete the questionnaire asking for background information about students.
4. Find the list of new material added to the site on a given date.
5. Find the URL of The Palace company and bookmark it.
6. Find the name and abbreviation of the primary protocol used on the Internet.
7. List the five major aspects of usability on a Web site.
8. List three required tasks on an optional Web development assignment.
9. Find the page that would be most useful to someone new to the Internet.
10. Describe the assignment due on a specific date.
11. Find the page that includes diagrams of three basic ways of using the World Wide Web for instruction.

Data

The data collected in the study included:

1. Background information on subjects from a survey.
2. Observations by the student assistant on whether students completed each task and how long it took.
3. Videotapes of subjects performing the tasks.
4. Satisfaction measures obtained from a follow-up survey.
5. Web server logs showing which pages each subject accessed and in which order.

These data sources were not uniformly useful and only specifically relevant data will be reported here.

RESULTS

Typically, usability studies have very small numbers of users. The usual belief among usability experts is that most problems can be uncovered with only a few subjects (Rubin, 1994). Recent studies may cast some doubt on that idea (Spool, 2001). Even so, this study did use only a small number of learners. As such it should be considered a preliminary study, which needs to be followed up with a larger sample. This is especially true since it compares two different course organizations, and the traditional rules of statistical inference apply here in a way that they may not apply in a usability study on a single site, whose purpose is to uncover problems that can be solved.

That said, the study does appear to have uncovered some differences in usability between two different course organizations. Table 1 shows the major results of the comparisons of the two courses in the objective data as well as the one survey question that showed a significant difference between the two courses. Most of the specific tasks showed no differences in time or number of mouse clicks between the two courses, although a few did. So far, no pattern has been seen in these tasks.

As shown in Table 1, there was no difference in either the number of tasks that the students completed successfully or in the number of mouse clicks they used to find the requested information. However, there was a statistically significant difference in the amount of time that people took to complete the full set of tasks ($t = 2.358$, $df = 18$, $p < .05$), with those who used the site that was organized according to the course assignments taking over 10 minutes less than those who used the site organized according to a content hierarchy. The one survey question that showed a significant difference between the two groups ($t = -2.449$, $df = 18$, $p < .05$) asked for ratings from 1 = Almost Never to 4 = Almost Always on the question, "Did you know where to click to navigate around the site?" The students using the assignment-organized site were clearly more likely to say that they generally knew what to click next, a finding that supports their lower overall times in actually finding the material. Apparently, although they made roughly the same number of mouse clicks, this group had to spend less time thinking about *what* to click.

Finally, correlations were computed among the various data items, although in this case both groups were treated as one. Lower overall times to find the material were significantly correlated with ratings on the questions, "How clear were the goals of this Web site?" ($r = -.641$, $p < .01$) and "How clear were the tasks you did today?" ($r = -.675$, $p < .01$). The results tend to support the findings above as well as the idea that people can usefully rate the usability of a site for themselves.

DISCUSSION

Usability is clearly an important issue for those designing and building instructional Web sites. No information or activities can teach any-

TABLE 1. Objective Usability Data on Two Course Organizations

	Content-Based Course Organization	Assignment-Based Course Organization
# of problems solved (out of 11 per user)	9.8	9.8
Length of time to find information (mean minutes)	36.2	25.4
Number of mouse clicks to find information (mean)	53.0	52.4
"Did you know where to click to navigate around the site?" (1 = Almost Never; 4 = Almost Always)	2.2	3.1

thing, if the students cannot find them or respond to them correctly. Usability has become a major problem in the ebusiness world, where large numbers of people apparently do not complete online transactions because they get frustrated and leave before finishing. Although in education we may sometimes appear to have a more captive audience for our instructional Web sites, we cannot ignore problems in this area. The more that students fail to find what they need in order to learn from our sites, the more they will have to resort to e-mail and other communications. The time we spend on communications about material that already exists is time that we cannot spend on more important instructional issues. Even if there were no other reasons to pay attention to usability (and there are many), this one would be sufficient to justify our time and effort.

The current study helps highlight two major things. First, it shows how usability testing can be applied to instructional Web sites. Second, it starts the process toward drawing general conclusions that can be used to design such sites in the future. Most usability studies done today are done for the internal use of the design teams for specific Web sites, whether commercial or instructional. These are aimed solely at identifying problems so that they can be fixed before the site "goes live." The hope is that many more research-oriented usability studies will begin to be conducted.

We must remember that most of those in educational settings who are building instructional Web sites are not professional designers, nor do they have teams of designers, usability specialists, programmers, and so forth to assist them. Often they are individual teachers or professors who are trying to improve the educational experiences of their students. They rarely have the time, the inclination, or, often, all the skills needed to design and test variations on sites to find the optimal ones for usability and teaching. Research results that people like this could use and apply would help immensely.

Implications for the Design of Instructional Web Sites

The current results are quite tentative. If, however, they are supported by future research, they suggest that course Web sites should be designed from a student-centered and assignment-oriented point of view for greatest usability. Often, teachers approach a topic with a bias toward the structure of the content itself. Although this appears to be especially prevalent at the college and university level, it can also occur among K-12 teachers. Students, of course, see it differently. They tend to come to a course wanting to find out what they have to do and how to do it. We may have the ideal that students should value learning for its own sake; many students may not share it.

The current study indicates that we should think of our site from the student point of view. In part, this may mean organizing the site according to the tasks that students will complete and using the pages to support those tasks. Doing so seems to lead to easier searches, less time spent looking for material, and, one hopes, more chances to concentrate on the educational content of our sites. Clearly, we need more usability research in order to verify these findings.

Usability Studies for All

Most people cannot be expected to do large-scale usability research studies (or even small ones such as this). It would improve most instructional Web sites, however, if designers were to do small studies to locate major problems that might interfere with student learning. The process need not be difficult or time-consuming, and the payoffs can be large. Most usability studies discover problems in even the most professionally designed sites. Eliminating them can reduce student frustration as well as your workload.

Here are some guidelines for running small-scale usability studies:

1. Use only a handful of people, say three to six. Although at least one study (Spool, 2001) seems to indicate that more might be needed, it concentrated on a large-scale commercial site, where

hundreds of potential usability problems were identified. Odds are that you can locate the major problems in a smaller instructional site with fewer people.

2. Develop a set of tasks for people to accomplish on the site during the test. Do not simply ask people to browse the site and see if it works well. Identify key pieces of information that a typical user might need to find or important activities that you want your students to complete online. Start them at your home page and ask them to do these tasks. Record how long it takes, whether they complete it, how many "errors" they make (such as looking in the wrong part of the site), and so forth. You might have them "think aloud" while they work and record what they say or take notes.

3. Gather as much data as you can, but do not go overboard. If you watch people going through the site, you might not need to videotape them as well. The Web server logs can help you gather data about which pages were viewed, but careful observation can give you much the same thing without the need for special software or lots of time.

4. Do not ask your students to redesign your site for you. When you ask them, either in person or using a survey, about their opinions of the site, concentrate on understanding their experience. They might not know how to make it better, although an awful lot of people have opinions on things like that. Use this data when you redesign the site and individual pages but do not relinquish your control to anonymous questionnaire responses or anything else.

Planning and implementing an effective usability study on your Web site will likely take only a few hours. Doing so will probably help you identify any major problems that your students might have in using your site. Rectifying them can mean the difference between your students finding the information and activities that will help them learn and your students missing out educationally. Going beyond mere usability to a more complete formative evaluation can have an even greater effect.

REFERENCES

Dick, W., Carey, L., & Carey, J. O. (2001). *The systematic design of instruction* (5th ed.). New York: Longman.

Ingram, A. L. (1999-2000). Using Web server logs in evaluating instructional Web sites. *Journal of Educational Technology Systems, 28*(2), 137-157.

Kim, H., & Hirtle, S. (1995). Spatial metaphors and disorientation in hypertext browsing. *Behaviour & Information Technology, 14*(4), 239-250.

Nielsen, J. (1993). *Usability engineering.* New York: Academic Press.

Nielsen, J. (1994) *Report from a 1994 Web usability study.* Retrieved October 29, 2001, from http://www.useit.com/papers/1994_web_usability_report.html

Nielsen, J. (1996). *Top ten mistakes in Web design.* Retrieved October 29, 2001, from http://www.useit.com/alterbox/9605.html

Nielsen, J. (1999). *"Top ten mistakes" revisited three years later.* Retrieved October 29, 2001, from http://www.useit.com/alertbox/990502.html

Peled, A., & Rashty, D. (1999). Logging for success: Advancing the use of WWW logs to improve computer mediated distance learning. *Journal of Educational Computing Research, 21*(4), 413-431.

Roberts-Witt, S. (2001, September 25). Site design as business decision. *PC Magazine iBiz, 29*(16), 6-8, 11-12.

Rubin, J. (1994). *Handbook of usability testing: How to plan, design, and conduct effective tests.* New York: Wiley.

Spool, J. M. (2001). *Eight is not enough:–UIEtips 06/05/01.* E-mail newsletter received June 5, 2001.

Spool, J. M., Scanlon, T., Schroeder, W., Snyder, C., & DeAngelo, T. (1999). *Web site usability: A designer's guide.* San Francisco: Morgan Kaufmann.

Paul G. Shotsberger

Mobile Wireless Technologies for Field-Based Teacher Interns and Their Partnership Teachers

SUMMARY. The project being reported in this article represented an effort to more thoroughly infuse technology into the undergraduate curriculum for prospective mathematics teachers, while strengthening the relationships that already existed between the university and its partnership public schools. A key component of the project was the use of mobile wireless technologies (computer and telephone), allowing pre-service and in-service mathematics teachers to be nearly anywhere and receive information, collaboration and support using productivity tools and Web resources. Usage data and survey results were used in order to address the primary questions of the investigation: Would the handheld PC be used in place of the desktop computer, or simply as a supplement? Which features of the handheld PC would prove most useful? Would there be a distinct difference in usage between pre-service and in-service teachers? The study concluded that mobile computing technology was used as a supplement to desktop technology, Web-browsing was by far the most useful feature, and the difference was clear-cut between pre-service and in-service adoption and employment of the mobile technologies. *[Article copies available for a fee from The Haworth Document Delivery Service: 1-800-HAWORTH. E-mail address: <getinfo@haworthpressinc.com> Website: <http://www.HaworthPress. com> © 2002 by The Haworth Press, Inc. All rights reserved.]*

PAUL G. SHOTSBERGER is Associate Professor, Department of Mathematics and Statistics, The University of North Carolina at Wilmington, 601 S. College Road, Wilmington, NC 28403-5970 (E-mail: shotsbergerp@uncwil.edu).

[Haworth co-indexing entry note]: "Mobile Wireless Technologies for Field-Based Teacher Interns and Their Partnership Teachers." Shotsberger, Paul G. Co-published simultaneously in *Computers in the Schools* (The Haworth Press, Inc.) Vol. 19, No. 3/4, 2002, pp. 49-65; and: *Distance Education: Issues and Concerns* (ed: Cleborne D. Maddux, Jacque Ewing-Taylor, and D. LaMont Johnson) The Haworth Press, Inc., 2002, pp. 49-65. Single or multiple copies of this article are available for a fee from The Haworth Document Delivery Service [1-800-HAWORTH, 9:00 a.m. - 5:00 p.m. (EST). E-mail address: getinfo@haworthpressinc.com].

49

KEYWORDS. Mobile wireless, mobile computing, partnership schools, pre-service, in-service, Web, just-in-time

MAKING THE CASE

A critical issue for teacher education today centers on the relationship, or lack thereof, between pre-service and in-service teacher education. There often is little attempt to make the connection between pre-service and in-service training, even though there exist many common needs. Partnership efforts such as Professional Development Schools (PDS) are one means of addressing this shortcoming (Goodlad, 1993). Additionally, advances in technology offer new opportunities for collaboration among pre-service and in-service teachers (e.g., Cifuentes, Sivo & Reynolds, 1997).

In particular, novice and experienced teachers can both benefit from using the information and communication resources of the World Wide Web. An abundance of useful information related to curriculum and pedagogy is easily accessible for classroom planning and implementation. Additionally, numerous opportunities exist for online interaction with other educators who have common concerns about important education-related issues. This kind of exchange benefits pre-service teachers by supporting the development of concepts and skills, while in-service teachers profit from multiple perspectives and continued opportunities for professional growth. The Web provides a flexible means of training that can be adapted to demanding work or student schedules for both of these groups of educators (Shotsberger, 2001).

Whereas the term *just-in-time* is used to describe this kind of computer support for teaching, the truth is that even as physical walls are being removed between teachers, time and resource constraints remain substantial barriers. The causes of these roadblocks range from limited availability of network connections at schools to the problem of scheduling collaborative meetings within the constraints of a full teaching schedule (even at the same school).

Mobile wireless technologies can be used to help meet the needs of educators (Berger, 2001; Dillon, 2001; Shotsberger & Vetter, 2001; Wilkes, 2001). For teachers in older school buildings where classroom wired network connections and telephone lines do not exist, or for teachers who are displaced from their classroom or who do not have a permanent room assignment, the capability of communicating via a handheld device could provide an excellent way for teachers to stay in touch with colleagues and parents. These teachers would not need to wait for access to a typically limited number of computers with Internet connections. Mobile wireless devices would allow them to research Web resources or send e-mail to parents or absent students from almost anywhere. Mobile wireless technologies would also enhance Web-based professional development by giving teachers immediate (as opposed to delayed) access to facilitators and other participants.

We are now beginning to see programs targeting the constraints of time and place in teacher education. The initiative detailed in this article was inspired in part by the LIVE Project, a three-year effort spear-headed by the Media Education Centre of the Department of Teacher Education at the University of Helsinki, Finland (Nummi, Ristola, Ronka, & Sariola, 1999). From the beginning, the LIVE Project incorporated mobile wireless technologies to create open and flexible learning environments for pre-service and in-service teachers and their students. Project researchers found that teachers regularly chose to employ a range of communications technologies, sometimes simultaneously, including telephone, e-mail, fax, and conferencing. Thus, a key aspect of establishing highly interactive, mobile learning environments is offering flexibility in terms of how to communicate, as well as intentionally honing participant skills in obtaining, managing, and communicating information and ideas. Results of the LIVE Project have led its researchers to wonder aloud: "Is the future of teacher education in digital nomadism?" (Nummi, Ristola, Ronka, & Sariola, 1999, p. 1092).

THE PROJECT

The project being reported in this article represented an effort to more thoroughly infuse technology into the undergraduate curriculum for prospective mathematics teachers, while strengthening the relationships that already exist between the University of North Carolina at Wilmington (UNCW) and its partnership public schools. A key component of the project involved the use of Jornada 720 handheld PC devices (Figure 1) and supporting equipment/access, including a mobile telephone to provide Wide Area Network (WAN) access. This technology adds a new dimension to just-in-time training and support by allowing pre-service and in-service mathematics teachers to be nearly anywhere and receive information, collaboration, and support using productivity tools and Web resources. The initiative stands as a unique field applica-

FIGURE 1. The Hewlett-Packard Jornada 720 Handheld PC

tion of mobile technology, in the spirit of the LIVE Project, which could potentially benefit not only universities and their students, but regional schools, teachers, and their students as well.

The Jornada 720 is a handheld, Windows-based, 206 MHz machine that comes standard with 32 MB of RAM, which was upgraded to 80 MB for the project. Standard software includes Microsoft Office (Word, Excel, PowerPoint, and Access), the Internet Explorer Web browser (with ChaiVM for Java support), a capability for sharing information with Microsoft Outlook (Inbox, Calendar, Contacts, Tasks), a Windows Media Player (audio and video), and the Inkwriter handwriting-recognition note taker. We also included the program IrcCE for participating in synchronous chats. The mobile telephone purchased was the SprintPCS Touchpoint 2100, along with a Web connection kit for each telephone.

The handheld PCs were purchased through an on-campus grant program during fall semester 2000 in anticipation of implementation during the pre-service teachers' practicum the following semester. The project involved six pre-service (intern) high school mathematics teachers paired with six in-service (partnership) teachers at area schools during spring 2001. Training was conducted in January regarding the functions and capabilities of the technology for research, communication, and reflection. Partnership teachers who expressed an interest were allowed to keep the devices past April 2001 (this was not an option for pre-service teachers due to graduation).

Online expectations for pre-service teachers included involvement in bi-weekly chats, submission of school observation forms, and submission of weekly e-journals. There were no formal online expectations for in-service teachers. Evidence of use included chat transcripts, form submissions, and telephone records of voice and Web minutes utilized (all participants had 500 total minutes available to them each month). Additionally, a survey was given to participants after the first 30 days and then again at the end of the semester to assess their overall impressions of the impact the technology had on their professional lives.

Ultimately what was desired was a comprehensive understanding of how teachers employed wireless technology on a daily basis and of the potential of the technology to transform classroom practice. Teachers generally do not lack for ideas of how to use technology such as the Web in their planning and teaching–they are constantly exposed to new practices through attendance at workshops and conferences. Rather, they suffer from an inability to implement new approaches due to a restrictive environment that includes limited time and resources. Therefore, the question of how extensively teachers would employ wireless technology placed in their hands was an open one. Would the handheld PC be used in place of the desktop computer, or simply as a supplement? Which features of the handheld PC would prove most useful? Would there be a distinct difference in usage between pre-service and in-service teachers? A primary feature of the project, then, would be negotiations between the participants and the technology, which would likely produce a number of unanticipated but desirable results along with the intended outcomes.

PROJECT OUTCOMES

Table 1 shows total telephone usage data for the three 30-day periods of the project, broken down by user (pre-service or in-service) and use (Web or voice).

The most obvious change over time was in pre-service Web minutes from the first month to the second and third. This did not result from a drop-off in enthusiasm, but rather was a function of some pre-service

TABLE 1. Total Telephone Usage for the Semester (minutes)

30-Day Period	Pre-service		In-service	
	Voice	Web	Voice	Web
First	586	2,770	334	171
Second	463	828	329	110
Third	818	840	444	119

teachers' having been warned about going over the total allotment of minutes for the month. Clearly, for the first two months, primary pre-service implementation tended to be Web-related. However, by the third month, voice usage was nearly equivalent to that of the Web. This was due to pre-service teachers feeling increasingly comfortable with calling parents and one another over the course of the semester. Another clear trend was the dominance of the in-service teachers' use of the technology for making voice calls, with the disparity between voice and Web minutes actually increasing as the semester continued. By the third month, pre-service teachers were using the Web at more than seven times the rate of the in-service teachers, with total minutes for the pre-service teachers nearly three times that of in-service. The reader should be aware that all pre-service teachers chose to use the Jornada for each of their bi-weekly chats, which represented using approximately 360 Web minutes per month. Nevertheless, a general observation was that pre-service teachers had more thoroughly integrated the mobile technology into their professional and personal lives. The survey data will be used to highlight possible reasons for this difference, as well as to detail particular functions and capabilities each group found valuable.

Appendix 1 is the initial survey given to participants at the end of the first month. Appendix 2 is the survey administered at the end of the semester. For the most part questions were repeated from the first survey to the second, although there were items that were included to tap into particular concerns at specific times of the semester. All 12 participants submitted initial surveys, while only 9 participants (6 interns and 3 partnership teachers) returned final surveys. Since the number of participants involved was small, results will only be presented in terms of frequencies, not percentages. The Jornada suite includes the Jornada handheld PC, the Touchpoint 2100 mobile telephone, and the connector cable.

Frequency of Use

Initially 7 of 12 said they used some portion of the suite "frequently," which included 4 of 6 interns. Of the remaining, one pre-service and two in-service teachers responded "infrequently," and one pre-service and one in-service teacher checked "rarely." At the end of the program, interns were equally split between "frequently" and "infrequently," while one partnership teacher each reported using the technology "frequently," "infrequently" and "rarely." Overall, there was not a lot of movement in this category from the initial survey to the final.

Primary Components

In the initial survey, 7 of 12 (including 5 interns) stated that they used "the entire suite"; whereas, 4 of 9 (all interns) reported using the entire suite in the final survey. Four respondents reported using only the telephone in the first survey, with the same number reporting phone-only use in the second survey. One participant in each survey reported using the Jornada by itself. Obviously, the interns were the major users of the Jornada-phone combination, which would enable a Web connection as well as use of the chat program.

Primary Location

The majority of respondents on the initial survey, 10 of 12, said that their primary location for using any component of the suite was "at home." However, by the time of the final survey an equal number of participants (four each) reported using the technology from home or while "commuting/traveling." This is compared to only one teacher using the technology on the road at the beginning of the semester. This migration in use appears to be due primarily to the partnership teachers, who represented three of the four identifying "commuting/traveling" in the final survey. This result speaks to the role of mobile technology, especially telephone, in addressing the needs of commuting teachers.

Primary Use for the Jornada

The majority of respondents in both the initial survey (8 of 12) and the final survey (7 of 9) said that they primarily used the Jornada for Internet access. For both surveys, the number using the handheld for this purpose included all six of the interns. Other responses included editing documents and writing/recording notes.

Ability to Synchronize

Although the ability to synchronize the Jornada with a desktop PC is a powerful feature that enables file and information sharing, very few participants utilized this feature. Three of four who indicated synchronization was "very useful" or "useful" at the beginning of the semester were still satisfied with it at the end, but no one began using the feature after the beginning of the semester, and one had become disillusioned with its use. The primary reason for the underutilization of this feature appeared to be the difficulty of loading the needed software and establishing a reliable partnership between machines. The author can attest to the fact that, whereas this feature is helpful and important in achieving true mobility in computing, it was nonetheless a daunting task to overcome the technical difficulties inherent in getting two very different kinds of computers to communicate with each other.

Overall Impression of the Jornada Suite

Most respondents were positive about the Jornada suite at the beginning of the program and remained positive throughout the semester. In the initial survey, 10 of 12 reported the suite was "easy to use" or was "some work, but worth it," while 8 of 9 gave one of these responses on the final survey. The only other response given on either survey was that it was "too much of a bother." So, apparently the Jornada and/or telephone proved to be a workable technology for the majority of teachers.

Disappointments/Worst Experiences

Disappointments expressed by teachers on the initial survey included every available response, with about half of the participants noting the lack of particular software features on the Jornada as compared to a typical desktop PC (e.g., no equation editor in Word, no ability to edit a PowerPoint presentation). Disappointments given by teachers changed little from the first survey to the second: getting and staying online (a problem more related to the Internet provider), the smaller screen and keyboard on the Jornada, the synchronization issues mentioned earlier, and limited telephone coverage in certain locations.

Best Experiences

Selected comments follow from both the initial and the final surveys.

> I got on-line during class to find Websites for the [classroom] project and the students were amazed. (Initial survey)

> While sitting in the car one afternoon, I was able to use the time to do an Internet search. (Initial survey)

> I really like the fact that I can work on a Word document on the Jornada and then transfer it to my [personal computer] to finish it at home. (Initial survey)

> One student was extremely disruptive to the point that I could barely teach one day. [My partnership teacher] called his parents right there during class for me (she stepped out into the hall). It was a bit of a shock to some students to see [my partnership teacher] and me pull out our cell phones right during class. (Final survey)

CONCLUSIONS

We now return to the motivating questions of the study in order to attempt some conclusions and provide direction for future research:

1. *Would the handheld PC be used in place of the desktop computer, or simply as a supplement?*

In general, it appears that participants favored use of a desktop PC over the Jornada, and therefore tended to use the handheld PC as a supplement. This is not to say that the Jornada did not serve an integral function in allowing teachers to do their work in a variety of settings, especially when desktop computing was not readily available. Perhaps the application in which the handheld PC competed most favorably with a desktop computer was in the area of Web access. One reason for this might be that surfing the Web requires very little typing or need for editing, and so the handheld PC format proved to be attractive, especially since the browser can handle most standard Web content.

2. *Which features of the handheld PC would prove most useful?*

As indicated, the most useful feature appeared to be the Web browser, along with the IrcCE chat program (for the interns). Use of both of these features was not without disappointment; however, difficulties seemed to center on the inability to get or stay online, which was a function of the Internet access, not the Jornada. One can imagine that, once technology such as General Packet Radio Service (GPRS) is in place, providing an "always-on" connection with substantially improved access speed, the Internet functions of the handheld PC will only take on greater importance. We are currently (fall 2001) using the Jornada with Local Area Network (LAN) cards while interns are still on campus, taking advantage of access points installed throughout campus and the greater access speeds they afford.

3. *Would there be a distinct difference in usage between pre-service and in-service teachers?*

This was perhaps the most striking feature of the project. Pre-service teachers immediately took to the Internet features of the Jornada, as well as pushing the envelope of the kinds of applications that were possible in the classroom. The primary usage limitation for pre-service teachers seemed to be software features that were lacking in the Jornada that they were accustomed to using on the desktop PC. This differed markedly with in-service teacher use, which seemed to be determined more by the level of technology available to them prior to the project. As an example, one teacher was using Microsoft Outlook for e-mail access before the start of the project; therefore her interest level was high about learning how to synchronize the desktop PC with the Jornada. However, most in-service teachers were using a dedicated e-mail software package at their schools and therefore could not take advantage of this feature. In general, the majority of in-service teachers viewed the handheld technology as simply "one more thing to learn."

Overall, the results of the study provide impetus for considering how this technology might be incorporated into teaching on a widespread basis. Clearly, some compatibility issues will need to be addressed before handheld PCs can be fully integrated into the classroom. However, given the near-reality of handheld PCs with GPRS capability, as well as an integrated telephone, one can imagine a time in the near future when use of this kind of technology will be seamless and consistently productive. An area of potential research is the use of handheld technology with in-class student assessment (Shotsberger & Vetter, 2001). This is a LAN application that employs a Web-based interface to provide immediate student feedback on a particular problem or situation posed by the teacher. Currently, handheld PC users are forced to choose between a LAN connection, using a nearby Internet connection point, and the kind of WAN application described in this article. To the extent that LAN function can be married with WAN usage, handheld PCs could soon begin to play a prominent role in classroom teaching and learning.

REFERENCES

Berger, C. (2001). Wireless: Changing teaching and learning "everywhere, everytime." *Educause Review, 36*(1), 58-59.

Cifuentes, L., Sivo, S., & Reynolds, T. (1997). Building partnerships between pre-service and in-service teachers: A project facilitated by interactive videoconferencing. *International Journal of Educational Telecommunications, 3*(1), 61-82.

Dillon, M. (2001). Enhancing learning with wireless networks. *Media and Methods, 37*(6), 31.

Goodlad, J.I. (1993). School-university partnerships and partner schools. *Education Policy, 7*(1), 24-39.

Nummi, T., Ristola, R., Ronka, A, & Sariola, J. (1999). Virtuality and digital nomadism in teacher education–The LIVE Project. In J.D. Price, J. Willis, D.A. Willis, M. Jost, & S. Boger-Mehall (Eds.), *Technology and teacher education annual, 1999* (pp. 1087-1092). Charlottesville, VA: Association for the Advancement of Computing in Education.

Shotsberger, P.G. (2001). Changing mathematics teaching through Web-based professional development. *Computers in the Schools, 17*(1/2), 31-39.

Shotsberger, P. G., & Vetter, R. (2001). Teaching and learning in the wireless classroom. *Computer, 34*(3), 110-111.

Wilkes, D. (2001). Wireless laptops in the classroom. *Media and Methods, 37*(4), 33.

APPENDIX 1. Initial Survey

Jornada Users Survey

Your name:

Today's date:

For the following questions, please choose or write the statement that best reflects your experience with the Jornada suite you were loaned at the beginning of the semester. The "Jornada suite" is defined to be the Jornada handheld PC, the Touchpoint 2100 mobile telephone, and the connector cable.

1. I am using some component(s) of the Jornada suite:

- ◌ frequently (more than twice a week)
- ◌ infrequently (once or twice a week)
- ◌ rarely (less than once a week)
- ◌ not at all

2. I tend to primarily use:

- ◌ the entire suite
- ◌ the Jornada handheld PC by itself
- ◌ the mobile telephone by itself
- ◌ no components of the suite

3. I tend to primarily use components of the suite:

- ◌ at school
- ◌ at home
- ◌ commuting/traveling
- ◌ not at all

4. My primary use for the Jornada handheld PC is for:

- ○ Internet access
- ○ editing documents (e.g., Word files)
- ○ writing/recording notes for myself
- ○ other. Please specify: [   ]
- ○ I am not using the Jornada

5. I am finding the ability to synchronize the Jornada handheld PC with my desktop PC to be:

- ○ very useful
- ○ useful
- ○ less than useful
- ○ ineffective
- ○ I have not used the synchronization feature

6. My impression of the Jornada suite to date is that it:

- ○ is easy to use
- ○ is some work, but worth it
- ○ is too much work for too little payoff
- ○ requires too much time to learn
- ○ is too much of a bother (either in terms of security or just being "one more thIng")

7. Probably the most disappointing thing about my experience with the Jornada suite so far has been:

- ○ the lack of phone coverage in certain places
- ○ the Jornada not operating properly/consistently
- ○ the inability to get online on a consistent basis
- ○ some software features (e.g., for editing documents) that my desktop PC has but which the Jornada lacks
- ○ I don't use any of the components

APPENDIX 1 (continued)

8. Though I haven't done it yet, I would like to work toward using the Jornada handheld PC for:

- ○ Internet access
- ○ editing documents (e.g., Word files)
- ○ presentations and/or demonstrations
- ○ other. Please specify: [   ]
- ○ I have no such plans

9. At this point I feel my greatest need related to the Jornada suite is for:

- ○ Dr. Shotsberger to work with me in person
- ○ Dr. Shotsberger to work with me over the phone
- ○ me to gain more experience with the suite working with my intern/partnership teacher
- ○ me to gain more experience with the suite on my own
- ○ me to be left alone

10. If you have used the Jornada suite during the past month, please write briefly about your best experience to date:

[text area]

11. If you have used the Jornada suite during the past month, please write briefly about your worst experience to date:

[text area]

[Submit] [Reset]

APPENDIX 2. Final Survey

Jornada Users Survey

Your name: [   ]

Today's date: [   ]

For the following questions, please choose or write the statement that best reflects your experience with the Jornada suite over the entire semester. The "Jornada suite" is defined to be the Jornada handheld PC, the Touchpoint 2100 mobile telephone, and the connector cable.

1. I have used some component(s) of the Jornada suite:

- ⚬ frequently (more than twice a week)
- ⚬ infrequently (once or twice a week)
- ⚬ rarely (less than once a week)
- ⚬ not at all

2. I tended to primarily use:

- ⚬ the entire suite
- ⚬ the Jornada handheld PC by itself
- ⚬ the mobile telephone by itself
- ⚬ no components of the suite

3. I tended to primarily use components of the suite:

- ⚬ at school
- ⚬ at home
- ⚬ commuting/traveling
- ⚬ not at all

APPENDIX 2 (continued)

4. My primary use for the Jornada handheld PC was for:

- ○ Internet access
- ○ editing documents (e.g., Word files)
- ○ writing/recording notes for myself
- ○ other. Please specify: |_____|
- ○ I did not use the Jornada

5. I found the ability to synchronize the Jornada handheld PC with my desktop PC to be:

- ○ very useful
- ○ useful
- ○ less than useful
- ○ ineffective
- ○ I did not use the synchronization feature

6. I found the color screen on the Jornada handheld PC (instead of black and white) to be:

- ○ very important
- ○ a nice feature
- ○ unimportant

7. My overall impression of the Jornada suite was that it:

- ○ was easy to use
- ○ was some work, but worth it
- ○ was too much work for too little payoff
- ○ required too much time to learn
- ○ was too much of a bother (either in terms of security or just being "one more thing")

8. Overall, I found the Jornada suite to be

- ○ more useful than I expected
- ○ about as useful as I expected
- ○ less useful than I expected
- ○ useless

9. When I have to return the Jornada suite, the thing I will miss most is:

- ○ wireless Web/e-mail access
- ○ using Office (Word, Excel, etc.) anywhere
- ○ the ability to make notes (handwritten, typed or audio) "on the fly"
- ○ the mobile phone
- ○ nothing

10. If you have used the Jornada suite during the semester, please write briefly about your best overall experience:

11. If you have used the Jornada suite during the semester, please write briefly about your worst overall experience:

12. Whether or not you used the Jornada during the semester, please provide a description of additional features (software or hardware) you think would make the Jornada more useful for supporting/providing classroom instruction:

13. Would you suggest interns and partnership teachers use the Jornada suite for practicum next year?

- ○ yes
- ○ yes, with modifications:
- ○ no

Submit | Reset

Doris L. Prater
Angus J. MacNeil

The Use of Collaborative Groups in Traditional and Online Courses

SUMMARY. This study investigates the relative merits of using learning groups in both traditional and online courses. Sixty-seven graduate students enrolled in a statistics and measurement course were taught by either an online or face-to-face delivery mode. Collaborative groups were used under both conditions. Responses to an attitude toward collaborative groups measure, performance on a comprehensive final examination, and journal comments were compared across groups. Results showed that both groups displayed an overall positive attitude toward the value of group work but their responses differed on two of the six questions. A significant difference in favor of the face-to-face groups was found when performance on the final examination was compared. Findings from this preliminary study appear to support the use of collaborative groups in both traditional and online courses if the groups have clear directions and if meaningful tasks are designed. *[Article copies available for a fee from The Haworth Document Delivery Service: 1-800-HAWORTH. E-mail address: <getinfo@haworthpressinc.com> Website: <http://www.HaworthPress.com> © 2002 by The Haworth Press, Inc. All rights reserved.]*

DORIS L. PRATER is Professor and Chair, Department of Educational Leadership and Cultural Studies, College of Education, University of Houston, 401 Farish Hall, Houston, TX 77204-5028 (E-mail: dprater@pioneer.coe.uh.edu).
ANGUS J. MACNEIL is Associate Professor, Department of Educational Leadership and Cultural Studies, College of Education, University of Houston, 401 Farish Hall, Houston, TX 77204-5028 (E-mail: amacneil@pioneer.coe.uh.edu).

[Haworth co-indexing entry note]: "The Use of Collaborative Groups in Traditional and Online Courses." Prater, Doris L., and Angus J. MacNeil. Co-published simultaneously in *Computers in the Schools* (The Haworth Press, Inc.) Vol. 19, No. 3/4, 2002, pp. 67-75; and: *Distance Education: Issues and Concerns* (ed: Cleborne D. Maddux, Jacque Ewing-Taylor, and D. LaMont Johnson) The Haworth Press, Inc., 2002, pp. 67-75. Single or multiple copies of this article are available for a fee from The Haworth Document Delivery Service [1-800-HAWORTH, 9:00 a.m. - 5:00 p.m. (EST). E-mail address: getinfo@haworthpressinc.com].

KEYWORDS. Collaborative groups, online instructions, student perceptions of collaborative groups, achievement in online courses, distance education

Distance education has become an attractive delivery system for courses in colleges and universities. It has been estimated that by the year 2007, almost 50% of the learners in post-secondary education will be taking part of their course work through some type of distance education delivery mode (Kascus, 1997). Today's students are active consumers, looking for flexible and cost-effective educational programs. They are comfortable with technology and expect online resources as part of their learning experience (Green, 1997). This new learning environment has institutions competing for a new, underserved population of learners.

In our haste to provide quality courses in this new, virtual environment, we must resist the temptation to simply dump traditional written material onto a Web site and let students figure things out for themselves. Clark and Sugrue (1988) suggest that media do not affect learning in and of themselves. Rather, some particular qualities of media may affect particular cognitive processes. Future research should aim at determining necessary conditions for learning. They contend that learning from well-prepared media presentations is due to three factors or types of variables: learning task type, individual learner traits, and instructional method.

In their review of research on instructional media, Clark and Salomon (1986) noted the paradigm shift from behavioral to cognitive theories and corresponding research questions in instructional media research. A cognitive theory of learning views learning as a constructive process, with the learner actively engaged in integrating new knowledge with old and in transferring knowledge and skills learned to a new situation. How can this be fostered in online courses? What particular activities foster this type of engagement by the learner?

One distinctive characteristic of distance is the clear separation of students in space and time from both teacher and fellow students. This separation can foster a sense of isolation in students. Current thinking in the field suggests that well-designed courses need to build in opportunities for students to actively engage with the text and to interact with other students and the instructor (Kiser, 1999). The use of collaborative groups is one mechanism frequently suggested for use in online instruction to build student-student interaction and reduce the sense of isolation (Palloff & Pratt, 1999). Well-designed group assignments also provide an opportunity for students to transfer knowledge and skills to a new situation.

This preliminary study was designed to examine the attitudes of online students toward the use of collaborative groups. To facilitate the active involvement of learners with content and provide an opportunity for transfer of knowledge to a new situation, collaborative groups were used for a major course assignment. It was believed that the group project would also promote interaction among students and reduce the sense of isolation. The group assignment required transferring knowledge and skills presented in the online units of study to a problem-based project. It was also felt that the project would provide practice for students in analyzing data. This practice should enhance performance on an end-of-course examination.

A seven-item questionnaire was designed to elicit students' attitude toward the effectiveness of collaborative groups in the course. In addition, performance on a final examination was compared. Students in a parallel section of the course taught in a traditional face-to-face lecture format by the same instructor were used as a comparison group. The following research questions were addressed:

1. Overall, did graduate-level students view learning groups as an effective instructional method? Did this vary across delivery modes?
2. Did participants feel that working in groups allowed them to develop a stronger product? Did this vary across delivery modes?
3. How did students view grading issues related to group work (individual versus group grades)? Did this vary across delivery modes?
4. Did students believe that time allocated for completion of the project was sufficient? Did this vary across delivery modes?
5. Did performance on an end-of-course examination vary across groups?
6. What overall suggestions and comments do students have regarding collaborative groups?

METHOD

Subjects

Subjects for the study were 67 college students enrolled in a three-hour master's level course in educational statistics and measurement. The course is a core course for all master's degrees and is one of two initial courses that students take in completing their degree. Thirty-eight of the subjects were enrolled in a traditional face-to-face section and twenty-nine were enrolled in the same course online. Subjects in both groups were assigned to collaborative work groups based on the subject and grade level in which they were presently teaching or aspired to teach.

Procedure

The online students were required to attend a three-hour orientation session in which the group project requirements were explained. They were provided one hour to become acquainted with their group and to discuss procedures for completing the task. Thereafter, they used chatrooms and e-mail to complete the assignment. Subjects in the traditional group were provided one hour of class time to become acquainted with their group and to plan the project. The remaining meetings were scheduled by the group outside of class.

The group project assigned was identical for both groups and counted for 30% of the class grade. The project was substantial and required the students to apply virtually all knowledge and skills that formed the course content. Specifically, the groups constructed a 20-item test, field-tested the instrument, conducted item analysis techniques on each item, established the reliability and validity of the instrument, and constructed a test manual that documented the process.

An attitude-toward-collaborative-groups measure was administered at the end of the course, and a face-to-face final examination was given to both groups. Group projects and relevant items on the final examinations were scored.

Data Sources

Student questionnaire. A seven-item measure was used to determine students' attitude toward collaborative groups. On six of the items, students responded on a five-point Likert-type scale. Subjects were asked to indicate the degree to which they agreed with statements related to the overall effectiveness of group projects as a means of instruction, the extent to which the final product was stronger because it was developed by the group, and the extent to which working in the group enhanced their learning. In addition, they were also asked two questions regarding their evaluation preference (group or individual grades) and whether or not group members should evaluate one another. They were also asked whether enough time was allowed for group work during the semester. The final question was open-ended and asked for comments on the collaborative group project.

Final examination. A final examination was given to both groups of subjects and consisted of multiple-choice items and computation of relevant formulas. Only items that reflected the concepts that students had applied in developing their collaborative project were used in the analysis. The range of scores on the final examination was 0 to 70 points.

RESULTS

Questionnaire Results

Six items from the attitude measure were compared across the two groups using separate *t*-tests for independent means. Significant differences across the groups were found on two of the six questions.

In response to the statement, *"All members of a group should receive the same grade,"* a significant difference was found, (t (65) = 2.84, $p <$ .01) was found. The online group means rating was 4.13 (slightly above "Agree") while the traditional group mean rating was 3.37, placing it at "Undecided."

Significant differences were also found in response to the statement, *"Sufficient time was allowed for the group project"* (t (65) = 2.32, $p <$ .02). The online group's mean rating of 3.89 was significantly lower than the mean rating of 4.34 for the traditional class. This was an interesting finding since no formal class time existed for the online group. The only restriction was that the project had to be completed during the course of the semester. No time constraints were put on the use of chatrooms and e-mail.

There were no significant differences across groups to the following statement, *"Group projects in EDUC 6032 are an effective means of instruction."* The online and traditional groups (t (65) = .04, $p >$ .05.) means were 4.137 and 4.132, respectively, placing the responses above "Agree."

In response to the statement, *"I developed a stronger final product by working with a group,"* no significant differences were found (t (65) = 1.05, $p >$ .05). Means were 4.17 and 3.92, respectively, for online and traditional groups, placing the responses slightly above and slightly below "Agree" on the scale.

There were no significant differences across groups for the statement, *"Having members rate each other's contribution is detrimental to the group's working relationship,"* (t (65) = .14, p > .05). Means of 3.06 and 3.02 for the online and traditional groups, respectively, placed the responses at "Undecided" on the scale.

Students in both groups agreed with the statement, *"I got to know my fellow classmates better because we worked in groups."* Means of 4.37 and 4.39 for the online and traditional groups, respectively, placed the responses between "Agree" and "Strongly Agree." These were the highest means (most positive) reported. No significant group differences were found (t (65) =. 10, p > .05).

The last item of the survey asked students to comment about the experience of working in groups. Comments from students in the online and face-to-face groups are shown in Appendix A. In general, these comments were positive for both groups of students. Numerous students in the online course mentioned predictable problems of sending documents to one another due to incompatibility of software and fear of viruses (in one instance an actual occurrence!). A number of students indicated that they felt that groups should be formed based on geographic proximity. And, several groups in the online class also indicated that they arranged to meet on several occasions face to face to complete the project. As courses extend beyond traditional geographic boundaries, however, this is not possible. Comments are provided in Appendix A.

Final Examination Data

Significant differences were found in favor of the face-to-face group on the final examination. The traditional lecture group outperformed the online group on the 70-item final examination (t (65) = 3.28, p < .01). The mean score for the traditional group was 62.64, while the online group mean was 57.21. The final examination required that students answer multiple-choice questions and calculate a variety of statistics involved in validation of a test. These included calculation of the measures of central tendency, measures of variability, item analysis, standard scores, percentiles, and correlation.

An inspection of the test items indicated that students across both groups had more difficulty with computation than with multiple-choice items; however, the face-to-face group did substantially better on the items. The traditional class setting may have provided more opportunity to practice calculation of formulas as they were introduced. Students in the online course, left on their own, may not have engaged as actively with the material. It is also possible that the division of tasks within the online group may have allowed students who most needed practice to yield to more mathematically adept students.

While the overall quality of the test manuals produced by the collaborative groups was not analyzed statistically, all were of high quality and earned group grades of A− or A. It appears that there were enough strong members within each of the groups to produce a strong product.

DISCUSSION

Information obtained from the attitude measure indicated an overall positive response to working in collaborative groups. Students felt that they produced a stronger product and got to know their classmates better by working in groups. The groups were split over whether students within a group should receive the same grade, with the online group disagreeing while the traditional class thought it was appropriate. This finding and comments within the journals provide some evidence that bonding was stronger in the traditional class where students see and interact firsthand with each other. Both groups were undecided if members should rate one another's work. Again, some journal comments indicated that students viewed this as divisive and worked against building group collegiality. Journal comments also indicated that the success of the group was dependent upon strong leadership emerging from the group, particularly for the online students. Interestingly, the online group felt that they did not have enough time to work on the project, although the semester was the same length for both groups.

While the overall quality of the projects did not vary across delivery mode, students in the face-to-face course performed better on the final examination, particularly when asked to perform calculations of statistical formulas. Since random assignment of subjects to conditions was not possible, initial differences may have existed across the groups; therefore, performance differences must be interpreted cautiously.

Overall, findings from this preliminary study appear to support the use of collaborative groups in both traditional and online courses if the groups have clear directions and if meaningful tasks are designed.

REFERENCES

Clark, R. E., & Salomon, G. (1986). Media in teaching. In M. Wittrock (Ed.), *Handbook of research on teaching* (3rd ed.). New York: Macmillan.

Clark, R. E., & Sugrue, B. M. Research on instructional media, 1978-1988. (1995). In G. J. Anglin (Ed.), *Instructional technology: Past, present and future* (2nd ed., pp. 348-364). Englewood, CO: Libraries Unlimited.

Green, K. C. (1997). Distance education. *AAHE Bulletin*, 5 (2) 3-6.

Kascus, M. (1997). Converging vision of library service for off-campus/distance education. *Journal of Library Services for Distance Education*, 1 (1). Available from the World Wide Web: http://www.westga.edu/library/jlsde/jlsdejlsdel.html

Kiser, K. (1999, November). Ten things we know so far about online training. *Training*, 66-74.

Palloff, R. M., & Pratt, K. (1999). *Building learning communities in cyberspace*. San Francisco: Jossey-Bass.

APPENDIX A

Comments from Online Class:

- It was difficult to come together as a group through a Web course. Sometimes systems weren't compatible so a great deal of work was done two or three times by different people.
- We were a virtual class so no class time was available.
- The group I was in was unusual. We all did pretty equal jobs; however, that is not always the case.
- I believe an announcement needs to be made that if anyone drops the course, they have to immediately notify the group.
- We had a great group. All my group experiences in online classes have been positive, but I can see where a bad experience could make you dislike group work.
- I thought online courses were hard on projects. Face- to-face contact was needed for this project due to the unreliability of electronic transferring of documents.
- I had a great group of people to work with. I learned a lot from them!
- Because we did not meet as a class, it was hard for people to get together online.
- Students should be grouped geographically.
- We should be allowed to do the project on our own.

Comments from Face-to-Face Class:

- I had a little difficulty getting the group to let me take some of the load. I realize this sounds very hard to believe, but it is true. Due to this, I believe everyone in the group should receive the same grade.
- We should get the same grade if we all contribute equally.
- It is difficult to assess peers when they all have their own priorities. In all groups, a few always carry the load and do most of the work.

- It is difficult to evaluate your peers because this can negatively affect a student's grade. Some people would rather work alone and this was an option.
- This course was a "piece de resistance."
- Allow smaller groups and independent choice of which group to be in. This may alleviate some tensions.
- I prefer to work alone on projects.
- My experience with group projects has not been positive in other classes, but I enjoyed this experience.
- I finally put it all together when we validated our test.
- It is not always possible to meet on campus. Place us with other students that live near us.
- I got to make new friends.

Gary T. Rosenthal
Barlow Soper
Richard R. McKnight
James E. Barr
Lamar V. Wilkinson
Walter C. Buboltz, Jr.
C. W. Von Bergen

Multimedia, It's How You Use It: Reflections on a Selected Computerized Teaching Technology

SUMMARY. The current study chronicles what one professor learned from teaching a distance education course with and without the aid of PowerPoint multimedia presentation software. It compares student ratings of three lectures from the same classes by the same professor; the

GARY T. ROSENTHAL is Professor of Psychology and Counselor Education, Nicholls State University, Box 2075 NSU, Thibodaux, LA 70310 (E-mail: psyc-gtr@nicholls.edu).
BARLOW SOPER is Professor of Psychology and Behavioral Sciences, Louisiana Tech University, Box 10048, Ruston, LA 71272 (E-mail: soper@latech.edu).
RICHARD R. MCKNIGHT is Professor of Psychology and Counselor Education, Nicholls State University, Box 2075 NSU, Thibodaux, LA 70310 (E-mail: psyc-rrm@nicholls.edu).
JAMES E. BARR is Distinguished Service Professor of Teacher Education, Nicholls State University, Box 2035 NSU, Thibodaux, LA 70310 (E-mail: te-jeb@nicholls.edu).
LAMAR V. WILKINSON is Associate Professor of Psychology and Behavioral Sciences, Louisiana Tech University, Box 10048, Ruston, LA 71272 (E-mail: lamar@latech.edu).
WALTER C. BUBOLTZ, JR. is Assistant Professor of Psychology and Behavioral Sciences, Louisiana Tech University, Box 10048, Ruston, LA 71272 (E-mail: buboltz@latech.edu).
C. W. VON BERGEN is Associate Professor of Management and Marketing, Southeastern Oklahoma State University, Box 4103, Durant, OK 74701 (E-mail: cvonbergen@sosu.edu).

[Haworth co-indexing entry note]: "Multimedia, It's How You Use It: Reflections on a Selected Computerized Teaching Technology." Rosenthal, Gary T. et al. Co-published simultaneously in *Computers in the Schools* (The Haworth Press, Inc.) Vol. 19, No. 3/4, 2002, pp. 77-86; and: *Distance Education: Issues and Concerns* (ed: Cleborne D. Maddux, Jacque Ewing-Taylor, and D. LaMont Johnson) The Haworth Press, Inc., 2002, pp. 77-86. Single or multiple copies of this article are available for a fee from The Haworth Document Delivery Service [1-800-HAWORTH, 9:00 a.m. - 5:00 p.m. (EST). E-mail address: getinfo@haworthpressinc.com].

first, a traditional lecture without any audiovisual aids; the second, a lecture supplemented by PowerPoint notes outlining the lecture; and finally, a multimedia lecture utilizing PowerPoint notes with pictures, music and animations. Students reacted no differently to any of the presentations when delivered by an experienced teacher. The students did, however, prefer PowerPoint multimedia to PowerPoint outline presentations. Suggestions for the optimal uses of presentation software are provided. *[Article copies available for a fee from The Haworth Document Delivery Service: 1-800-HAWORTH. E-mail address: <getinfo@haworthpressinc.com> Website: <http://www.HaworthPress.com> © 2002 by The Haworth Press, Inc. All rights reserved.]*

KEYWORDS. Teaching, distance education, computers, PowerPoint, presentation software, multimedia

Educators are being urged to integrate computer technologies into their teaching to make it "more efficient" and "more fun." Lectures are supposed to give way to "multimedia presentations," and professors are being urged not to be left out of the revolution in teaching technology. Reinhardt (1995), for example, claimed that "explosive growth in . . . multimedia, and collaborative software environments is fueling a new wave of better teaching tools. This generation of technology promises more than an improvement in educational productivity: It may deliver a qualitative change in the nature of learning itself" (p. 50). Gatlin-Watts, Arn, and Kordsmeier (1999) wrote: "[I]nstructional delivery systems using multimedia can be the exponential tool that will transform education in the same manner the tractor transformed agriculture and the airplane transformed transportation" (p. 190).

In his book *High Tech Heretic* computer expert Clifford Stoll (1999) voiced a dissenting opinion. He noted that putting a computer into the hands of every student was not the panacea that many teachers hoped. Stoll stated that, contrary to manufacturers' claims, having a particular computer or software program did *not* necessarily make learning "more efficient" or "more fun"; and, despite computers being hyped by business and governmental agencies, not all classroom problems could be solved by a computer.

How helpful the computer will be to education is yet to be determined. However, it is unlikely to be any more of a quick fix or panacea than the miracle tools or "magic bullets" of the past (Stanovich, 1998).

The present study is an attempt to determine initial student impressions of one computerized multimedia teaching technology–that is, Microsoft's PowerPoint presentation software. PowerPoint is frequently used in local and distance education settings. Three types of presentations were compared within the same courses presented by the same professor. The first, a traditional lesson in lecture format (lecture lesson) without any audiovisual aids; the second, a different lesson with a series of PowerPoint slides outlining the main ideas (PowerPoint notes lesson); and finally, a lesson utilizing a PowerPoint multimedia outline, including pictures, music, and animations (multimedia lesson).

Following the presentations, students in the two psychology classes completed an After-Class Rating Sheet (ACRS), evaluating each type of lesson. The primary hypothesis was that the three types of lessons would be rated differently by the students in terms of instructor quality, presentation, and student involvement/understanding. A second hypothesis was that the two types of PowerPoint lessons (PowerPoint notes and multimedia) would be rated differently on ACRS questions specific to those presentations.

METHOD

Participants

Participants were students in either a developmental or a social psychology class at a small rural southern university. Both classes were sophomore level. As part of the ACRS survey, students were asked to generate their own "identifier," a word to enable matching their responses during statistical analysis. Based upon the number of unique identifiers, all 75 students (74 undergraduate and 1 graduate) originally registered for the classes rated at least one of the lessons, and 50 students completed rating sheets for all three types of lessons. Of the original enrollment, 63 were females and 12 were males. Since there was a preponderance of females, gender differences were not explored. A total of 72 students received a grade at the end of the semester.

All 75 participants were volunteers. The most common classification (31 students or 41%) was sophomore. Most of the students (34 or 45%) were nursing majors. Only 6 students (8%) were psychology majors.

Materials

After-Class Rating Sheet (ACRS). The ACRS consists of 14 Likert-type items and two open-ended questions about the lesson. The ACRS is provided as Appendix A. The Likert-type items are based on the university's end-of-the-semester student evaluation of instruction. All Likert-type items are scaled ranging from 1 (*strongly disagree*) to 7 (*strongly agree*), except for item 7. The scale for item 7 was 1 (*strongly negative*) to 7 (*strongly positive*).

The 14 scalar items fall into four categories. The first consists of "instructor items" such as "The instructor was well prepared for this lecture." The second category is comprised of "presentation items" such as "The presentation of today's material was clear." The third category is "multimedia items" such as "The multimedia materials (materials presented on television via LCD projector) contributed to your interest in this class." If PowerPoint was not used, students were instructed to leave these items blank. Finally, the fourth category contained "self-items" focused on the students' reactions (e.g., "I felt that I was involved in today's class").

The ACRS concludes with two open-ended items: The first is "The thing that I liked most about today's class was:"; the second item, "The thing that I liked the least about today's class was:"

Procedure

The ACRS was administered during the last five minutes of each 50-minute class period immediately following the lesson. To avoid contaminating the ratings, the instructor stressed that ratings would remain anonymous and have no effect on students' grades. Students were encouraged to take as much time as necessary and to be truthful. Participation did not garner extra credit.

The four instructor items were summed to yield an "Instructor Total Score" (ITS) for each respondent. A similar procedure was used to calculate a "Presentation Total Score" (PTS) based upon ACRS's five presentation items and a "Self Total Score" (STS) based upon the three self-items.

The ACRS contained two multimedia items. The first was "The multimedia materials contributed to your interest in today's class" (MMIN). The second was "The multimedia materials made the presentation more clear" (MMCL). These items were analyzed separately from each other.

Analyses

A ceiling-effect was apparent in all ACRS items (and derived scores); the distributions were negatively skewed. Therefore, analyses consisted of a series of nonparametric tests. Since each respondent could generate an ITS, a PTS, and an STS for all types of lessons (lecture, PowerPoint notes, and multimedia), a Friedman test for repeated measures was performed with these scores. Given the preliminary nature of the study, an alpha level of .05 was the significance criterion for each test.

Since respondents generated only two measures of multimedia effectiveness (MMIN for interest and MMCL for clarity), a Wilcoxon matched-pairs signed-ranks test was deemed appropriate.

RESULTS

Table 1 presents the medians, semi-interquartile ranges, and n's for the 14 scalar items on the After-Class Rating Sheet (ACRS) for each of the three types of lessons. Some individuals did not complete an ACRS for all three types of presentations; therefore, only 61 of the sheets rated the lecture, while 64 rated the PowerPoint notes lesson, and 64 rated the multimedia lesson. The medians, semi-interquartile ranges, n's, and statistical analyses for the Instructor Total Score (ITS), Presentation Total Score (PTS), and Self Total Score (STS) are presented in order, followed by the multimedia items. The open-ended items will be discussed at the conclusion of this section.

Instructor Total Score. The ITS compares students' ratings of instructor preparedness, concern, attentiveness, and enthusiasm during the lecture, PowerPoint notes, and multimedia lessons. The medians and semi-interquartile ranges were as follows: for the lecture, $MD = 28.00$, semi-interquartile range was 1.5; for the PowerPoint notes lesson, $MD = 28.00$, the semi-interquartile range was 1.5; for the multimedia lesson, $MD = 28.00$, the semi-interquartile range was 1.0. The Friedman test statistic (corrected for ties) of $\chi^2 (2, n = 50) = .540, p > .05$ was not significant. Students' ratings of the instructor did not vary significantly over the three lesson formats.

Presentation Total Score. The PTS compares students' ratings of presentation clarity, ability to hold their interest, overall quality, clarity of objective, and speed of presentation during the lecture, PowerPoint notes, and multimedia lessons. The medians and semi-interquartile ranges were as follows: for the lecture, $MD = 33.00$, semi-interquartile range was 2.5; for the PowerPoint notes lesson, $MD = 34.00$, semi-interquartile range was 2.5; for the multimedia lesson, $MD = 33.50$, semi-interquartile range was 1.5. The Friedman test statistic

TABLE 1. Medians (Mdn), Semi-Interquartile Ranges (SiR) and N's of Items on the After-Class Rating Sheet

	Item	Lecture		PowerPoint Notes		Multimedia	
		Mdn	SiR	Mdn	SiR	Mdn	SiR
1.	Instructor is well prepared.	7	0.13	7	0.50	7	0.00
2.	Presentation clear.	7	0.50	7	0.50	7	0.50
3.	Presentation interesting.	6.5	0.50	7	0.62	7	0.50
4.	Multimedia made interesting.	*	*	7[a]	1.00	7	0.00
5.	Multimedia made clear.	*	*	7	0.75	7	0.25
6.	Instructor concerned.	7	0.50	7	0.50	7	0.00
7.	Rating of the presentation.	7	0.50	7	0.50	7	0.00
8.	Objective presented.	7	0.50	7	0.50	7	0.50
9.	Instructor attentive.	7	0.50	7	0.13	7	0.50
10.	Presentation rate.	7	0.50	7	0.00	7	0.50
11.	Instructor enthusiastic.	7	0.13	7	0.50	7	0.00
12.	I understood.	7	0.00	7	0.13	7	0.50
13.	I was involved.	6	1.00	6	1.00	6	1.00
14.	I was interested.	7	0.50	7	0.50	7	0.50

Note: [a] Statistics for items 4 and 5 are based on $N = 49$, as 49 participants completed the ACRS for PowerPoint notes and multimedia. All other statistics are based on $N = 50$, as 50 participants completed the ACRS on all three occasions.

(corrected for ties) for this variable, $\chi^2 (2, n = 50) = 3.288, p > .05$, was not significant.

Self Total Score. The STS compares students' ratings of their understanding, involvement, and interest during the lecture, PowerPoint notes, and multimedia lessons. The medians and semi-interquartile ranges were as follows: for the lecture, $MD = 19.00$, semi-interquartile range was 1.5; for the Power Point notes lesson, $MD = 19.00$, semi-interquartile range was 2.0; for the multimedia lesson, $MD = 19.50$, semi-interquartile range was 1.5. The Friedman test statistic (corrected for ties) of $\chi^2 (2, n = 50) = .623, p > .05$ was not significant.

Multimedia Interest and Clarity. The MMIN and MMCL measures examined whether students found the PowerPoint notes lesson more interesting (MMIN) or clearer (MMCL) than the multimedia lesson, or vice versa. Medians and semi-interquartile ranges for the MMIN variable were as follows: for the PowerPoint notes lesson, $MD = 7.00$, semi-interquartile range was 1.0; for the multimedia lesson, $MD = 7.00$, semi-interquartile range was 0.0. The Wilcoxon matched-pairs signed-ranks test statistic (corrected for ties) of the interest variable was $Z = -3.19$, $p < .001$, n = 49. Results indicated that students felt the multimedia lesson held their interest better than the PowerPoint notes lesson.

The medians and semi-interquartile ranges for the MMCL variable were as follows: for the PowerPoint notes lesson, $MD = 7.00$, semi-interquartile range was 0.75; for the multimedia lesson, $MD = 7.00$, semi-interquartile range was 0.25. A Wilcoxon of the MMCL variable (corrected for ties) indicated that students also felt that the multimedia lesson was significantly clearer than the PowerPoint notes effort ($Z = -3.19$, $p < .001$, n = 49).

The Open-Ended Items. The final two items of the ACRS were the open-ended questions, "What did you like most. . . ." and "What did you like least. . . ." Of the 189 ACRS scales completed, 131 forms had a "liked most" comment, a "liked least" comment, or both. A total of 43 students had positive comments concerning the lecture; 29 had positive comments concerning the PowerPoint notes class; and finally, 59 students commented positively about the multimedia class. On the liked least item, 5 students commented negatively on the lecture; no negative comments followed the PowerPoint notes class; and 9 students commented negatively on the multimedia class.

A positive theme that reoccurred through different lesson types concerned the use of humor, good examples, and doing something different in class (e.g., a demonstration, audience participation, singing). Negative reoccurring themes included the necessity for taking notes, getting off topic, and pacing (not enough or too much material covered). Most comments concerning integrating PowerPoint into lessons were positive, although some students disliked using PowerPoint.

DISCUSSION

With respect to the primary hypothesis, there was no evidence that students react more or less favorably to traditional lectures versus lessons with PowerPoint outlines or lessons with PowerPoint and multimedia when delivered by an experienced teacher. This is true regarding student ratings of the presentation, the instructor, and students' own reactions. The data are congruent with Lookatch's (1995) conclusions that "research to date has never verified that using a computer or any other technology improves learning" (p. 4). With respect to the second hypothesis, the data provided clear evidence that these students thought that PowerPoint multimedia presentations were more interesting and clear than those that merely outlined what was being said.

What may be concluded about multimedia presentations? To paraphrase the English actor Edmund Gwenn, "Dying is easy . . . multimedia is hard." Creating and integrating even simple slide outlines into class presentations is a time-consuming, labor-intensive task. Much more so when one adds multimedia components (e.g., a 15-second animation may take hours to prepare).

There is substantial pressure to "get with the program" and integrate multimedia into the classroom, as if doing so will cure academic ills. While innovation is often laudable, "innovation for innovation's sake" is dubious. There is no clear evidence that multimedia can make a bad teacher good, or even a good teacher better. It may be argued that a novice teacher might be better served by innovating and developing a personal presentation style and skills before making the considerably sizable leap to multimedia. There are certain principles of sound pedagogy that transcend the media. To misquote McLuhan, "The media *is not* the message," but rather a "conduit" for the message (McLuhan & Fiore, 1967, title page).

While "the sound and the fury" of multimedia are flashy, the teacher should adopt a healthy skepticism about them. We are reminded of the unfulfilled promise of previous technologies (e.g., educational television and programmed instruction) that were also supposed to cure all of our teaching woes; we are still waiting.

Given that multimedia will continue to be incorporated into education, the following provide suggestions for its effective use.

1. Utilize sounds and graphics with a multimedia presentation; that's what makes it *multi*media. Data from our second hypothesis confirm this. The most common mistake in using presentation software like PowerPoint is under- or non-utilization of the programs' sound, graphics, and animation capabilities, resulting in a series of slides that are no different than an automated series of overhead transparencies and often less legible. Is a limited presentation convenient? Sometimes; but it is far from making full use of even the simplest multimedia software.

2. Do not become so focused on the multimedia program or hardware that one disconnects from students. Instructors can use their notes as a buffer between themselves and students; wonder of technological wonders, some can now fiddle with PowerPoint to pretend students are not really there! When teachers fail to no-

tice that their students are getting lost, bored, frustrated, or downright angry because the teacher is focusing the LCD display, fumbling with hardware, or looking for the missing slide, very little positive occurs.

3. Remember, multimedia is a tool–and sometimes tools fail to work. Plan for disaster, and have a ready backup. A good teacher can teach by candlelight if necessary. Lessons should not stop because of a computer glitch. It may be suggested that teachers adopt a policy whereby if the hardware/software cannot be made to work in the first five minutes of class, start teaching–by "candlelight" if necessary. *But start teaching!* Interminable delays occasioned by technological poltergeists are inexcusable; and, worse, once some classes are lost, it can be very difficult to bring them back on track.

4. Do not become so enamored by a multimedia program that it becomes an "end-in-and-of-itself." What's wrong with the following dialog? Professor to a colleague, "Wow. I've a great set of slides and animations on spurious correlation." Colleague to professor, "Great! Are your students understanding it better?" Professor to colleague, "I don't know, but the slides are sure neat!"

CONCLUSION

When all the hype has abated multimedia will occupy a proper place in the classroom, be it locally or at a distance, not as the savior of modern education, nor as a pariah, but as one of many tools that good teachers use as appropriate. Integrate such technology wisely. Teachers need to ask whether each picture, sound, or video clip furthers student learning or is extraneous fluff. We remind our colleagues and ourselves that an unorganized, boring lesson with animated multimedia is still an unorganized, boring lesson.

REFERENCES

Gatlin-Watts, R., Arn, J.V., & Kordsmeier, W.F. (1999). Multimedia as an instructional tool: Perceptions of college department chairs. *Education, 120*(1), 190-196.
Lookatch, R.P. (1995, November). Technology for teaching? The research is flawed. *The Education Digest, 61*, 4-8.

McLuhan, M., & Fiore, Q. (1967). *The medium is the message: An inventory of effects.* New York: Bantam.

Reinhardt, A. (1995, March). New ways to learn. *Byte, 20,* 50-72.

Stanovich, K.E. (1998). *How to think straight about psychology* (5th ed.). New York: Longman.

Stoll, C. (1999). *High tech heretic: Why computers don't belong in the classroom and other reflections of a computer contrarian.* New York: Doubleday.

APPENDIX A

Lecture Evaluation
Please Print your Identifier: Today's Date:

1. The instructor was well prepared for this lecture.[1]
2. The presentation of today's material was clear.
3. The presentation contributed to your interest in today's class.
4. The multimedia materials (materials presented on television) contributed to your interest in today's class. (If no multimedia was used please darken this circle.)
5. The multimedia materials (materials presented on television) made the presentation more clear. (If no multimedia was used, please darken this circle.)
6. The instructor was concerned that students learn today's material.
7. Overall rating of the presentation for today's class.[2]
8. The objective of today's lecture was clearly presented.
9. During today's presentation the instructor was attentive to students and their needs.
10. The presentation was at a reasonable rate.
11. The instructor displayed enthusiasm about today's material.
12. I understood the material in today's class.
13. I felt that I was involved in today's class.
14. I felt that I was interested in today's class.
15. The thing that I liked the most about today's class was:
16. The thing that I liked the least about today's class was:

[1] The scale for all items (except item 7) was 1 = Strongly Disagree to 7 = Strongly Agree.
[2] The scale for this item was 1 = Strongly Negative to 7 = Strongly Positive.

GENERAL ARTICLES

Amy S. C. Leh
Andrianna Jobin

Striving for Quality Control
in Distance Education

SUMMARY. From 1995 to 1998, the use of Internet-based courses grew from 22% of institutions to 60%. It is estimated that by the year 2006 enrollment in distance education learning programs will increase by 1.5 million students. In light of this rapid growth, many educators wonder whether the learning in these new courses is of the same value as in traditional courses. The authors of this article share their thoughts on this topic by first talking about distance education and online instruction, including its benefits and drawbacks, and then discussing the quality of product, learning, and technology. Lastly, they illustrate how to control the quality of online instruction. *[Article copies available for a fee from The Haworth Document Delivery Service: 1-800-HAWORTH. E-mail address: <getinfo@haworthpressinc.com> Website: <http://www.HaworthPress.com> © 2002 by The Haworth Press, Inc. All rights reserved.]*

AMY S. C. LEH is Associate Professor, Instructional Technology, College of Education, California State University, 5500 University Parkway, UH 40137, San Bernardino, CA 92407 (E-mail: aleh@csusb.edu).
ANDRIANNA JOBIN is a masters student, Instructional Technology, California State University, 5500 University Parkway, UH 40137, San Bernardino, CA 92407 (E-mail: andriachan@cs.com).

[Haworth co-indexing entry note]: "Striving for Quality Control in Distance Education." Leh, Amy S. C., and Andrianna Jobin. Co-published simultaneously in *Computers in the Schools* (The Haworth Press, Inc.) Vol. 19, No. 3/4, 2002, pp. 87-102; and: *Distance Education: Issues and Concerns* (ed: Cleborne D. Maddux, Jacque Ewing-Taylor, and D. LaMont Johnson) The Haworth Press, Inc., 2002, pp. 87-102. Single or multiple copies of this article are available for a fee from The Haworth Document Delivery Service [1-800-HAWORTH, 9:00 a.m. - 5:00 p.m. (EST). E-mail address: getinfo@haworthpressinc.com].

KEYWORDS. Distance education, quality control, online learning, Web-based, hybrid courses, supplemental learning, online instruction, instructional methods, educational technology

Technology is drastically transforming education, especially distance learning in higher education. "In just three years–from 1995 to 1998–the use of Internet-based courses grew from 22[%] of institutions to 60[%] . . . more than 1.6 million students were enrolled in distance education courses in 1997-98" (American Federation of Teachers [AFT], 2001, Introduction section, para. 2). It is estimated that in 2002 about 85% of two- and four-year colleges would offer distance education programs and that by the year 2006 enrollment in distance education learning programs would increase by 1.5 million students (Lane, 2001). These numbers clearly reveal an educational paradigm shift.

During the past few years, terms such as online courses, completely online courses, Web-based courses, Web supplement courses, Web enhancement courses, and hybrid courses have frequently appeared in professional literature and discourse. The number of presentations concerning Web-based courses in conventions sponsored by professional associations has also been dramatically increasing. Questions such as "How many online (Web-based) courses does your program offer?" or "How often do I have to come to campus for my coursework?" have been asked much more frequently than ever before, and answers to such questions have become factors for learners in selecting their institutions and for institutions in attracting their students.

Educators have varied opinions toward these changes. Some educators highly regard such courses because they think the courses offer opportunities to people who otherwise could not receive education. Some view them as an alternative that provides learners with more options for learning. Some even expect virtual classrooms to be the future of education. Meanwhile, other professionals doubt the value of such education and strongly question its quality. In the midst of these changes, we should ask ourselves, What is the mission of education and how can we serve a greater number of learners in a variety of ways without lowering the quality of education? As educators, have we taken advantage of current advanced technology or have we been driven by technology rather than our educational missions?

In this article, we first discuss distance education and online instruction, including its benefits and drawbacks. We then discuss quality of distance learning, within the rubrics of quality of product, learning, and technology. Lastly, we illustrate how quality of distance education can be controlled. It is our hope that this article will stimulate educators to reconsider the effective practices within distance education.

DISTANCE EDUCATION AND ONLINE INSTRUCTION

Distance education is not new. During the 70s, Moore (1972) defined it as "the family of instructional methods in which the teaching behaviors are executed apart from the learning behaviors . . . so that communication between the learner and the teacher must be facilitated by print, electronic, mechanical or other devices" (p. 76). In general, distance education refers to instruction that takes place when a teacher and student(s) are separated by physical distance, and technology such as voice, video, data, and print is used to bridge the instructional gap. Although the concept of distance education remains the same, technology developed during the past few years makes distance education delivery appear very different. At present, online or Web-based instruction plays an important role in distance education.

Benefits

Why does online instruction attract many learners? Online instruction provides learners with appealing benefits. One such benefit is convenience. Students can study at a flexible time (time-shifted communication) and from different places (place-shifted communication). Sometimes, start and finish dates can be flexible. Other conveniences are the abilities to get more help outside of class hours, organize projects, search for specific information, and access the course outside of class. Distance learners also may be freer to learn actively, work at their own pace, and review materials more frequently. Sherry and Morse (1995) note that there are numerous advantages for using telecommunications in education: It promotes collaboration and cooperative learning, improves communication skills, enhances multicultural education, increases motivation, saves trees, increases access to experts, eliminates phone tag, provides current information, reduces isolation, increases self-esteem, supplies faster communication, and aids in administrative tasks.

Drawbacks

Along with the benefits of online instruction, there are some drawbacks. Significant challenges for both students and faculty stem from reduced class interaction and lack of nonverbal clues. In addition to this, faculty face the predicament of distance assessment and the time and learning involved in adapting materials to the media. Due to these limitations, program administrators are confronted with additional training needs and a high dropout rate.

First, it is difficult to assess students at a distance. Distance education is better suited for some subjects than others because it is easier to assess the success of instruction in those subjects. Distance education is valuable for competency-based subjects such as languages and job skills for which the motivation to learn is intrinsic and improvement can be easily tested. However, it is difficult to assess the quality of learning at a distance in intellectual disciplines such as psychology. How can an instructor know whether students got the idea or are intellectually stimulated?

In addition, a persistent problem of distance education assessment is how to ensure that candidates are in fact the authors of their work. New concerns such as virtual impersonation exacerbate existing ones such as cheating and plagiarism. This does not concern some instructors who feel that students are ultimately responsible for their own learning. Nevertheless, this does not absolve the instructor of responsibility for ensuring the quality of credits and grades. Features such as logins, timers, question randomizers, and blocking multitasking are effective only in a supervised lab environment.

Second, the lack of nonverbal communication is a disadvantage to students who are not linguistically oriented, especially in courses relying heavily on discussion boards and assigned reading. Unfortunately, many distance education courses are text-based and do not fully use the potential of multimedia to enhance learning. Rosenberg (2001) notes that instructors often cannot or do not use simulation techniques, such as experiments, role-plays, and guided practice. Many of them still use formats such as the lecture model that are less effective at a distance (Gold, 2001, Quality, para. 1). Moreover, the lack of communicative social cues such as facial expressions and gestures may cause misunderstanding, frustration, or even communication breakdown.

Third, the most criticized drawback of distance education is its impersonality and limitations for learning. A recent survey by vault.com found "37[%] of HR [Human Resources] officials reluctant to accept online graduate degrees" (Elearning, 2001, para. 16). Many prestigious universities are reluctant to offer distance degrees out of fear that they will devalue their traditional degrees. Professionals think that distance education is too limited to facilitate learning and note, "You can do business skills training online but you cannot really engage learners" (Cambridge e-MBA, 2001, para. 3).

Some programs have taken an all-or-nothing approach to going online. Gradually, educators are looking for middle ground. For instance, for nearly 800 years Cambridge has maintained a rule requiring all students to reside in the town of Cambridge, England (Cambridge e-MBA, 2001). Last year the university ended this 800-year-old tradition to begin the university's first Internet-enabled program, a global MBA. Although the rule was revoked, Cambridge still hesitates to offer a purely online program. They therefore require a residency of two to four weeks preceding each four-month learning module:

> The idea is to offer the same MBA, with the same admissions criteria and the same learning outcomes as on campus but to deliver some of it online. Sixty-five percent of the program will still take place face-to-face. . . . You can do business skills training online but you cannot really engage learners. You can't get the spirit going without residential periods. (Cambridge e-MBA, 2001, para. 1-3)

Cambridge is not alone; the American Federation of Teachers (2001) reported that one-third of courses include a requirement to come to the campus or meet with the instructor at least once.

Fourth, the time and training involved in adapting materials to the media are demanding. Distance delivery of multimedia content enables teachers to reinforce their messages in different ways and appeal to different learning styles. This great potential is contingent on the instructors' abilities to add multimedia or to access multimedia specialists. Although the performance of faculty is the overwhelming arbiter of distance education quality (Husmann & Miller, 2001, Discussion section, para. 3), little attention is paid to faculty training and satisfaction. Care and Scanlan (2001) introduce findings that underprepared instructors bear the burden of providing quality in distance courses:

> All faculty participants agreed that designing distance courses was time consuming and impacted upon their ability to fulfill other scholarly responsibilities. . . . Most faculty reported that designing courses for distance delivery was carried out in addition to their

regular teaching assignments. A related issue which affected faculty receptiveness to take on course conversion to distance delivery was the belief that this activity was not fully recognized or seen as a priority for promotion and tenure purposes. (Findings section, para. 2)

In a multidisciplinary survey (AFT, 2001), faculty members concurred that they spend more time preparing courses, communicating with students, and grading assignments. "Faculty members teaching Web-based courses, for example, must prepare, in advance, highly structured written materials and graphics covering every detail of the course. Some estimates range anywhere from 66% to 500% longer" (The Standards section, item 2). How can we expect faculty members to deliver such courses of quality if they are not well trained and rewarded for their efforts and innovations?

These drawbacks inherent in current distance education courses contribute to a high dropout rate–estimated at 32% by the Institute for Higher Education Policy (IHEP, 1999). Comparing this to the 4% dropout rate for traditional courses, the IHEP dismissed the optimism about distance education as based blindly on a lack of large-scale or scientific research. Given the statistics, they concluded distance education is currently unsuitable for many students.

Nonetheless, the alarming dropout rate does not negate the many advantages of distance education and the opportunities it creates for many students who would not otherwise have access to or be able to attend a traditional class. Nor does the dropout rate reflect student performance. In a survey of 200 teachers practicing distance education in higher education, "respondents rated the performance of distance education students about the same (54%) or better (27%) than their classroom-based students. At the same time, a substantial proportion (over 42%) reported higher dropout rates in their distance education courses" (AFT, 2001, The Standards section, item 4).

The IHEP report admitted that reasons for the dropout rate were not evident, despite the high numbers. In exploring these reasons, distance education programs can improve their quality through restructuring and advances in telecommunications. Respondents to the AFT study were also asked to speculate on reasons, causes, or solution for the higher dropout rate. The responses recommended "self-paced courses" and flexible deadlines, a "mechanism to promote regular work and interaction," clear expectations and expected competencies published in a syllabus before the class, online community building, and reviews sheets for evaluating one's peers and oneself. Many also discussed the attributes of successful distance learners, including self-motivation, the ability to work independently, technical competency, and readiness for academic coursework (AFT, 2001, Appendix section, item 7B). It seems that institutions that attend to the problem can improve their dropout rate. For example, UCLA now "boasts an online-course-completion rate of 87[%]" for the 1,300 students who take online courses each semester, up from a 50% dropout rate at inception several years ago (Carr, 2000, para. 16).

QUALITY CONTROL

Distance education carries benefits and drawbacks, just as traditional instruction does. Nevertheless, professionals, especially educators in higher education, are much more concerned about quality of the former than the latter. Why?

The main reason is the inferiority of distant communication as compared to face-to-face communication. In a traditional classroom, instructors and students can afford to take a more individual approach to quality; instructors can see when students are struggling, exchange non-verbal feedback, and have more latitude for improvisation. As to assessment, instructors can always ensure that students perform tasks by themselves. Although in a traditional classroom a student might turn in a paper or project conducted by others, oral presentations, defenses, etc., can help to reveal student abilities instantly. In contrast, such communication is limited in the distance-learning environment.

The second reason that educators are more concerned about the quality of distance education is that distance learners have additional characteristics and needs from traditional learners. Compared with the students in traditional classrooms, distance education students tend to be older, have more professional experience, and often have families and careers to juggle. Many of them are not merely interested in obtaining a degree, but in gaining the competence and knowledge necessary to rise within their professions. Therefore, instructors need to monitor quality from not only an academic standpoint, but also a professional one. Because the learners have many responsibilities–careers, families, and studying–their academic performance sometimes might be influenced by those obligations. Instructors need to maintain high standards while being understanding about student challenges.

The third reason is that distance education has something to prove–its effectiveness. Higher education needs to prove that course credits obtained at a distance are as valuable as the ones obtained in traditional formats. Degree-granting institutions must be especially sensitive to the need for consistent quality because learners will not purchase an education that they do not perceive to be legitimate. A major factor in recruiting students is accreditation. Charlotte Thomas, editor for *Peterson's*, (as quoted in Kathawala & Abdou, 2001) said, "Accreditation is the number 1 verification of the quality of a higher-education distance education provider" (para. 3).

Quality control concerns institutions of higher education: quality of educational product, quality of learning, and quality of technology. The quality of the educational product is an objective matter that can be standardized and put into numbers, and the quality of learning is dependent upon learners' involvement. Both rest on the foundation of technology in distance education.

Quality of Product

Objective measures of quality are important in the accreditation process, which requires standards for credits and grades. Two main indicators are academic standards and faculty qualifications. As mentioned earlier, many distance education learners are reentry and working students. They tend to be less interested in theory than practical skills, but opt for degrees that carry good reputations. In choosing a program, they look for academic reputation; but, in their courses, they look for practicality. By catering to less academic motives, could institutions maintain their academic standards? Do or would some of them lower their standards? Additionally, would the qualifications of instructors in distance education change? In some fields, academically qualified faculty members avoid teaching via distance. Would more technologically proficient but less academically qualified instructors be hired to teach distance education? Would more professionally qualified instructors (practitioners) be hired instead of academically qualified ones? How would these issues influence the quality of education?

Quality of Learning

The quest to measure product quality leads to an overemphasis on instructional materials. Sound pedagogy may transform quality materials to quality learning. Do we have sound pedagogy for distance education?

Berge and Collins (1995) note that new media enable but do not supply new models of education; the overriding question is not controlling the technology or the performance, but the "perennial problem . . . of instructional content and design" (p. 4).

There are three distinct aspects of instructional design: the formats available, the messengers, and the pedagogical approach. Formats are lectures, text documents, slide shows, graphics, and charts. The messenger, or the medium of delivery, can be a person, book, radio, TV, computer, personal digital assistant (PDA), etc. The media in distance education have rapidly advanced during the past years; however, our pedagogies do not seem to catch up with the technological innovations. Heretofore, distance education curricula have been driven more by the technology than by pedagogy; that is, educators have focused more on the educational materials and formats made possible by the technology than on student learning. Let us look at student self-direction in distance education models.

The earliest model, the correspondence model, used mailed documents and radio. This model was famously limited in interaction and student choice of direction. Given the huge time delay in two-way communication, it was not feasible to communicate sufficiently to have a give-and-take relationship between student and teacher. Yet, even after TV and audio/video conferencing made two-way communication possible, neither of the ensuing models involved many student choices. The multimedia approach primarily exploited the audiovisual features of multimedia for enriching course content. Although the student chose the time, place, and pace, uniform material was chosen by the teacher and administration. The most promising approach, telelearning, used the conferencing features to expand opportunities for communication, but it generally simulated a teacher-directed classroom rather than encouraging student independence and autonomy (Berge & Collins, 1995). Unilateral models hinder students from taking initiative in their learning. A pedagogy that involves the participation of students will improve the quality of learning and the quality of feedback to course designers.

Quality of Technology

Technology affects quality in four main areas: hardware, software, Internet access, and training. Some distance programs expect students to provide their own equipment, and course designers consider students' equipment, especially unsophisticated equipment, when they develop distance education courses. This consideration could consequently limit a course in taking advantage of telecommunications. Some programs fail to set realistic minimums for required technologies. This could make a frustrating experience for the learner accessing a course designed for better technology. Moreover, both students and faculty are not adequately prepared for effectively using distance technologies. It is frustrating to a learner to be figuring out the course management software and other software instead of learning the material at hand. The lack of technical support for home-based users only compounds that frustration.

How to Control Quality?

There are four main areas in which to control quality: prerequisites, instructional design, support systems, and program design.

Prerequisites

Before courses begin, students should be required to meet minimum technology requirements and complete training. This includes entry requirements for technical competency and training for distance-specific technologies. Entry requirements should include not only technical abilities, but also computer system requirements. Realistic minimums need to be set for hardware and Internet bandwidth. Equipment recommendations–such as specific models of sound cards, PC cameras, etc.–will facilitate troubleshooting and training. Choosing specific software programs will help instructors provide software-specific directions. Money not spent on standardizing computers or preparing users translates into time wasted. When the inadequate technology preparation affects student accomplishments and satisfaction, it will affect faculty and institutional reputations. Setting entry requirements also allows instructors to know what limits they have in using technologies. Prerequisites also help avoid "the tyranny of expertise syndrome" where "once one has mastered CMC, it is hard to remember how confusing it is for beginners" (Lewis, Whitaker, & Julian, 1995, p. 27).

The act of quality control via prerequisites may exacerbate the problem of the digital divide: technology requirements may exclude poorer students. In a 1999 report, the College Board (as cited in "Distance education," 1999, para. 5) wrote, "While education is the great equalizer, technology appears to be a new engine of inequality. Those with limited computer experience will be handicapped in their ability to access knowledge and avail themselves of the ever-increasing variety of learning experiences." Public institutions in particular should consider ways to provide technology and training for these students. If necessary, state laws regarding equal education opportunities should also account for access to technology.

Instructional Design

In evaluating students in online courses, instructors should distinguish the quality of instruction from the quantity of information (Rosenberg, 2001) and emphasize the former over the latter. One way to do this is to adopt a constructivist approach, which engages learners in the process of constructing knowledge rather than simply receiving it. This entails focusing more on the learning process than exact outcomes. Salmon (2000) suggests that instructors:

1. Look at the process of learning rather than testing the content transmitted
2. Accept diversity of outcomes rather than demanding uniform learning
3. Consider whether knowledge is being created and disseminated rather than information merely communicated (p. 120).

Contexts in which students can apply learning include: virtual fieldtrips, interactive essays, supervised apprenticeships, and group projects. Using rubrics for evaluation and formative assessments can be beneficial.

Collaboration could lead to work of high quality because group members apply and feel pressure to contribute. Informing students that group members and apprentice supervisors will evaluate their performance may encourage students to seek feedback from their peers and supervisors along the way.

Accepting diverse rather than uniform outcomes requires rethinking assessment. Student contracts allow students to set their own goals in conjunction with instructor standards. They may also be valuable during accreditation. A constructivist approach may alleviate the problem of cheating by eliminating the need for fact-based assessments. Morgan and O'Reilly (2001) assembled case studies of a number of innovative alternatives for formative assessment. These include:

1. Online debates with peers
2. Volunteer internships with written reflection journal

3. Team projects providing real consultant services to a company
4. Weekly critiques followed by live discussions
5. Collaborative problem solving
6. Essays that include reflections on peer discussions
7. Researched debates via videoconferencing, and
8. Audiotaped interviews.

In a case study by Tony Dunn of Charles Stuart University in Australia, he argues that the "audiotape medium has proven to be extremely reliable. It is virtually impossible to fake a tape. The realism of the task prevents any short cuts, and unprepared interviews show up clearly because they are too short or too confused" (C. Morgan, 1999, p. 205). Incremental writing and writing based on experience are also controls against cheating and may demonstrate growth of knowledge. Students cannot have someone else write their papers unless that same person also participated in peer discussions. Another technique is to have students verbally record, not write, their assignments.

A constructivist approach allows learners to decide for themselves what they want to read to fulfill course requirements. An instructor may give students a range of high quality materials from which they choose to conduct discussions of interest to them via computer-mediated communication. For example, discussion boards can thread conversations according to topic and sender. Learners can select those messages that pertain to their own situations.

In addition to using a constructivist approach, fostering personal interaction is important for distance education. The American Federation of Teachers (2001) strongly urges distance education programs to include in-person communication because "the simultaneous visual and verbal interaction of individuals in the same place working together toward a common educational goal" and "the resources of the campus–from classrooms, laboratories and libraries to social and performance spaces" (Standard 5) are valuable for learners. Morgan and Thorpe (1993) further discuss benefits of residential components such as time to concentrate on a topic, engage in an in-depth approach to learning, and access experts and qualified tutors. Surely, not all distance courses can require a residential component. Nonetheless, it may be possible to incorporate fieldwork at approved sites or regional centers to which the students may commute periodically. Alternatives include a site visit, a class conference, or a weekend retreat.

Support Systems

Who is going to make all of these curricular innovations to support the quality of distance education and the quality of instruction? Instructors are on the front line. In a survey conducted by Husmann and Miller (2001), administrators rated most strongly the need to "provide additional support for faculty development of course materials" (Results section, para. 3). They note a need for reward systems that acknowledge and promote faculty participation in distance education. Offering special grants to faculty and assuring faculty recognition or compensation for innovative and creative efforts are crucial.

Similarly, the American Federation of Teachers (2001) points out that institutions must support faculty with training, higher compensation commensurate with work, and institutional rewards such as promotion. It also suggests that it is counterproductive to the development of the necessary skills to coerce faculty into teaching distance courses. Training and enticing existing faculty make more sense than hiring instructors based on their technical expertise. Furthermore, training existing faculty may actually improve student satisfaction. Gold (2001) studied a two-week training course for college teachers who were veterans in their fields but novices in online education. He found that "teachers exposed to the course significantly changed their attitudes toward online instruction seeing it as more participatory, and interactive than face-to-face instruction" (Abstract, para. 4).

Although instructors of distance education are on the front line, they alone cannot make distance education successful. Collaboration and division of labor may improve quality by providing several areas of expertise. Media specialists and technology coordinators should be hired to train and assist instructors who are experts on the content.

> [A] media specialist . . . can help with the technical aspects of embedding video, audio, and advanced graphics as well as the visual design of the course. After the course is developed and up and running, a person who manages the server and the related software is needed in addition to technical support personnel available to answer both student and faculty questions. (Schweizer, 1999, p. 103)

Faculty in the survey conducted by Care and Scanlan (2001, Findings, para. 2) said that they would have liked to collaborate with more experienced distance education instructors to reduce the time and frustration of struggling alone through trial and error. Care and Scanlan suggest forming a team involving a content expert, a media specialist, an instructional designer, a faculty representative, an administrative director, and a student representative to collaborate on developing courses.

Program Design

As institutions improve the quality of their educational products, they should distinguish more between professional development (certificate) and academic programs (degree). Quality control of a professional certificate is different from that of an academic degree. If institutions wish to maintain a reputation for quality, they should reconsider the granting of degrees for essentially professional development or technical training. Building more transfer between technical and academic aspects might allow academic and professional requirements to be more clearly distinguished while minimizing the tension between them. One model is to allow professionals to enter the certificate program with the option of applying the work to a master's degree later. In this way, professional experience and technical training can be a scaffold for academic work. Lewis, Whitaker, and Julian (1995) suggest that we revise our concepts of academic standards for this new market by finding ways to account for prior learning and alternatives for faculty credentialing. The more instructors can reward knowledge and the sharing of it, the more learning will occur. One way to reward sharing knowledge is to grant credit for coursework demonstrating an area of expertise. Researching and writing about areas of professional interest can meet academic standards. Of course, program design must satisfy accreditation, but this is exactly the kind of planning that is essential in quality control and instrumental in improving the reputation of distance education.

CONCLUSION

Educators concerned with quality control in distance education face a variety of parties to simultaneously satisfy, collaborate with, and assess. Unraveling the complex issues detailed in this article requires the oldest of educational virtues–patience and perseverance. Distance education is such a new field that educators should prepare for some failures and learn from mistakes. Meanwhile, distance education has great potential to serve a larger number of learners in a variety of ways. As educators, we should carry out our mission and continue steering distance education toward or keeping it on the right direction until pedagogies and technology are shoulder to shoulder, and academic degrees carry their deserved value.

REFERENCES

American Federation of Teachers: Higher Education Program and Policy Council. (2001, November). Distance education: Guidelines for good practice. *USDLA Journal, 15*(11). Retrieved April 7, 2002, from http://www.usdla.org/html/journal/ NOV01_Issue/ (Original work including Appendix published May 2000. Retrieved April 7, 2002, from http://www.aft.org/higher_ed/technology/

Berge, D., & Collins, M. (Eds.). (1995). Introduction: Computer-mediated communication and the online classroom in distance education. *Computer mediated communication and the online classroom: Vol. 3. Distance learning.* (pp. 1-12). New Jersey: Hampton Press.

Cambridge eMBA breaks 800 year-old tradition. (2001, February). *Virtual University Gazette.* Retrieved December 2, 2001, from http://www.geteducated.com/vug/ feb01/vug0201.htm

Care, D., & Scanlan, J. M. (2001). Planning and managing the development of courses for distance delivery: Results from a qualitative study. *Online Journal of Distance Learning Administration, 4*(2). State University of West Georgia, Distance Education Center. Retrieved December 2, 2001, from http://www.westga.edu/distance/ ojdla/summer42/care42.html

Carr, S. (2000, February 11). As distance education comes of age, the challenge is keeping the students. *The Chronicle of Higher Education: Information Technology.* Retrieved March 28, 2002, from http://chronicle.com/free/v46/i23/23a00101.htm

Distance education questioned in US. (1999, May 20). *Daily Bulletin of the University of Waterloo.* Retrieved April 7, 2002, from http://www.adm.uwaterloo.ca/bulletin/ 1999/may/20th.html

Elearning–the other white meat? Industry wide promotion campaign takes shape. (2001, October). *Virtual University Gazette.* Retrieved December 2, 2001, from http://www.geteducated.com/vug/oct01/vug1001.htm

Gold, S. (2001). A constructivist approach to online training for online teachers. *Journal of Asynchronous Learning Networks, 5*(1). Retrieved December 27, 2001, from http://www.aln.org/alnweb/journal/Vol5_issue1/Gold/gold.htm

Husmann, D. E., & Miller, M. T. (2001). Improving distance education: Perceptions of program administrators. *Online Journal of Distance Learning Administration, 4*(3). Retrieved December 28, 2001, from http://www.westga.edu/~distance/ojdla/ fall43/husmann43.html

Institute for Higher Education Policy. (1999). What's the difference? A review of contemporary research on the effectiveness of distance learning in higher education. Retrieved April 7, 2002, from http://www.ihep.com/Pubs/PDF/Difference.pdf

Kathawala, Y., & Abdou, K. (2001). Strengths, weaknesses, opportunities, and threats for the on-line MBA programs: A literature review for its future. *USDLA Journal, 15*(9). Retrieved December 22, 2001, from http://www.usdla.org/ED_magazine/ illuminactive/SEP01_Issue/article03.html

Lane, K. (2001, September 17). Report examines shortfalls of distance education. *Community College Week, 14.* Retrieved December 2, 2001, from http://www.ccweek.com/ index.html

Lewis, J., Whitaker, J., & Julian, J. (1995). Distance education for the 21st century: The future of national and international telecomputing networks in distance education. In Z. L. Berge & M. P. Collins (Eds.), *Computer mediated communication and the online classroom: Vol. 3. Distance learning* (pp. 13-30). New Jersey: Hampton Press.

Moore, M. (1972). Learner autonomy: The second dimension of independent learning. *Convergence, 5*(2), 76-88.

Morgan, A., & Thorpe, M. (1993). Residential schools in open and distance education: Quality time for quality learning. In T. Evans & D. Nation (Eds.), *Reforming open and distance education: Critical reflections from practice* (pp. 72-87). New York: St. Martin's Press.

Morgan, C., & O'Reilly M. (1999). *Assessing open and distance learners. Open and distance learning series.* London: Kogan Page.

Morgan, C., & O'Reilly, M. (2001). Innovations in online assessment. In F. Lockwood & A. Gooley (Eds.), *Innovation in open and distance learning: Successful development of online and Web-based learning* (pp. 179-188). London: Kogan Page.

Rosenberg, M. J. (2001). *E-learning: Strategies for delivering knowledge in the digital age.* New York: McGraw-Hill.

Salmon, G. (2000). *E-Moderating: A guide to teaching and learning online. Open and distance learning series.* London: Kogan Page.

Schweizer, H. (1999). *Designing and teaching an on-line course: Spinning your Web classroom.* Needham Heights, MA: Allyn & Bacon.

Sherry, L., & Morse, R. (1995). An assessment of training needs in the use of distance education for instruction. *International Journal of Educational Telecommunications, 1*(1), 5-22.

Lisa A. Heaton
Rudy Pauley
Ron Childress

Quality Control
for Online Graduate Course Delivery:
A Case Study

SUMMARY. Marshall University has a 29-year history of delivering graduate education to in-service teachers. In 1997 the college began using Internet-based courses as a means of reaching an expanding service area. Currently the Graduate School of Education and Professional Development has over 300 courses developed for Internet delivery. During any given semester, approximately 80 online graduate courses are offered. As the emphasis on Web-based delivery has increased, the college has addressed the issue of quality control at several levels, including student surveys, online course evaluations, faculty surveys, faculty peer reviews, and a course approval process. This paper will present a case study of the evolution of our efforts to improve the quality of course development and delivery. *[Article copies available for a fee from The Haworth Document Delivery Service: 1-800-HAWORTH. E-mail address: <getinfo@haworthpressinc.com>*

LISA A. HEATON is Assistant Professor, Elementary and Secondary Education, Graduate School of Education and Professional Development, Marshall University, 100 Angus E. Peyton Drive, South Charleston, WV 25303 (E-mail: heaton@marshall.edu).
RUDY PAULEY is Program Director, Elementary and Secondary Education, Graduate School of Education and Professional Development, Marshall University, 100 Angus E. Peyton Drive, South Charleston, WV 25303 (E-mail: rpauley@marshall.edu).
RON CHILDRESS is Dean, Graduate School of Education and Professional Development, Marshall University, 100 Angus E. Peyton Drive, South Charleston, WV 25303 (E-mail: rchildress@marshall.edu).

[Haworth co-indexing entry note]: "Quality Control for Online Graduate Course Delivery: A Case Study." Heaton, Lisa A., Rudy Pauley, and Ron Childress. Co-published simultaneously in *Computers in the Schools* (The Haworth Press, Inc.) Vol. 19, No. 3/4, 2002, pp. 103-114; and: *Distance Education: Issues and Concerns* (ed: Cleborne D. Maddux, Jacque Ewing-Taylor, and D. LaMont Johnson) The Haworth Press, Inc., 2002, pp. 103-114. Single or multiple copies of this article are available for a fee from The Haworth Document Delivery Service [1-800-HAWORTH, 9:00 a.m. - 5:00 p.m. (EST). E-mail address: getinfo@haworthpressinc.com].

103

KEYWORDS. Quality control, distance education, assessment, program evaluation, in-service, teachers, peer review

The rapid growth of distance education in U.S. colleges and universities has challenged traditional models for ensuring quality instruction by institutions of higher education. According to one 1997 study, nearly 90% of institutions with an enrollment greater than 10,000 were involved in distance education efforts (Gibson, 1998). Many programs have grown so rapidly that institutions have struggled in their efforts to provide appropriate models of quality control. In other instances, distance education efforts have gone unchecked because of a lack of appropriate quality control models, tools, and techniques.

Concrete evidence of this concern about the quality control of distance education is readily available when one catalogs the recent rash of distance education reports and standards. The American Federation of Teachers, for example, released a report suggesting that the lack of quality control in distance education could greatly jeopardize an institution's effort to implement a quality distance education program (*Chronicle of Higher Education*, 2001). Likewise, the Canadian Association for Community Education and the FuturEd Consulting Education Futurists are creating a set of quality standards for online learning products and services (*Distance Education Report*, April 1, 2001). Other organizations, such as the Southern Regional Education Board (SREB), have created sets of quality guidelines. The SREB's "Principles of Good Practice" constitutes a checklist of criteria for an effective online program (SREB, 2001).

In response to this need, this paper will describe a comprehensive quality control model for delivering online graduate programs and courses. Evolving over the past several years, the model represents one graduate school of education's attempt to ensure quality in its online instruction.

THE SETTING

Marshall University (MU), located on West Virginia's border with Kentucky and Ohio, is a 154-year-old state-supported university with a regional focus. Marshall has an undergraduate enrollment of approximately 12,000 students and a graduate enrollment of approximately 4,000 students. The Graduate School of Education and Professional Development (GSEPD), a unit within Marshall University's College of Education and Human Services, has been actively involved in distance education for over 30 years. Initially, the school began with faculty driving to outlying locations to deliver classes. The evolution of the technological focus of the distance education commitment of the school can be traced from audio phone bridges to satellite links, compressed video, and most recently, the use of the Internet to offer coursework. Since beginning to pursue computer-mediated education in 1997, MU has established over 800 courses residing on its distance education server and has provided over 16,000 student accounts for access to computer-based courses. Over three hundred of these courses are designed as graduate courses for the in-service teaching professional. Target populations that are served by the distance education effort include elementary and secondary education teachers, reading specialists, special educators, school administrators, school counselors, and school psychologists.

Each semester several new courses are created as additional faculty users begin to use the Internet to serve a growing population of interested students. MU has made a tremendous commitment to provide resources that allow the faculty to post course content in a variety of formats such as audio, video, and text. MU has constructed three new libraries since 1998, with a large portion of each dedicated to electronic delivery of information to students. The commitment of the faculty, administration, and support staff to distance education has allowed the GSEPD to expand its outreach to all 55 counties in West Virginia and surrounding states.

THE QUALITY CONTROL DOMAINS

The quality control model that has evolved at MU is one that involves a multi-faceted approach working within three domains: course development, course delivery, and course evaluation. The distinctions between the domains are often blurred, as many of the quality control variables blend into more than one domain. The model has developed into a continuous system of checks and balances that is best represented by Figure 1. The quality control variables interact and combine to create the model. The domains and points of interaction for the variables are represented in Figure 2.

The variables interact with differing levels of frequency in each domain (see Figure 2). The 10 variables discussed in this paper are those that are most often observed and measured within the domains at MU.

Faculty Development

Faculty development plays a critical role in organizing quality control measures for distance education programs. Quality in course development and quality in course delivery are also critical variables affecting any online program.

The GSEPD supports the development of faculty as informed users of distance education techniques in a variety of ways. One primary resource available to faculty using technology in course delivery is funding for attending state, regional, national, and international conferences pertaining to distance education. During 2000-2001, the school funded conference attendance for over 30 faculty members. Faculty members attend conferences, often presenting, and return to the college to report their findings to the faculty users group (discussed later). This constant input of new ideas is a valuable resource that contributes to quality course delivery at MU.

FIGURE 1. Quality control domains.

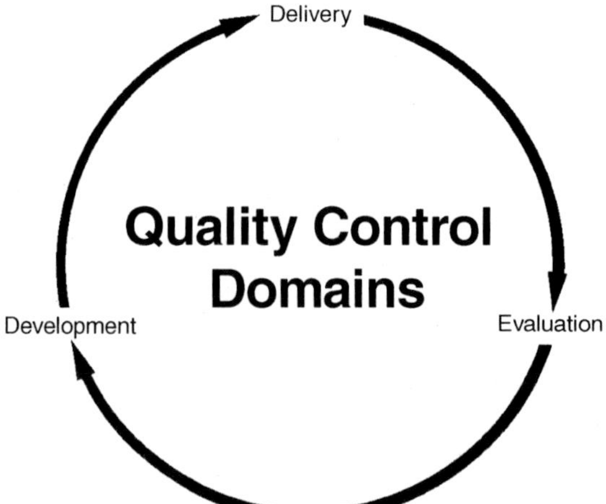

FIGURE 2. Domains and variables and points of interaction.

		Domains		
		Development	Delivery	Evaluation
Quality Control Variables	Faculty Development	•	•	
	Course Approval Process	•		
	Library Services	•	•	
	External Reviews		•	•
	Institutional Assessment			•
	Course Evaluations	•	•	•
	Single Delivery Platform	•	•	
	Faculty and Student Surveys			•
	Student Performance		•	•
	Faculty Users Group	•	•	•

In addition to faculty attending and presenting at conferences, for the past several years the university has sponsored a statewide conference for computer users on delivering distance education. This annual conference typically attracts over 100 participants from higher education and K-12. The two-day event offers attendees the opportunity to network and share ideas with professionals in their field. The showcasing of Internet courses by faculty from our institution and others allows each participant to assess the quality and usability of each course presented.

Each year the school downlinks satellite-delivered panel discussions concerning distance education and makes the proceedings available to the faculty. This is another rich source of new information that allows faculty to remain up to date on the latest techniques in computers in education and to compare their techniques to those of other institutions.

Each semester the Center for Instructional Technology at MU prepares a series of workshops targeted for the developer of Internet courses. These workshops cover a variety of topics and serve to update faculty skills. Web-authoring techniques, delivery platform updates, and adult learning styles have been some of the most recent seminar topics.

Perhaps the single most powerful faculty development tool in place is the faculty mentoring process. Each new user of technology is assigned (either formally or informally) to a faculty mentor. This mentor serves as a sounding board and guide for the new user of technology. The mentoring process provides the new developer of electronic coursework with a constant source of support during development and delivery.

Course Approval Process

In order for a new course to be offered online, approval from several levels must be received. This quality control measure helps to maintain a consistency that is vital to the total program. Initially the faculty member proposing a new Internet-based course must receive departmental approval. This "review" serves to determine the need for a particular course to be developed for online delivery as well as the viability of the content.

Distance education programs and courses are also subject to qualitative assessment through administrative oversight. This second level of approval comes from the GSEPD dean's office, where the legitimacy of the requested online course is either accepted or rejected. The dean relies heavily upon the faculty users group (discussed later in this report) to help guide the overall program at the school. Typically, the dean requests that the new course be presented to the third tier of oversight, the faculty users group, that consists of faculty and instructional technologists. The users group serves as a quality control unit that ensures that the course is usable, understandable, and of graduate school quality.

Finally, prior to offering a course to students, the Center for Instructional Technology checks the course template. This involves assuring that the course utilizes the institutional delivery platform in a manner that facilitates student access and participation in the course without undue difficulty. All courses at the university must contain several common links to areas such as the library and help desk.

Once a course has proceeded through this network of approval, it may be placed on the schedule for delivery the following semester. It is important to note that the process flows freely from one area to the next, and faculty developers are given feedback at each juncture. The end result is typically a well-planned, high-quality graduate course.

Library Support

The MU library system consists of the Drinko, Morrow, Health Science and Music Libraries in Huntington and the Graduate College Library in South Charleston. Together, the University Libraries' holdings include 1.7 million volumes and 3,000 periodical titles. The integrated library catalog and a variety of indices and full-text databases are accessed electronically from the library's Web page.

Specific databases used by graduate students in education are *ERIC, Mental Measurements Yearbook, Dissertation Abstracts International, PsycINFO, Academic Search, Education Abstracts, Education Law: Abstracts and Statistics, Social Sciences and Psychology,* and *Business.* These resources are all available to MU students online, allowing remote and simultaneous access. The library subscribes to full-text databases when possible and links to many full-text research resources.

Marshall University Graduate College has provided library support to graduate and doctoral students in education for more than 25 years. As a result, the library collection is especially strong in this discipline. Approximately two-thirds of the library's collection of 725 journals is related to educational research. Because of the college's historical mission to support distant and nontraditional learners, the library offers a document delivery service.

MU is working very closely with the West Virginia Academic Library Directors Group to facilitate access to resources in all 22 college and university libraries in the state, both private and public. Combined, the academic libraries in West Virginia represent a collection of 2.5 million volumes (1.7 million volumes belonging to MU) and 10,000 journal titles.

The online library service offered by MU is an important variable in the quality control model. All Internet-based courses at the university use a common delivery platform, and each course has a link to the MU library page that connects the student to the above mentioned features. Each semester library services personnel contact the faculty members using online delivery and ask for input to enhance the library's online support. Each instructor is encouraged to conduct an electronic library information seminar at the beginning of each class. Conducting educational research and reading current literature from remote sites are made possible through the use of the electronic library.

External Reviews

Distance education courses and programs are also subject to external review every five years by the state higher education governing board. The West Virginia Board of Education conducts a similar review of all educational licensure programs on the same cycle.

Annually, the professional education unit must file progress reports with both the state licensing agency and the National Council for Accreditation of Teacher Education (NCATE). Both reports require that any change in the unit technology plan be addressed.

All professional education programs are also subject to periodic review by NCATE and, where applicable, specialized accrediting groups (e.g., NCTM, IRA, and CEC) that focus on specific content areas. Most of these accrediting groups have standards or guidelines related to distance education and the use of technology.

Institutional Assessment

Distance education courses and programs are subject to several internal institutional assessments. All new courses must be reviewed and approved by the program/departmental faculty, the Dean, the college's Graduate Program Committee, and the university's Graduate Council. In preparation for external program review, each degree program prepares a self-study and program assessment every five years. This self-study is subject to both faculty and administrative review. Programs must then submit an annual report of progress toward accomplishing the goals and objectives of the plan.

Course Evaluations

Course evaluations have been used extensively as a quality control measure in traditional courses, and most colleges and universities have a standard course evaluation form that students complete for each class at the conclusion of the semester. Using the "Survey Tool" within the online course delivery software, distance education faculty can gather anonymous feedback from students in the same manner that was previously completed using a scantron questionnaire.

The system for implementing the electronic course survey provides another example of the benefit of the faculty users group and the faculty development support system within the GSEPD. This particular movement started with one faculty member digitizing the course evaluation form and demonstrating, during a faculty users group meeting, the resulting feedback obtained from one semester of student reviews. Discussion was then conducted about the viability of this format as opposed to attempting to distribute and retrieve paper copies through mail or other means. Once it was decided that the format provides students with the same opportunity to submit anonymous feedback, the process was implemented through a faculty development session.

Many of our instructors have found the electronic format even more beneficial than the traditional paper-and-pencil format. With the online course evaluation, student feedback can be accessed and compiled by the instructor within seconds of submission. Student feedback can then be used to update courses in a more timely fashion (i.e., faculty can use the data for course improvement before repeating the course the following semester).

Another unanticipated outcome of the online surveys seems to be the increased likelihood for students to provide anecdotal comments. These typed comments from students can serve as valuable feedback about what worked and did not work in relation to the technical makeup and delivery of a course. With the online format, instructors also have the option of including additional questions related to certain assignments or new and innovative delivery media that may have been incorporated on a trial basis within a given course.

Single Delivery Platform

The university's dedication to a single delivery platform (WebCT) has been beneficial in maintaining quality control and consistency during all facets of the program. One essential aspect in relation to this is the consistency in delivery. Students have a single point of access to all online courses, and there is consistency in the tools they are required to use for communication, assignment submission, and navigation throughout the duration of a course or series of courses.

Using a single delivery platform facilitates the process of setting university-wide standards for course appearance, maintaining the server, and administering the online program. While each faculty member who develops an online course has some flexibility with layout and arrangement of materials, there are prescribed elements that are built in to the template at the beginning of any new course. These elements include the university logo as a header on the home page of each course and the use of the officially adopted "Marshall" green as the universal color for the navigation bar. A standard footer includes links to WebCT Help, the instructor's e-mail, the course syllabus, library resources, and MUOnline (which serves as an access point for student services such as admissions, financial aid, course listings, online registration, university bookstore, and university calendar). While instructors can customize many elements of a course, the consistent use of these items makes the identity and ownership of every course quickly recognizable. Student feedback has indicated that one attraction to the online courses is the ease of transitioning from one course to the next.

Faculty and Student Surveys

Each summer for the past three years surveys have been mailed to all students who were registered for a Web-based course during the previous fall and spring semesters. Student responses provide demographic data (age, gender, location), program data (number of Web courses completed, number of face-to-face meetings desired), technical data (whether the student received training, technical problems accessing a course or using course tools), and instructional data (overall quality of content and instructional strategies). Results from student surveys are reviewed and discussed by the faculty users group for the purpose of re-evaluating course development and delivery strategies. One example of this feedback is that students have indicated a desire to meet three times each semester in a face-to-face format. Having this information, most instructors have adopted the "three-live-meeting" format, with face-to-face class sessions at the beginning, middle, and end of the term.

A survey of faculty users, including full-time and part-time faculty, was also conducted at the beginning of the spring 2001 semester. Questions were designed in a similar format to gather demographic information (number of years in higher education, number of Web courses developed), technical data (Web tools used, faculty development needs), and instructional data (instructional strategies used, quality of student work). Results of this evaluation effort have been used as topics of discussion during faculty users group meetings to identify faculty development needs and as an additional evaluation tool in examining the quality of the online teaching and learning experience.

Student Performance

A frequent topic of debate related to computer-based instruction is the question of impact on student learning (Gibson, 1998; Simonson, Smaldino, Albright, & Zvacek, 2000): Do students participating in an online course perform as well as their traditional counterparts? At any level of education, the question cannot be ignored. While several sources are used to gather data on this topic, including questions on both the faculty and student surveys, results from state and national certification and licensing exams provide the most promising evidence.

In 1998 the Leadership Studies Program within the GSEPD compared the achievement of an online cohort with that of a traditional delivery cohort and found that the online group performed better on the nationally normed Praxis exam. Faculty surveys indicate that the online students within our programs appear to be performing as well if not better than the traditional students. Student surveys also suggest that the online courses offer as much or more instructional value as the traditional courses.

Faculty Users Group

The faculty users group started with two faculty members who wanted to share information and resources as they were learning to use the online course delivery tools. Bates (2000) states, "Putting too much emphasis on formal organizational structures can be dangerous. Staff willing to work collaboratively will often work around or across organizational boundaries, and perfect organizational arrangements will not work if petty jealousies and conflicting ambitions get in the way" (p. 181). The faculty users group has an extremely active membership that echoes Bates' thoughts. The group includes university faculty, administrators, the school's instructional technologist, and computer services personnel. Faculty members from across disciplines (leadership studies, elementary and secondary education, school counseling and psychology, special education, humanities, and engineering) come together to discuss common issues related to online course development, delivery, and evaluation.

Monthly meetings are used to discuss issues such as software updates, faculty development needs, student training issues, new technology applications, and teaching strategies. The typical meeting includes a combination of discussions and demonstrations. Demonstrations are offered by faculty volunteers interested in gathering feedback about a newly developed course, or to share a new technical element or teaching strategy that has been integrated into a course. The faculty users group has been pivotal in the checks-and-balances process of establishing and implementing quality control measures throughout the three domains of the model.

CONCLUSION

The development and implementation of a quality control system for online course delivery is a "work in progress" and will continue to evolve in the foreseeable future. For change related to technology integration to occur, instructors must not only acquire new skills, but they must also change attitudes and behaviors in order to function successfully in the electronic classroom (Fullan, 1993; Hanna et al., 2000; Rogers & Shoemaker, 1971). In many ways, the issues and concerns are the same as they are with traditional classroom-based instruction. At the same time, assessing and ensuring the quality of online instruction requires a rethinking of some of our traditional approaches to quality control.

We suggest that any institution seeking to develop a comprehensive quality control system for online course delivery address multiple issues within the three key domains–development, delivery, and evaluation. We believe that four essential elements within this process include administrative support, faculty development, a course review and approval process, and a system for gathering feedback from student and faculty users.

REFERENCES

Bates, A.W. (2000). *Managing technological change.* San Francisco: Jossey-Bass.

Canadian organization develops e-learning comparative guidelines. (2001). *Distance Education Report, 5(7).*

Fullan, M. (1993). *Change forces: Probing the depths of educational reform.* London: Falmer Press.

Gibson, C. C. (1998). *Distance learners in higher education: Institutional responses for quality outcomes.* Madison, WI: Atwood.

Hanna, D. E., Dede, C., Poley, J., Tallman, J., Olcott, D., Schmidt, K., & Brown, G. (2000). *Higher education in an era of digital competition: Choices and challenges.* Madison, WI: Atwood.

Rogers, E. M., & Shoemaker, F. F. (1971). *Communication of innovations: A cross-cultural approach* (2nd ed.). New York: The Free Press.

Simonson, M., Smaldino, S., Albright, M., & Zvacek, S. (2000). *Teaching and learning at a distance: Foundations of distance education.* Upper Saddle River, NJ: Prentice-Hall.

Southern Regional Education Board. (2001). *Principles of good practice.* Atlanta, GA: SREB.

Union offers warning on distance education. (2001, September 14). *The Chronicle of Higher Education*, p. A39.

Raymond G. Taylor
Ellen Storey Vasu
Michael Lee Vasu
Jane D. Steelman

Cost-Income Equilibrium
for Electronically Delivered Instruction

SUMMARY. This article presents a basic cost-income model for electronically delivered instruction (EDI) (Jewett, 1999; Karelis, 1999). Systematic elaborations on the basic model are presented that explain the financial problems associated with EDI, and suggest strategies for making EDI financially viable. The basic model presented in the first figure includes dollars, enrollment, and hypothetical delivery systems and start-up costs. The second figure adds income and crossover points. The third figure adds the market share concept. The fourth figure simplifies the third. Seven solutions for moving the crossover to the left of the market share are presented and discussed: Increase income per enrollment,

RAYMOND G. TAYLOR is Professor Emeritus, North Carolina State University, P.O. Box 339, Bristol, ME 04539 (E-mail: rtaylor@profsonline.edu).
ELLEN STOREY VASU is Department Head and Professor, North Carolina University, Instructional Technology, Department of Curriculum and Instruction, Box 7801, North Carolina State University, Raleigh, NC 27695-7801 (E-mail: Ellen_Vasu@ncsu.edu).
MICHAEL LEE VASU is Director of Information Technology and Associate Professor, North Carolina State University, Department of Political Science and Public Administration, Box 8101, North Carolina State University, Raleigh, NC 27695-8101 (E-mail: Vasu@social.chass.ncsu.edu).
JANE D. STEELMAN is Assistant Professor, Instructional Technology, Department of Curriculum and Instruction, Box 7801, North Carolina State University, Raleigh, NC 27695-7801 (E-mail: jane_steelman@ncsu.edu).

[Haworth co-indexing entry note]: "Cost-Income Equilibrium for Electronically Delivered Instruction." Taylor, Raymond G. et al. Co-published simultaneously in *Computers in the Schools* (The Haworth Press, Inc.) Vol. 19, No. 3/4, 2002, pp. 115-128; and: *Distance Education: Issues and Concerns* (ed: Cleborne D. Maddux, Jacque Ewing-Taylor, and D. LaMont Johnson) The Haworth Press, Inc., 2002, pp. 115-128. Single or multiple copies of this article are available for a fee from The Haworth Document Delivery Service [1-800-HAWORTH, 9:00 a.m. - 5:00 p.m. (EST). E-mail address: getinfo@haworthpressinc.com].

115

decrease the start-up costs, decrease the marginal cost, improve market share, change mode of delivery, and reduce fixed costs. *[Article copies available for a fee from The Haworth Document Delivery Service: 1-800-HAWORTH. E-mail address: <getinfo@haworthpressinc.com> Website: <http://www.HaworthPress.com> © 2002 by The Haworth Press, Inc. All rights reserved.]*

KEYWORDS. Distance education, electronically mediated instruction, electronically delivered instruction, online courses, economics of instruction, cost-income equilibrium for instruction, accountability, Web-based courses

Every undergraduate student of economics is introduced to standard diagrams that help explain certain economic relationships, such as supply-demand and cost-income. Typically these diagrams, or models, show some point of equilibrium where costs equal income, or supply equals demand. They are instructive, especially with regard to elementary theory, although they do not mimic reality very well. Take, for example, the classic model that shows income being pushed against costs. Dollars are represented by the vertical axis and volume of sales by the horizontal axis. Income rises diagonally, starting at the origin, showing a simple linear gain in income as sales increase. Costs are broken down into two parts, fixed and variable. The fixed costs are represented as a horizontal line. Variable costs are shown as a diagonal line intercepting the vertical axis at the level of fixed costs. This model is meant to show that, if marginal income is higher than marginal costs, eventually the income and cost lines will cross and that any region to the right of that crossover represents profit.

The criticisms of such a model are as basic as the model itself: In real life, fixed costs are not normally flat, variable costs are usually discontinuous (i.e., have steps), and income usually is not linear. Nevertheless, this classic little diagram has taught unnumbered thousands of students the underlying ideas behind costs, income, and the crossover into a region of profitability.

We were pleasantly surprised to discover how well the cost-income model teaches important lessons regarding the economics of electronically delivered instruction (EDI). A set of systematic elaborations on the model not only explain some of the financial problems associated with EDI, but these elaborations also suggest strategies for making EDI financially viable. It is important to insist at the beginning of this article that there are many reasons why an institution of higher education might want to participate in EDI over and beyond any desired financial benefits–having increased access and a larger geographic cachement, providing convenience to students and faculty, keeping up with trends, exploiting the electronic medium, maintaining enrollments, and so on. However, the present article deals with EDI strictly from the standpoint of its economic viability. It is assumed that, in the long run, *EDI must rest on a sound economic base or else it will fall into disrepair and disuse.*

Also, at the outset, we acknowledge that we have elaborated and expanded on a fundamental idea that was not invented by us, but rather by Charles Karelis (1999), director for the Fund for the Improvement in Secondary Education. Further, Karelis acknowledges that he used, with permission, the basic income-cost diagram provided earlier by Jewett (1999). Compared to these earlier works and Vasu, Vasu, and Taylor (2000), the present article differs somewhat in perspective, provides elaboration on the work Karelis published, and goes on to nearly double the number of suggested strategies for improving the viability of EDI.

The cost portion of the basic model is important. Figure 1 shows the axis-labeling scheme, which remains constant throughout this discussion–dollars on the vertical axis and enrollments on the horizontal axis. Costs are broken down three ways: fixed, start-up, and variable. Start-up costs are not included in the fixed costs because they change depending upon the mode of delivery (e.g., the specific accessibility costs incurred when the mode of instruction is Web-based). Figure 1 shows five hypothetical delivery systems, A to E, each with a different start-up cost and each with a different marginal (i.e., variable) cost. Note that Figure 1 is idealized in the sense that, as A, B, C, and D are compared, the marginal costs (the slopes) go down as a greater investment is made in the start-up. Obviously, a very poor economic choice would be to select a delivery mode, as represented by cost line E that has high start-up costs and high marginal costs. Unfortunately, this is exactly what many institutions have done by making large investments in electronically linked classrooms and by using them in a totally synchronous fashion. Synchronous communication is that in which members of the class meet online at the same time to engage in real-time communications. Chat rooms and interactive video conferencing are examples of synchronous communications.

Figure 2 adds an income line and the crossover points. (Practically speaking, cost line E never crosses the income line because its slope is so steep.) As Karelis (1999) points out, so far this is a happy picture be-

FIGURE 1. Basic cost model.

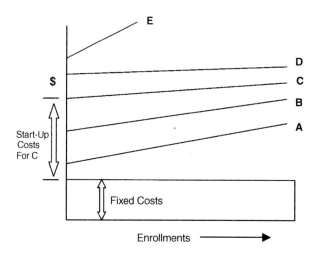

FIGURE 2. Cost-income crossover.

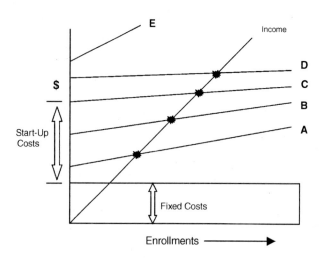

cause all that has to be done is enroll students until the crossover is reached; thereafter, EDI is not only economically viable but is actually profitable. He also shatters this good news by adding what he calls a "scale barrier." We have substituted "market share" because it is more intuitive and better represents the suggested strategies.

Figure 3 adds the market share and shows that, if enrollments are held back to the market share level as drawn, some of the EDI modes will be viable (only A in this case) and some will not (B, C, D, and E). Where the market share line is located is dependent upon many things. Sometimes it is idiosyncratic to the policies of the institution. For example, "We will only offer three sections of this course, and each will be limited to an enrollment of 25, regardless of demand." Sometimes it is a reflection on the relative demand for the course (Math 101 versus Russian 420). Sometimes it is a function of the student's perception of how amenable a particular course is to electronic delivery (Stat 501 versus Counseling 501).

Finally, market share is obviously affected by competition from within and from without the institution, and this competition is becoming more intense every day. Figure 3 shows that a certain course being delivered electronically will only be viable economically if the crossover can be reached, and it will not be reached if the crossover falls to the right of the market share line. In preparation for the discussion of strategies, which dominate the rest of this paper, Figure 3 has been simplified and the result presented in Figure 4. From Figure 4, seven solutions or strategies for moving the crossover to the left of the market share are developed and presented in the text that follows.

SOLUTION ONE: INCREASE INCOME PER ENROLLMENT

Simply put, the first solution presented in Figure 5 shows: "Charge more tuition and keep your fingers crossed that the laws of supply and demand will not undo your intention to produce more income." As shown in Figure 5, increasing the income slope can move the crossover to the left of the market share. The obvious risk is that the market share line will also shift left as students find similar and less expensive courses at other universities or as they drop out of courses and programs due to increased tuition. It is a risky strategy both economically and politically and is, in most circumstances, best used gently and in combination with other strategies.

FIGURE 3. Market share concept.

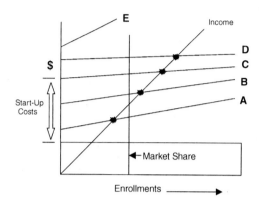

FIGURE 4. Generalization of the model.

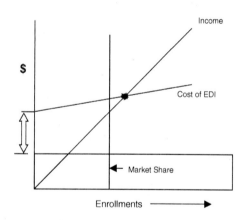

SOLUTION TWO: DECREASE THE START-UP COSTS

The second solution, presented in Figure 6, is to decrease start-up costs. This solution obviously applies best to modes of delivery that have relatively high initial costs. As Karelis (1999) pointed out, one of the ways this is being done is through cooperation between institutions and by cooperative support systems within single institutions. Our uni-

FIGURE 5. Solution one: Increase income per enrollment.

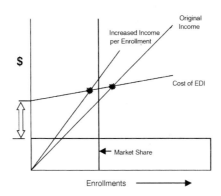

versity offers a variety of services, courses, and technical assistance plans to instructors and departments to help them get started with EDI with the lowest possible investment in time and equipment. In other cases, several large consortiums of universities, typically combinations of institutions within a state system, pull together to create an electronic university. Or, less formally, one faculty member may make significant progress with EDI and then share the experience with other faculty either within the department or through social affiliation. Figure 6 shows how a reduction in start-up costs can move the crossover to the left without any changes in income or market share. Further, it might be argued that one of the advantages of high levels of cooperation is that they not only lower start-up costs but also may increase market share by providing an electronic interface that is consistent across courses and thus more user-friendly for the student.

SOLUTION THREE: DECREASE THE MARGINAL COST

The third solution, presented in Figure 7, is to decrease the marginal cost (variable cost per student). Of course, before this strategy is employed, it is assumed that the institution has not wed itself to modes of delivery that have excessive and virtually unchangeable high marginal costs. Remember cost line E from Figures 1, 2, and 3! We return to an earlier criticism of synchronous, linked classrooms, where instructors

FIGURE 6. Solution two: Decrease the start-up costs.

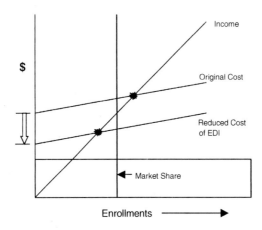

Enrollments ⟶

and students all have to be interacting at the same time–albeit in dispersed locations. *All of the costs of regular classroom instruction apply to this mode plus the enormous costs of equipment and communications links.* One might argue that there are some pedagogical advantages to this mode of delivery, although in an interview with faculty from a large northern U.S. university, the senior author observed that instructors who have used this mode are generally negative about its effectiveness and their comfort with the instructional environment. Further, there is clearly no economic viability to be found here.

Consider Figure 7 again, wherein the crossover is moved left by lowering the slope of the cost line–that is, by lowering the marginal cost. With "mode E" set aside, how can the marginal costs of EDI be reduced? James Bruno (1998) suggested one way wherein he described a vision of the future university. In this vision there are expert professors who create courses to be delivered electronically. These courses are broadly shared among universities but for a fee both to the employing institution and to the author. The campus is populated with students and mentors. The students take the courses electronically but meet only with mentors, who are presumably paid far less than the relatively few surviving professors. The courses not only have the benefit of the most up-to-date research, and the maximum degree of polish, but the marginal cost of their delivery is relatively low.

FIGURE 7. Solution three: Decrease the marginal cost.

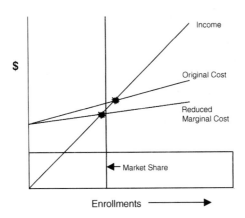

Unfortunately, as the senior author knows so well, one of the temptations of EDI is for the instructor and/or the institution to accept a very large number of students into an online course section–far more than one would accept in the classroom. This certainly lowers the marginal cost, but ultimately exploits the faculty and eliminates individual attention to student problems and questions. This individual attention does not need to be eliminated. At our university, a professor was interviewed who provided EDI in which the course enrollment was limited to what would normally be found in a face-to-face learning environment. The students expressed a high degree of satisfaction, a feeling of connectedness, and were pleased with the timely response of the instructor to their e-mail or netforum questions. Clearly, this can be accomplished with the smaller student-professor ratio, but doing this increases the marginal cost contrary to the scenario presented in Figure 7.

SOLUTION FOUR: IMPROVE MARKET SHARE

As Figure 8 suggests, the crossover can be moved to the left of market share by the obvious technique of diminishing the barriers to enrollment. The strategies for doing this depend upon the factors that originally set the market share. If they are internal and policy-oriented barriers, then some reconsideration of those policies or practices is in order. In many cases, however, the strategy of improving market share comes down to the same issues as it does for business–effective advertising and other marketing strategies.

SOLUTION FIVE:
ALLOW MARGINAL COSTS TO BE CURVILINEAR

Solution five is to de-linearize marginal costs as shown in Figure 9. Although this solution may at first appear to be little more than a trick with the diagram, it does, in fact, hold considerable promise. The strategy dictates that the marginal costs be lower at the beginning of a new course offering and that they be allowed to rise if the course is successful. This approach is analogous to a business limiting its investment in a new product or service until after a trial period proves its viability. The problem with this approach is that if the start-up and marginal costs at the beginning of a new endeavor are held too low, the experiment may be doomed to failure when it would have otherwise succeeded. It does make sense, however, when the market share is unknown, to test the market with a modest investment before providing higher levels of marginal funding. Thus, if a new course proves to be popular, class sizes can be lowered and the mode of delivery can be made marginally more expensive if warranted.

FIGURE 8. Solution four: Improve market share.

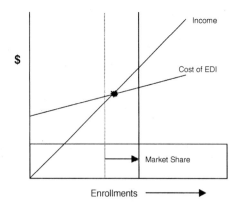

FIGURE 9. Solution five: Allow marginal costs to be curvilinear.

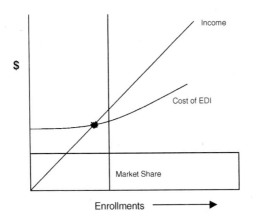

SOLUTION SIX: CHANGE MODE OF DELIVERY

The sixth solution, changing the mode of delivery to one with a lower start-up cost and/or a more favorable marginal cost, is rather obvious, but frequently ignored. Once a course is established with a particular mode of EDI, the temptation is to stay with that mode, even if the course is not economically viable. Perhaps this happens largely because the faculty member who developed the course sees his/her time and effort as a sunk cost and therefore does not want to "reinvent" the course in a more economically viable EDI mode. In any case, it is apparent from Figure 3 that a change in the mode of delivery can have a salutatory effect on the economics of EDI.

SOLUTION SEVEN: REDUCE FIXED COSTS

Solution seven is to reduce fixed costs as shown in Figure 10. There are two distinct situations to which this solution may apply–the first is much easier to deal with than the second. In the first situation, a university, from its very beginning, is established to deliver all of its programs by way of EDI. Thus it avoids all of the costs associated with a university that offers both EDI and traditional classroom instruction. It has fewer levels of administration, a differently constituted faculty, far fewer facilities (no classroom buildings, parking lots, dormitories, football stadium, etc.), no campus police or transportation department, and so on. Thus, the fixed costs of the University of Phoenix, for example, must be far lower than those of a traditional university.

The second situation applies to all other schools. Here, lowering fixed costs is somewhat of an accounting trick. Typically a separate EDI "college" or "university within a university system" is set up as a cost center. This special unit is isolated from the rest of the larger university with respect to its costs and income. Ideally, the unit holds down its fixed costs to those that are essential only to EDI. Typically, as departments grow and classroom space becomes unavailable, EDI becomes more attractive as a cost-efficient strategy for providing instruction. At that point, the cost of developing EDI becomes more cost-effective than building new classroom space or renovating existing spaces.

The greatest difficulty with the seventh solution arises for colleges and departments that are fully a part of a traditional university and thus have overheads that can range from 40 to 60% or more. These units and their faculty are under pressure to develop EDI, but the only way they can do this economically is with financial incentives, either from university subsidies, outside grants, or more typically from legislative mandates and support. The problem with all of these methods of funding is that they are temporary and are likely to be in place only long enough to establish the EDI presence. In the long

FIGURE 10. Solution seven: Reduce fixed costs.

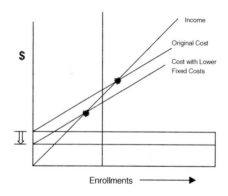

run, legislative resolve diminishes as EDI becomes commonplace, special funding dries up, and new money moves on to more glamorous endeavors. This appears to be true with every new program in the university and, thus, in the long run, *EDI must be self-sufficient.* When the subsidies end, any lack of financial viability within EDI will become an unsustainable liability for the sponsoring department or college.

SOLUTION EIGHT: WAIT OR DO NOTHING

"Solution" eight is to do nothing. This strategy, or lack thereof, was also offered by Karelis (1999), but in the present paper it is expanded into several versions. One version is simply that an institution doubts either the effectiveness or the viability of EDI and therefore does not participate in it. Although we are committed to EDI, we have days when the frustrations of failed electronics make us long for a piece of chalk and neat rows of students. A second is that an institution simply does not like the "look and feel" of EDI. Although to most outsiders this may label the institution as a den of Luddites, there may well be conflicts between the perceived culture of EDI and an institution's deeply held commitment to provide personal responsiveness and direct instruction to students. The reasoning is that, when a large number of students are in an online course section, no matter how hard one tries to make EDI friendly, it lacks the warmth and coziness of the small classroom or of the seminar setting. In an interview with a student participant of four courses delivered as EDI at our university, it was found that certain strategies may be employed that will make the student feel more connected and less isolated. But, as we discussed earlier, doing so increases the marginal costs, since a smaller student-professor ratio would most likely be required. A third version comes closer to strategy, "The technology is changing, improving, and coming down in price, so we will go slow. When the technology settles down and works more reliably, we will catch up." Of course the corresponding argument against this is that the market is being quickly absorbed by the existing EDI institutions, and no market share may be left for late arrivals. Karelis (1999) claims that another argument against this strategy is that the costs of traditional classroom instruction are simultaneously going up and that such costs could get out of hand for institutions that have developed no EDI alternatives.

CONCLUSION

The fundamental income-cost model from Economics 101 is especially useful for understanding the underlying economics of EDI. The model not only provides an explanation of the basic financial realities of this new and rapidly emerging set of delivery systems, but it also suggests a suite of strategies for making EDI economically viable.

REFERENCES

Bruno, J. (1998, May). UCLA Seminar Series, Los Angeles, CA.

Jewett, F. (1999). *Case studies in evaluating the benefits and costs of mediated instruction and distributed learning.* [Online]. Available: www.calstate.edu/special_projects.

Karelis, C. (1999). Education technology and cost control: Four models. *Syllabus,* 12(6), 20-28.

Vasu, E., Vasu, M., & Taylor, R. (2000, November). *Economic, technical and pedagogical factors related to distance education.* Paper presented to the International Conference of Computers in Education, Taipei, Taiwan.

Ananda Mitra
Amelia Hall

Distance Education
as a Discursive Practice:
Voice, Discourse, and Pedagogy

SUMMARY. Distance education has taken on a new shape with the introduction of new digital technologies that have made the process of interaction between the teacher and student a far more vibrant process. This change, and the fact that distance education often takes place with the use of text-based systems, leads to the re-thinking of the distance education "classroom" as a discursive space where the voices of the teachers and students take on unique qualities. Using the construct of "voice" this paper argues that the role of the teacher and the student is constantly changing as multiple voices can be heard in the discursive pedagogic space of distance education. *[Article copies available for a fee from The Haworth Document Delivery Service: 1-800-HAWORTH. E-mail address: <getinfo@haworthpressinc.com> Website: <http://www.HaworthPress.com> © 2002 by The Haworth Press, Inc. All rights reserved.]*

KEYWORDS. Distance education, Internet, voice, discourse, ethics, pedagogic practice

ANANDA MITRA is Associate Professor, Department of Communication, Wake Forest University, Box 7347 Reynolda Station, Winston-Salem, NC 27109 (E-mail: ananda@wfu.edu).
AMELIA HALL is a graduate student, Department of Communication, Wake Forest University, Box 7347 Reynolda Station, Winston-Salem, NC 27109 (E-mail: hallam1@wfu.edu).

[Haworth co-indexing entry note]: "Distance Education as a Discursive Practice: Voice, Discourse, and Pedagogy." Mitra, Ananda, and Amelia Hall. Co-published simultaneously in *Computers in the Schools* (The Haworth Press, Inc.) Vol. 19, No. 3/4, 2002, pp. 129-142; and: *Distance Education: Issues and Concerns* (ed: Cleborne D. Maddux, Jacque Ewing-Taylor, and D. LaMont Johnson) The Haworth Press, Inc., 2002, pp. 129-142. Single or multiple copies of this article are available for a fee from The Haworth Document Delivery Service [1-800-HAWORTH, 9:00 a.m. - 5:00 p.m. (EST). E-mail address: getinfo@haworthpressinc.com].

Distance learning has been a part of education since the development of technologies that allowed for the affordable and efficient transmission of the voice of a teacher to students who were far flung from the location where the teacher was teaching (Carpenter, 1978; Hezel, 1980; Lewis, 1961). Over the years the technologies of distance learning have changed, and researchers and educational policymakers have shown a keen interest in understanding the way in which distance learning can impact a student's learning outcome. Numerous case studies exist in the literature where teachers and scholars have explored the effects of distance learning through empirical research in trying to understand how the technologies of distance learning and the process of distance learning can have tangible and measurable results (Chapanis, 1983; Denton, Clark, Rossing, & O'Connor, 1984; Peters, 1993).

Here we argue that the time has now come when the new digital technologies that can be used for distance learning need to be thought of in fundamental terms. The focus needs to be both on the outcomes that can be quantified as well as on outcomes that remain at the ontological level. To be sure, the technologies and process of distance learning can transform who we are as human beings living in the learning space, and the way in which we can express ourselves within the new relationships of power that are being made possible as we are going online with distance learning. In this article we present an argument to consider the fundamental implications of the very idea of distance learning enhanced by digital technologies. We do not present a case study but attempt to provide a theoretical framework within which current and future case studies could be framed and interpreted.

DISTANCE EDUCATION, TECHNOLOGY, AND VOICE

There is enough evidence in the literature on technology and education over the past two decades that academic institutions from the K-12 level to higher education have embraced various forms of pedagogic technology to reach various students (Archee & Whitty, 2001; Smith, Waby, Neville, & Dalloway, 1999; Williamson, 2001). In recent years, many journals and magazines have sprouted that deal specifically with the functions and use of technology in teaching. Indeed, the classrooms of the twenty-first century cannot be imagined without the use of some form of technology to assist in teaching. Consequently, several areas of research have considered the impact of technology-assisted distance learning. Research has examined the way in which the combination of technology and distance learning has impacted teacher training, student learning outcomes, and the effect of gender. Online teacher training has proven effective and cost-efficient. Student learning outcomes have tended to vary with age and gender. There are reports that females and older adults tend to work quite well in online courses, but males and younger adults tend to require the structure and discipline provided by the traditional classroom setting (Davidson-Shivers, 2001; Ladewski, 1996; Young, 2001a; Young, Dewstow, & McSporran, 1999). The research has been inspired by the intensive expansion in using technology. This expansion itself can be traced to various roots. It is useful to consider some of that history to frame our key argument: Technology changes the way in which the pedagogic discourse is carried out with the various voices that can be heard within that discourse.

Essentially, it is possible to identify three different thrusts in using technology in education. First, the development of television, particularly cable television, offered the opportunity to take the classroom lecture outside the confines of the classroom and narrowcast the lecture to students who could not be in the classroom. This opened up the opportunity for distance education where it was possible for the teacher's voice to be heard in many different locations. In many ways, television opened up the possibility of distance education, and the opportunity was embraced by educational institutions across the globe (Carlisle, 1974; Charles, 1986). The interest in the developmental theories of communication also helped to theoretically frame and endorse the use of television for educational purposes (Schramm, 1964). There was, however, one significant drawback to this technology–the lack of interactivity between the student and the teacher. While the technology allowed students to experience the "presence" of the teacher, the students often had no voice in the pedagogic process, particularly when the students were so geographically distant from the teacher that there was little opportunity for interpersonal interaction.

The lack of interactivity in television-aided distance learning led to the second technological thrust, which was to develop methods by which the students could also gain a voice in the pedagogic process with the use of interactive video technology. The analog video technology that was available for the pioneers of distance education, however, was too cumbersome to allow for high-quality interactivity. In the initial stages, even the most advanced form of interactivity was restricted to the "head and shoulder" shot of the teacher teaching in one location, and students with a camera pointed at them vying for the attention of the teacher, who would be equipped with an array of monitors attempting to respond to the students who appeared on the video screens. The pedagogic experience was not of a high quality. Nevertheless, early studies demonstrated that even a rudimentary form of interactivity was preferred over the complete lack of interactivity (Mitra, 1988).

The use of analog video technology continued for a long period until it was evident that digital technologies had become sophisticated and affordable enough that educational institutions could deploy them in high volumes and apply the technology to pedagogic settings. The development of affordable personal computers and the simultaneous development of the Internet as a global communication network have now opened up the third level of technology. At this level the new technologies bring a very sophisticated level of interactivity and global reach, changing the landscape of distance education (Anderson, 2001; Strickland, 2001). This paper focuses on the consequences of the new notion of interactivity presented by digital technology.

It is important at this juncture to briefly develop the idea of voice as used in this argument. In recent scholarship on the notion of voice, there are two things that have been considered to be of particular importance. First, it is argued that voice constitutes agency (Mitra & Watts, in press). In other words, the fact that someone has a voice suggests that the person or the institution is able to produce an utterance, making that person an agent within the public sphere. This necessarily provides a certain degree of power to the agent in shaping the specific public sphere within which the agency is actualized. Paradoxically, the strength of agency is particularly palpable when it is absent, as in the cases where a particular group does not have a voice, and thus the agency is denied (Mitra, 2001; Spivak, 1988). Classrooms where teachers demand silence, and noninteractive analog video technology that disallows response are examples where the student's agency is stripped, thus completely altering the face of the specific public sphere of the classroom. Voice, as a public occurrence, thus provides the agency and consequent power to the speaker. Technologies that enhance that process are therefore the ones that offer the agent an opportunity to speak and to be heard.

The second key component of voice is the notion of being "heard." Hyde and Rufo (2000) have argued that voice opens up the potential of dialog. Indeed, when a student speaks up, there is a necessary assumption that a response is expected. The process of pedagogy, when examined from the perspective of voice, is composed of a dialog where the student and teacher can have their own voices and can expect to be heard and responded to. This model of pedagogy, which is intrinsically dependent on interaction, is what the earlier technologies of distance education were unable to provide efficiently. Consequently, the issue of voice was indeed a moot point and required little examination. However, new technologies offer a heightened level of interaction that remains novel to teaching. This increased interactivity needs to be explained and understood with the use of specific theoretical lenses that can help to understand how the technologies of distance education can begin to transform the pedagogic space. The transformation is eventually dependent on the way in which the new technologies are being used in the educational environment because it is that usage pattern that determines who has what kind of voice.

THE MODALITIES OF TECHNOLOGY USE

The digital technologies made available with the use of the personal computer and the Internet have many different characteristics, all of which have an impact on the way in which they are used by teachers and students in teaching and learning. To begin with, the new technologies offer the possibility of rethinking the notions of space and time within a completely interactive environment. It is first useful to examine the notion of interactivity.

Digital technologies offer the opportunity for users to interact with one another through various media (Barker, 2001; Hudson, 1998; Najjar, 1996; Sullivan, 2001). At the most basic level, the new technologies offer the opportunity of one-to-one asynchronous interaction with the use of electronic mail. It has been demonstrated that, under many circumstances, electronic mail offers a nonthreatening mode of communication in a networked institution where the traditional channels of communication can be bypassed, resulting in a "flattening" of the hierarchical system. This outcome can have far-reaching consequences in the teacher-student relationship, which has traditionally been particularly hierarchical. The introduction of electronic mail can indeed increase the amount of interaction between teacher and student. However, when electronic mail is coupled with asynchronous opportunities, such as through a list serve or a bulletin board, interaction increases as students and multiple teachers can participate in an ongoing dialog (Akahori, 2001; Collins, 1998; Young, 2001b). However, electronic mail is only the starting point for more complex forms of interaction where both at the synchronous and asynchronous level, students and teachers can interact with one another by exchanging sound and images. This ongoing discourse can eventually transform the entire teaching and learning experience.

The enhanced opportunities for interaction also need to be placed within the context of the recasting of the notions of time and space. Digital technologies alter the way in which interaction takes place on the time axis and in geographic spaces. Synchronous communication results in situations where teachers and students can find themselves interacting in real time, even though they are separated by great geographic distances (Anderson, 2001; Davidson-Shivers, Muilenburg, & Tanner, 2000; Davidson-Shivers, Muilenburg, & Tanner, in press; Draper, 2001; Roxin, 2001). The combination of the speed of the Internet and its global reach has made it possible to have chat rooms and other synchronous communication tools that allow students and teachers, who are physically separated, to have real-time discussion. Numerous case studies report the use of such technologies where chat rooms, in combination with streaming video and white board technologies, have reshaped the face of distance learning (see e.g., Gerhardt, 2000; Wittlich & Rubens, 2000). To be sure, the whole notion of distance has been changed by the fact that both space and time shrink with the use of the Internet. Consequently, within the context of distance learning, the new technologies are beginning to redefine what distance is. What used to be restrictive teaching within the reaches of narrowcast television has now exploded to global classrooms where distance is no longer a barrier.

The changes in interactivity and ideas of distance that result from the new technologies are expected to have different kinds of outcomes in dismantling some of the traditional notions of distance learning that were based on analog technologies. As Negroponte (1995) points out, when we become digital, new benefits and burdens become evident that can be thought of as different orders of effect as also suggested by Sproull and Kiesler (1992). However, what remains fundamental to the altered distance learning landscape in using digital technologies is that the most pervasive use of the technology remains in the area of changing modalities of communication among the different players in the pedagogic scenario. It is this emphasis on communication that justified the argument that the new distance learning environment can be theorized using a basic construct within the study of human communication: voice. The various technological innovations that can be applied to distance learning can have well-defined, measurable outcomes in learning and attitude toward teaching and learning, but more fundamentally, these technologies can alter the relationship that exists between the different players and their voices.

VOICES IN THE PEDAGOGIC SPACE

The idea of voice, when applied to the process of technology-assisted distance education, begs the question of whose voices can be heard in this space. For an institution to be able to claim successful networking, it must allow the free flow of communication between the various elements that are networked (Sproull & Kiesler, 1992). The new climate of distance education provides such a networked environment where the players can claim to operate within a networked education organization. To be sure, within that environment the networking can be extremely robust and efficient, allowing for broadband synchronous communication with the simultaneous use of text, image, and sound (Natan & Barkai, 2001). Such technological opportunities make it possible to create a unique pedagogic discourse, and a teaching discursive space, where the teachers and students can take up roles that are different from traditional classroom roles. Existing data suggest that, within these technological circumstances, the voices of the previously quiet members of the discursive community can suddenly be heard (Sproull & Kiesler, 1992).

Research on interpersonal communication, communication apprehension, and the opportunities provided by digital communication has demonstrated that, first, more voices can be heard on synchronous (and asynchronous) educational communication tools such as teaching chat rooms (Walther, 1992, 1994, 1996). This is particularly significant, because these are often the voices of the people who were quiet in the traditional classroom. Thus, in answer to the question of whose voices can be heard, it is safe to suggest that the students' voices are the ones that are most conspicuous when technology is applied to the distance learning (or even traditional learning) scenario. This tendency can also be traced in the case of asynchronous communication tools with potential distance learning applications. Using a tool such as e-mail to communicate with the instructor is often accompanied by an increasing burden on the teacher to respond to all the electronic letters that arrive with missives and voices of the students who are often the quiet ones in the classroom. The reason for this phenomenon can be traced within the literature on communication apprehension, but the consequences of this phenomenon within the context of digital learning with enhanced technology is the focus of attention in this paper.

To start with, the possibility offered by the new technologies can lead to a condition where many of the participants in the pedagogic arena are able to speak together. For instance, in a chat room class the students and the teachers are all able to speak together and can engage in a discussion around an issue that might have been treated as "lecture" material in the traditional classroom either in the face-to-face situation or in a video-enhanced distance learning environment. The digital option, however, offers the opportunity to all participants to interact in real time. Since this technology often helps to overcome communication anxieties, it is also often the case that, independent of location, more people can actually participate in the discussions. To be sure, such a phenomenon can lead to conditions where the discussion can become unwieldy, given the fact that many more people participate in the discussion. Most research on chat room environments indicates that the lurking habit is insignificant in the synchronous chat room as compared to the asynchronous list services and Usenet bulletin boards. Consequently, a Babel of voices can be heard in the chat room. Yet such a collection of voices demonstrates that more agents are using the opportunity provided by the technology to utter their point of view using their own voice instead of either being silent or having someone else speak for them. In this new pedagogic space, the very act of utterance becomes a determinate moment, since it demonstrates that anyone has the right and ability to speak in this geographically distributed classroom and that location and status could disappear in the nonhierarchical teaching situation (Mitra, Chesner, Burg, & Ferebee, 2000).

Indeed, the shift from being spoken for by a class representative or even by the teacher could disappear in the technology-enhanced distance learning environment where traditional determinants of speaking capital are removed. In the past, with video technology, the teacher would have a group of students in a face-to-face classroom and a different set of students in the distant classroom. Often the physical proximity to the teacher and the easier interactivity offered in the face-to-face classroom gave those students a certain advantage in gaining the teacher's attention. However, the digital classroom removes such biases, since in cyberspace the teacher and all the students are equidistant from one another, and no particular voice has any advantage based on geographic placement. This is true both for synchronous and asynchronous distance learning technologies. It can be argued that in the asynchronous technologies that use electronic mail or Web-based tools, every voice is equitably placed in terms of distance. Indeed, the classroom in such cases becomes "ageographic," since the presence of the other students and teachers are felt in the voices and texts that appear on the ubiquitous computer screen of the student and the teacher. Here, momentarily, the technology of the computer erases the traditional relationships between voice and physical location, giving each player an equal voice.

This egalitarianism is also related to the way in which the teacher can exercise control in allowing or disallowing certain voices to be heard. As suggested earlier, the power attached to the teacher has often been the result of the physical structure of the classroom. In the case of distance learning environments, where teachers would be teaching before a video camera and the students would be watching a television monitor, the teacher takes on the role of the narrator and the teacher's voice necessarily becomes more powerful. The teacher becomes the authoritative voice that is broadcast over closed-circuit television or by videotapes sent to students. However, in the digital situation, such technological and spatial advantages do not exist and the teacher often has fewer tools available to control the flow of the discourse. The natural advantage attached to spatial arrangement is lost, but the teacher and the students are required to mobilize their discursive strategies to assure their voices are heard. Indeed, within a distance learning scenario where the teacher does not occupy a predefined position of power, it is possible that, instead of being a teacher, the person has to become a moderator to control the flow of the discourse rather than supervise who has a voice in that discourse. When considering the pedagogic condition from the perspective of voice, it becomes clear that the role of the teacher in the discursive environment changes, since it is the voice that becomes more important than a presence that is dependent on pre-existing power vectors. In the electronic distance learning classroom, the speaking capital determines the teaching process rather than the capital attached to other determinants such as school year, teacher status, or even the physical set up of the classroom.

It is clear that the new technologies are transforming the relations of power between the various voices that compose the new digital learning space that can well be spread over great distances. Changing power relations, first, places unique strains and demands on the teacher, whose voice has traditionally been the authoritative one. In the cyber classroom of distance learning, a new space begins to emerge–a cybernetic space–where the power relations of cyberspace and the power relations of real space begin to merge (Mitra & Schwartz, 2001). The voices of the students, who could well have been marginalized in the past, now take on importance, for instance, in a chat-based classroom. Those voices now demand to be heard. Not acknowledging those voices can have far-reaching outcomes both for the teacher and the student(s) who might go unacknowledged. This is particularly true in the cybernetic space where the teacher and student both create their presence by uttering their voices. The primary mode of interaction within the digital classroom is with the use of the texts and discourses that the voices produce. Consequently, the teachers must be able and willing to acknowledge the presence of the voices as well as moderate their density so that a few do not monopolize the discourse. Thus, there are two new demands that digital technology places on the teacher–to acknowledge and to moderate. In the end, the way in which a teacher is able to attend to the voices can shape the second key transformation that results from the use of digital technology in the distance teaching environment–the emphasis on teaching as a discursive process.

That voice can be considered central in thinking about the new technology also opens up the opportunity to consider the new pedagogic space primarily as a discursive space where the centrality of discourse and dialog is emphasized. As mentioned earlier, the teaching process is more acutely a discursive act in contemporary distance education. Here, what is voiced, how it is acknowledged, and the response it elicits creates a pedagogic dialog that is more akin to the traditional "discussion" session in the traditional classroom. However, it is also the case that, in the progress of the dialog, the various voices can take on equal amplitude, and the teacher's voice becomes less important. This focus on discourse and dialog, while empirically observable in the new environment of distance education, can perhaps be better managed and understood when it is possible to bring in the idea of voice to the analysis of digitally enhanced distance learning. Indeed, by focusing on voice, it can be argued that the new distance learning process must engender the process of dialog and discourse to take maximum advantage of the new technologies that are available now.

The distance learning classroom now becomes a discursive space and the way in which the space is constructed is dependent on the way the discourse is created and managed. With the disappearance of the traditional relations of power, the eloquence of the voices of the discursive space of the distance classroom could determine who actually "teaches." A teacher who is not eloquent could easily see his or her "authoritative voice" being usurped by a more eloquent student.

CONCLUSION

The use of enhanced technology in the distance learning scenario opens up a series of pedagogic opportunities that go far beyond the options provided by the traditional analog technologies that were introduced for teaching students geographically distant from the teacher. However, as suggested in this article, these new opportunities can also transform the relationships between teachers and students and those changes can have far-reaching implications on the effectiveness of technology use. It is certainly possible and necessary to understand these effects in terms of measurable outcomes, such as those of grades, scores, and learning outcomes. However, it is also important to be able to understand how these technologies can begin to transform the learning space and the learning experience. Often the transformations in the process of learning are not easily measured by the "objective" measurements such as those of grades and scores. Yet, the difficult-to-measure transformations can have a strong role to play in the way students learn.

In this analysis we have suggested that these second- and third-order transformations, as suggested by Sproull and Kiesler (1992), can be conceptualized in terms of voices of the different agents who populate the emerging cybernetic learning space. When considered from the perspective of voice, these spaces can also be thought of as discursive spaces, where the different voices are expected to enter into a dialog with one another thus creating a pedagogic discourse where the traditional determinants of power and authority are called into question. However, the transformations of power and authority make it necessary to "measure" these changes because the tracking of the changes can eventually offer clues about the way in which the roles of the teacher and student change in the new spaces created by these technologies. The measurement here may well be done using qualitative measures such as those of participant observation, focus groups, and ethnographic tools, but the findings from such analysis could offer directions for policy decisions about what the new teacher-moderator is expected to do and what the active student agent is supposed to be doing. The new technologies thus not only call for the development of new forms of content presentation of courses but also the way in which the various players speak. The perspective of voice offers the opportunity to examine the modalities of speaking. Indeed, as we voice ourselves in this emerging space, going online to teach what comes online is the way we manage the discourses that make up the teaching and learning experience.

REFERENCES

Akahori, K. (2001). *Improvement of university classes introducing topics-based discussion using the Web bulletin board.* Paper presented at the annual World Conference on Educational Multimedia, Hypermedia and Telecommunications, Tampere, Finland.

Anderson, L. (2001, August 13). E-learning in Barcelona news from campus. *Financial Times.*

Archee, R., & Whitty, M. (2001). *Enhancing student access to the university: The integration of online and course-based material for the visually impaired.* Paper presented at the annual World Conference on Educational Multimedia, Hypermedia and Telecommunications, Tampere, Finland.

Barker, P. (2001). *Creating and supporting online learning communities.* Paper presented at the annual World Conference on Educational Multimedia, Hypermedia and Telecommunications, Tampere, Finland.

Carlisle, R. D. B. (1974). *College credit through TV: Old idea, new dimension.* Lincoln, NE: Great Plains National Instructional Television Library.

Carpenter, R. L. (1978). Multipoint closed circuit interactive television as a response mode to the need for inservice training in special education. *Educational Technology, 18,* 6-19.

Chapanis, A. (1983). *Interactive communication: A few research answers for a technological explosion.* Paper presented at the Annual Convention of the American Psychological Association, Ontario, Canada.

Charles, J. (1986). Interactive television: Use your imagination and help your students. *Audiovisual Instruction, 21,* 23-25.

Collins, M. (1998). The use of email and electronic bulletin boards in college level biology. *Journal of Computers in Mathematics and Science Teaching, 17*(1), 75-94.

Davidson-Shivers, G.V. (2001). *Gender and online discussions: Similarities or differences?* Paper presented at the annual World Conference on Educational Multimedia, Hypermedia and Telecommunications, Tampere, Finland.

Davidson-Shivers, G.V., Muilenburg, L., & Tanner, E. (2000). *Synchronous and asynchronous discussion: What are the differences in student participation?* Paper presented at the annual World Conference on Educational Multimedia, Hypermedia and Telecommunications, Montreal, Quebec, Canada.

Davidson-Shivers, G.V., Muilenburg, L., & Tanner, E. (in press). How do students participate in synchronous and asynchronous online discussions? *Journal of Educational Computing Research.*

Denton, J. J., Clark, F. E., Rossing, R. G., & O'Connor, M. J. (1984). Assessing instructional strategies and resulting student attitudes regarding two-way television instruction. *Journal of Educational Technology Systems, 13*(4), 13.

Draper, N. (2001). *Net-based learning.* Paper presented at the annual World Conference on Educational Multimedia, Hypermedia and Telecommunications, Tampere, Finland.

Gerhardt, K. J. (2000). A doctoral degree in audiology offered through distance-learning. In D. G. Brown (Ed.), *Teaching with technology* (pp. 129-133). Bolton, MA: Anker.

Hezel, R. T. (1980). Public broadcasting: Can it teach? *Journal of Communication, 30* (3), 173-178.

Hudson, B. (1998). Group work with multimedia: The role of the computer in mediating mathematical meaning-making. *Journal of Computers in Mathematics and Science Teaching, 4*(2/3), 181-201.

Hyde, M. J., & Mitra, A. (2000). On the ethics of creating a face in cyberspace: The case of a university. In V. Berdayes & J. Murphy (Eds.), *Computers, human interaction and organizations* (pp. 161-188). New York: Praeger.

Hyde, M. J., & Rufo, K. (2000). The call of conscience, rhetorical interruptions, and the euthanasia controversy. *Journal of Applied Communication Research, 28,* 1-23.

Ladewski, B.G. (1996). Comparing and contrasting four systems. *Interactive Multimedia Learning Environments, 15*(1/2), 173-197.

Lewis, P. (1961). *Educational television guidebook.* New York, NY: McGraw-Hill.

Mitra, A. (1988). *The use of interactive television in the place of classroom lectures.* Paper presented at the annual convention of the American Evaluation Association, New Orleans.

Mitra, A. (2001). Diasporic voices in cyberspace. *New Media and Society, 3*(1), 29-48.

Mitra, A., Chesner, C., Burg, J., & Ferebee, M. (2000). Computer-mediated communication and face-to-face instruction: An integrative perspective for a changing society using a case study approach. In D. G. Brown (Ed.), *Teaching with technology* (pp. 220-224). Bolton, MA: Anker.

Mitra, A., & Schwartz, R. L. (2001). From cyberspace to cybernetic space: Rethinking the relationship between real and virtual spaces. *Journal of Computer Mediated Communication, 7*(1). [Online]. Available: http://www.ascusc.org/jcmc/vol7/issue1/mitra.html

Mitra, A., & Watts, E. (in press). Theorizing cyberspace: The idea of voice applied to the Internet discourse. *New Media and Society.*

Najjar, L.J. (1996). Multimedia information and learning. *Journal of Educational Multimedia and Hypermedia, 5*(2), 129-150.

Natan, N., & Barkai, I. (2001). *Concept maps: E-learning environment.* Paper presented at the annual World Conference on Educational Multimedia, Hypermedia and Telecommunications, Tampere, Finland.

Negroponte, N. (1995). *Being digital.* New York: Knopf.

Peters, O. (1993). Understanding distance education. In K. Harry & M. Hohn (Eds.), *Distance education: New perspectives.* London, UK: Routledge.

Roxin, I. (2001). *Broadband multimedia for distance education via satellite.* Paper presented at the annual World Conference on Educational Multimedia, Hypermedia and Telecommunications, Tampere, Finland.

Schramm, W. (1964). *Mass media and national development.* Stanford, CA: Stanford University Press.

Smith, R , Waby, P., Neville, P., & Dalloway, J. (1999). *Adaptive technology and communication for blind and sight impaired users: Its impact on education and work opportunities.* Paper presented at the Disability in Education Conference, Otago University, New Zealand.

Spivak, G. C. (1988). Can the subaltern speak? In C. Nelson & L. Grossberg (Eds.), *Marxism and the interpretation of culture* (pp. 217-313). Urbana, IL: University of Illinois Press.

Sproull, L., & Kiesler, S. (1992). *Connections: New ways of working in the networked organization.* Cambridge, MA: MIT Press.

Strickland, A.W. (2001). *Creating Web-based programs for international delivery: Curriculum and faculty concerns.* Paper presented at the annual World Conference on Educational Multimedia, Hypermedia and Telecommunications, Tampere, Finland.

Sullivan, F.R. (2001). *Constructing the on-line classroom: Interaction in the synchronous chat room.* Paper presented at the annual World Conference on Educational Multimedia, Hypermedia and Telecommunications, Tampere, Finland.

Walther, J. B. (1992). Interpersonal effects in computer-mediated interaction: A relational perspective. *Communication Research, 19*, 52-90.

Walther, J. B. (1994). Anticipated ongoing interaction versus channel effects on relational communication in computer-mediated interaction. *Human Communication Research, 20,* 473-501.

Walther, J. B. (1996). Computer-mediated communication: Impersonal, interpersonal and hyperpersonal interaction. *Communication Research, 23,* 3-43.

Williamson, D.M. (2001). *Distance education creating an environment for all: Content accessibility–tools, techniques, and methods.* Paper presented at the annual World Conference on Educational Multimedia, Hypermedia and Telecommunications, Tampere, Finland.

Wittlich, G. E., & Rubens, E. (2000). Computing environment at Indiana University. In D. G. Brown (Ed.), *Teaching with technology* (pp. 25-28). Bolton, MA: Anker.

Young, S. (2001a). *Confident men-successful women: Gender differences in online learning.* Paper presented at the annual World Conference on Educational Multimedia, Hypermedia and Telecommunications, Tampere, Finland.

Young, S. (2001b). *Innovative use of bulletin boards in undergraduate and masters level online courses.* Paper presented at the annual World Conference on Educational Multimedia, Hypermedia and Telecommunications, Tampere, Finland.

Young, S., Dewstow, R., & McSporran, M. (1999). *Who wants to learn online? What types of students benefit from new learning environment?* Paper presented at the National Advisory Committee on Computing Qualifications Conference, Dunedin, New Zealand.

Heidi Schweizer
Joan Whipp
Carrianne Hayslett

Quality Control in Online Courses: Using a Social Constructivist Framework

SUMMARY. There has recently been increased interest in the quality of online courses. Faculty from the School of Education at Marquette University suggest using social constructivist theories in the design and development of online courses and in the training and pedagogy of online instructors to ensure quality in online courses. Quality can be designed into online courses by focusing on complex tasks, using multiple perspectives, establishing a learning community, encouraging the social negotiation of meaning and providing assistance for learners at various levels. While good design can go a long way to ensure quality in online courses, the quality of the instructor is equally critical. Training instructors to establish a supportive climate, provide constructive feedback, and ask critical and probing questions leads to high quality online instruction. *[Article copies available for a fee from The Haworth Document Delivery Service:*

HEIDI SCHWEIZER is Assistant Professor of Education and Director, Center for Electronic Learning, Marquette University, School of Education, P.O. Box 1881, Milwaukee, WI 53201 (E-mail: Heidi.Schweizer@marquette.edu).
JOAN WHIPP is Assistant Professor of Education and Co-Chair, Educational Policy and Leadership, Marquette University, School of Education, P.O. Box 1881, Milwaukee, WI 53201 (E-mail: Joan.Whipp@marquette.edu).
CARRIANNE HAYSLETT is a doctoral student, Educational Policy and Leadership, Marquette University, School of Education, P.O. Box 1881, Milwaukee, WI 53201 (E-mail: Carrianne.Hayslett@marquette.edu).

[Haworth co-indexing entry note]: "Quality Control in Online Courses: Using a Social Constructivist Framework." Schweizer, Heidi, Joan Whipp, and Carrianne Hayslett. Co-published simultaneously in *Computers in the Schools* (The Haworth Press, Inc.) Vol. 19, No. 3/4, 2002, pp. 143-158; and: *Distance Education: Issues and Concerns* (ed: Cleborne D. Maddux, Jacque Ewing-Taylor, and D. LaMont Johnson) The Haworth Press, Inc., 2002, pp. 143-158. Single or multiple copies of this article are available for a fee from The Haworth Document Delivery Service [1-800-HAWORTH, 9:00 a.m. - 5:00 p.m. (EST). E-mail address: getinfo@haworthpressinc.com].

143

1-800-HAWORTH. E-mail address: <getinfo@haworthpressinc.com> Website: <http://www.HaworthPress.com> © 2002 by The Haworth Press, Inc. All rights reserved.]

KEYWORDS. Quality online courses, social constructivist, asynchronous, Marquette University, pedagogy, distance learning, e-learning, online course design, teaching online

Despite the explosive growth of online courses in higher education in recent years from 753,640 students enrolled in 1994-95 to 1.6 million in 1997-98 (U.S. Department of Education, 1999), questions about the quality of these courses are only beginning to surface (American Federation of Teachers, 2000; Carnevale, 2000; Robbin, 2000). Much of the popular and practitioner-oriented literature on online courses emphasizes their virtues: quick and remote access to information and instruction, convenience, speed of communication, instant feedback, potential for interactivity, ability to reach large audiences, and cost savings for students (Eamon, 1999; Hantula; 1998; Koch & Gobell, 1999; Pychyl, Clarke & Abarbanel, 1999; Vodanovich & Piotrowski, 1999). This literature tends to minimize difficulties in routinely providing high quality courses or assessing whether students are learning from them (Hara & Kling, 2000; Neuman, 1995).

Research studies have done little more to illuminate the issue of quality in online education because of flawed methodology (Dillon & Gabbard, 1998). Several studies focus on the effectiveness of online courses compared to traditional, face-to-face instruction (Robbin, 2000); however, often these studies rely on standardized tests as the outcome measure, basing assessment of quality on a mere acquisition of facts (Brower & Klay, 2000). Other studies only focus on learner satisfaction, most often determined by student self-reports in end-of-course evaluations.

Further clouding any comprehensive assessment of online course quality are the widely disparate methods, media, and terms used to deliver and talk about these courses. Any review of literature on online learning will call up closely related but dissimilar reports that interchange the terms "distance learning," "online learning," "Web-based learning," "e-learning," and older terms like "computer-mediated conferencing," "computer-assisted learning," and "correspondence courses." Platforms for delivery of partial or completely online courses can vary greatly and include asynchronous course management systems, synchronous Webcasts, videoconferencing, Web pages, instructional videos, listservs, and/or Web-based chat rooms. Furthermore, visions of learning and instruction guiding these courses can range widely among behaviorist, information-processing, constructivist, and socially oriented models (Koschmann, 1996). It is important, then, in any discussion of quality in distance education to clarify precisely what type of learning at a distance is being discussed and what principles of learning and teaching are guiding design and delivery.

THEORETICAL FRAMEWORK
FOR ONLINE COURSE DESIGN AND DELIVERY

For the past five years we have taught online staff development and graduate education courses in technology, curriculum planning, learning theories, teacher research, and teacher leadership to more than 600 practicing teachers. Typically, these courses meet face-to-face for the first and last sessions; the rest are conducted online in a course management system developed by either Lotus Learning Space or BlackBoard. In both the design and delivery of these courses, we have tried "to create the kind of learning community that can arise in a good graduate seminar" (Hiltz, 1998, p. 2).

To do this, we find that social constructivist theories (Rogoff, 1990; Salomon & Perkins, 1998; Wertsch, Del Rio, & Alvarez, 1995; Vygotsky, 1978), with their focus on complex and authentic activities, social interaction, intentional learning communities, and guided assistance to learners, offer frameworks for course design, teaching, and training of faculty to teach online. In particular these principles guide our work:

1. *Complex environment and authentic tasks.* Learning must take place in rich environments that engage learners in real-world problems and activities rather than artificial exercises (Duffy & Cunningham, 1996). Students need to look at problems in complex ways and use a variety of means to represent their understanding.

2. *Social negotiation of meaning.* What counts as knowledge and how one thinks about and expresses ideas about that knowledge come from interactions with others in a variety of learning communities, both formal (academic classrooms, scholarly disciplines) and informal (social groups sharing a common interest, families, neighborhoods). Putnam and Borko (2000) suggest that

these communities "provide the cognitive tools–ideas, theories, and concepts–that individuals adopt as their own and use to make sense of their experience" (p. 5). Through extended dialogue and collective problem solving with others who have both greater and lesser expertise than they do, learners move from what they currently know to more complex understandings (Brown, Collins, & Duguid, 1989; Salomon & Perkins, 1998).

3. *Intentional learning communities.* Building an intentional learning community where there is a shared sense of purpose around the generation and sharing of new knowledge is critical to more formal learning environments. The learners are in control, continually diagnosing their own learning needs and identifying what they will do next. Learning is collective as students jointly create a product rather than simply summarize their individual understandings (Scardamalia & Bereiter, 1996).

4. *Assistance for learners at varying zones of proximal development.* Instead of imparting blocks of knowledge to passive learners, the teacher creates an environment where teachers and learners can jointly construct knowledge and become more self-aware and self-directed in their learning process. Through modeling and feedback, both teachers and learners nudge each other to higher levels of understanding.

In this article, we demonstrate how we are using these social constructivist principles for both design and delivery of an online graduate course, Teacher as Leader. The course focuses on leadership development for practicing teachers who want to remain in the classroom but also assume leadership roles in their schools.

DESIGN OF ONLINE COURSES

Complex Environment and Authentic Tasks

We begin the course design process with lengthy conversations about what we want our students to know and be able to do when they complete the course. Essential to this conversation is how the course content can be connected in ways that are meaningful, challenging, and relevant to the teachers who take our courses. Our conversations then focus on the development of clear learning outcomes and authentic assessments that set rigorous expectations. For example, in the Teacher as Leader course we expected the learners to:

1. Describe and critically evaluate the leadership roles they have or may potentially have in the classroom, team, school, or organization.
2. Demonstrate basic knowledge of human relation principles, communication skills, and motivational theory as applied to leadership in several educational settings.
3. Apply the skills of an effective leader to a collaborative group process that results in meaningful change in one's school, district, or organization.

To assess these outcomes, we ask students to participate in weekly discussions that focus on the analysis of readings and multimedia presentations and include applying this information to their own experiences in schools. Additional assessments include collaborative analyses of leadership dilemma case studies and a major leadership project. Students initiate, collaborate, and lead others in the planning and initial implementation of a project that can potentially lead to a significant instructional or organizational change in their schools.

When designing online learning environments, we constantly consider ways to provide a variety of options for students to access information, interact with the information, and finally represent the knowledge they have constructed. Technology in general and the online environment in particular provide unique and ever-expanding opportunities to engage the learner in a learning process that honors multiple forms of intelligence–abstract, textual, visual, musical, social, kinesthetic, and inter personal. As designers and teachers of online courses, we have learned to incorporate articles, Web sites, guest lectures, textbooks, videos, audio clips, lecture notes, CD-ROMs, music, peer reviews/reactions, interviews, projects, animation, discussions, reflective journals, PowerPoint presentations, desktop publishing, simulations, case studies, and interactive games into our online courses resulting in a rich online learning environment. An example of an assignment in Teacher as Leader that allows for multiple modes of expression is found in Figure 1.

Establishing a Learning Community

Online discussions and projects. We see the students in the online classroom as a collection of creative "authors" and project teams. Early in the course, student project teams are given the opportunity to name themselves, which they often do with nicknames like Techno Chics,

FIGURE 1. Online assignment.

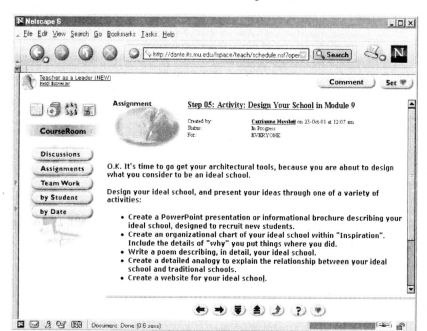

Gamma Quadrant, or Midnighters. Each week students engage in on-line discussions or projects that focus on problems or situations that they may be facing as teacher leaders in their schools or organizations. They use a variety of course materials to look at those problems or situations from multiple perspectives. At the end of many discussions a student on each team synthesizes the group discussion and "publishes" it in the online discussion room so that other teams can read and react to it. Team projects are also made public in the discussion room and become an ongoing record of the joint knowledge building in the learning community.

Small discussion groups and teams. We divide classes of 15-20 into smaller discussion groups to promote a common belief and experience that "six" minds jointly constructing meaning really are better than one. We encourage each member of the group to take on a specific role in the group, and we also encourage group members to alternate these roles from week to week. These roles can include discussion leader, summarizer, devil's advocate, technician, encourager, and muse. The discussion leader begins the week's discussion and periodically poses questions to the group. The summarizer synthesizes highlights of the group discussion at the end of the week and publishes it in the discussion room. The devil's advocate continually raises questions, challenges assumptions, and poses counter-positions. The technician offers support to those experiencing technical problems. The encourager monitors participation and sends a supportive e-mail to anyone not participating. The muse offers inspiration to the group, whether it be with humor, quotations, or new resources.

Social Negotiation of Meaning

Activities and discussion prompts. We carefully design question prompts, assignments, and activities to create an environment that actively engages students to collectively construct meaning. Through document sharing, asynchronous discussions, and attachments, students debate issues, assume positions and counter-positions, role play, persuade others to take a position, invent solutions to problems and assess the efficacy of those solutions. For example, in Teacher as Leader we ask students to debate whether management and leadership are the same thing, to take on the roles of specific types of leaders, to face the challenge of trying to reach a consensus by role playing, and to suggest solutions to problems faced by a school in one of the course readings. We ask students to look critically at relevant literature on topics such as equitable funding in education, academic freedom versus accountability and centralization, and the value of multicultural education. Students assess theoretical and research literature on these issues and then draw connections between readings and their own experiences.

Discussion rubric. It is difficult to design and harder to sustain an environment in which every member of the online learning community is held accountable for advancing the dialogue. To reach this goal, we require participation in the learning community, basing a portion of the course grade on active involvement in the class. Furthermore, to scaffold these discussions beyond simple chat, we use a discussion rubric (Figure 2). The rubric offers the online student specific criteria that address not only the frequency and timeliness of contributions but also the quality of his or her contributions to the discussions. We have discussed this rubric with our students and revised it over time. As we have developed more specific guidelines for online discussions, we have found that the quality of those discussions has improved.

FIGURE 2. Rubric for asynchronous discussion.

Discussion Rubric

Frequency of Discussion Responses

___(5) interacts at least three times with instructor and/or other students

___(3) interacts at least twice with instructor and/or other students

___(1) interacts once with either the instructor or other students

Timeliness

___(5) All three entries submitted on time (lst by Wednesday; remaining by Saturday)

___(3) All submitted but some submitted late

___(1) All submitted late or at least one not submitted

Evidence of Critical Thinking

___(5) Takes a fully developed critical position; analyzes, synthesizes, or evaluates information or responses of others

___(3) Some evidence of analysis, synthesis, or evaluation but not fully developed

___(1) Summarizes information or response(s) of others

Development of Ideas

___(5) Well-developed (at least a full paragraph) and introduces new ideas; uses specific details from readings/experience as support

___(3) Some weakness in development/use of supporting detail but introduces new idea

___(1) Very weak development/use of supporting detail; does not add to discussion

Interactivity

___(5) Makes specific reference to one or more postings and presents counter-positions to issues raised by others

___(3) Makes some reference to one or more postings of others

___(1) Makes no reference to other postings

Assisting Learners at Varying Zones of Proximal Development

Throughout our work with online courses, we have surveyed our students about the challenges they face in this learning environment and what kinds of supports they need. In addition to the invariable technical challenges in any online course, our students tell us that procrastination and time management issues, isolation, and writing anxiety pose the greatest problems. To support our students in these areas of need, we have built several features into our course design.

Supports for time management. We provide schedules, calendars, and time completion charts; these tools seem to assist many students to organize their time and maintain regular participation in the course. We set consistent deadlines for initial discussion input and replies to others during weekly discussions; these deadlines seem to support interactivity and encourage greater depth and breadth in discussions.

Supports to reduce isolation and increase interactivity. We build into all courses an announcement or welcome page for instructors to easily highlight special information and with options for using pictures, jokes, and anecdotes that personalize the course for students. We find that changing this page frequently keeps students appropriately updated and helps to maintain student interest. We include a private portfolio for each student, where instructors can provide constructive feedback about his or her work and notification of current grade standing in the class. In each of our courses we also create a Cyber Cafe as an informal area where students can pose questions, share ideas and resources, or initiate conversations.

Supports to reduce writing anxiety. For all course topics, we provide optional resources such as Web sites, articles, or audio clips that can encourage students with less experience or knowledge to build understanding and write about more difficult topics. For example, in Teacher as Leader, we ask students to debate the differences between management and leadership. To assist them in their discussion, we include optional readings, Web sites, and case studies for those without management or leadership experience. We also include design templates and model projects for major assignments that assist in guiding and encouraging less experienced or more reluctant students to aim for higher levels of quality in their work.

TRAINING AND PEDAGOGY

Good design can contribute greatly to the quality of an online course; however, the quality of the instruction is equally critical (Berge & Collins, 1995; Palloff & Pratt, 1999; White & Weight, 2000). For this reason, we assure that all online instructors have time to practice and reflect on effective online teaching practices.

Before each semester, we conduct a four-day on-campus seminar for new and returning online instructors. In addition, we offer online instructors an optional four-week online course, "Facilitating Your Online Classroom." By asking them to participate in asynchronous discussions, submit assignments, and harness the power of distance technologies, this course encourages instructors to put themselves in the place of online learners and to think about how to teach them.

Again, guided by social constructivist principles, both instructor training experiences focus largely on what instructors need to do to create a complex online learning environment where students actively engage each other in challenging discussions and joint projects and where they are also challenged to become more self-aware and directed in their learning process. In particular, we have found that online instructors need to (a) establish and nurture a collaborative and supportive climate and (b) use probing questions and modeling to scaffold discussions to deeper and more complex levels.

Establishing and Nurturing a Collaborative and Supportive Climate

In an environment where students can initially feel uncertain or isolated, it is critical that online teachers make the environment an inviting one. In our training sessions, we help them create personal Web pages in the course so that they can immediately establish a presence and connection with their students. On the Web page, instructors include a picture; background information about experience, interests, family, and hobbies; and links to other personal information. Figure 3 shows one instructor's Web page created for the Teacher as Leader course.

We use models from previous courses to help each instructor create a welcome letter that is sent out to students before class begins and a "welcome" Web page that becomes the first page students see when they enter the course. We show instructors how they can use color, graphics, and animation on this Web page to create an invitational climate for learning and how they can change this page on a weekly basis. Again, using samples of interactions between teachers and students in previous online courses, we work with new instructors on practicing ways to set an approachable and encouraging tone in their interactions through a friendly, informal writing style that addresses students by first names and that acknowledges student strengths:

> Tina, I want to chime in to support your candor, but I also want to thank you and others who are doing this–for making a direct connection between your experience and specific concepts in the reading. It seems as though we're getting particularly "rich" discussions from people's willingness to share personal experiences that compliment the readings, and people's willingness to voice divergent ideas and personal experiences that contradict the readings. I, personally, find both interesting and illuminating.

FIGURE 3. Personal Web page for an instructor.

Helen, thank you for your honesty and openness. You should not feel any embarrassment at all. You have shown a great deal of courage by coming back to the second face-to-face "help" session and also getting this journal assignment done. Please contact the tech people or me as soon as you feel you might be confused about something so that you don't have to feel frustrated when things don't go the way you anticipated.

Prompt and helpful feedback in an online environment is particularly important because otherwise students can feel alone or ignored. For this reason, we ask that instructors respond to students within forty-eight hours of each posting and to be more specific in their feedback than "nice job" or "I really like what you are saying." Feedback needs to reflect that "students need to know what they know in order to focus their learning. Students need help in assessing existing knowledge and performance, in addition to having opportunities to get suggestions for improvement. They need to reflect on what they have learned, what they still need to learn, and how to evaluate the learning process" (White & Weight, 2000, p. 167).

In the training sessions we offer instructors a variety of additional materials and strategies that they can use to set and maintain a climate that encourages student collaboration and the development of a learning community: icebreaker activities, team building and cooperative learning activities, personal Web pages for students, and private e-mail and phone calls to individual students who need extra support or encouragement, especially during the first few weeks of class.

Using Probing Questions and Modeling

In the design process, we focus on creating question prompts, assignments, and activities that provoke thoughtful and social construction of new knowledge. A provocative prompt is important, but unless it is followed up with prompt and helpful feedback, a learning community is not likely to develop. An important part of providing meaningful feedback includes critical questioning that can help to continually move the conversation to deeper and richer levels and also model for students the critical thinking, social negotiation of ideas, and self-reflection important to the learning process. Using transcripts of actual online discussions, we spend time in these training sessions helping instructors practice posing questions that:

1. *challenge assumptions or sources of information* (What have you seen to support your belief that students learn by doing? Have you noticed a difference in students' understanding or performance on assessments when you use traditional versus experiential learning?)
2. *ask students to ground claims in theory* (Can you relate your comments, "I sometimes don't bring everything I know to the table, sometimes I don't know as much as I think I do, and sometimes I assume that everyone understands" to the discussion of communication styles in our text?)
3. *move students toward self-evaluation and reflection* (You say, "Hmmm, looks like I don't think much about inborn characteristics or authority as sources of leadership abilities." How does this response compare with the class as a whole? What does it say about your own leadership experiences?)
4. *look for further clarification, examples, or more detail* (I'm not following your connection between biblical stereotypes and the

Civil Rights Movement. Would you please explain and describe it further? I found your comment about a problem-solver being a person who doesn't start controversy interesting. It seems as though you see problem-solvers as people who do not raise issues that need to be solved, but only apply themselves to issues raised by others. Is that a fair translation of your statement?)

5. *offer contrasting perspectives and counter-positions on issues* (If power comes from the interdependence of a group, isn't it equally likely for anyone in the group to have power? How come it's not uncommon for some people to consistently have power positions and some people to consistently not have power positions if power arises out of group interdependence?)

6. *challenge students to consider solutions* (Talk about direct pressure on dissenters! Your example really illustrates one way a leader can almost guarantee groupthink. Has anyone ever effectively voiced an opposing opinion around this person in your school? If so, how did they do it and what happened?)

7. *ask students to apply what they are learning to a real-life situation* (Do you think this novel idea has any hope of being adopted in education? If it were your job to get parents, other teachers, administrators, and politicians to support this kind of education, do you think you could do it? What might be some obstacles? What arguments might you use to overcome those obstacles?)

We also spend some time with the instructors discussing how they can take advantage of different levels of expertise in their online class and accommodate a wide range of cognitive needs. They can encourage more knowledgeable and experienced students to offer examples, metaphors, and life experiences that will scaffold the understanding of more complex concepts for those less knowledgeable and experienced. Instructors can also assign "expert" or "devil's advocate" roles early in the course to certain students so that they can share with others their knowledge and experiences and model the kind of critical questioning that supports social negotiation of meaning.

CONCLUSION

Interactive, self-directed, intentional, and complex learning environments set rigorous and quality online courses apart from those courses that require not much more than rote learning in impersonal, isolated, and simplistic electronic settings. In our experience, social constructivist theories have offered useful frameworks for the design and teaching of such courses. However, these theories need to be more widely used to frame rigorous and systematic studies of online learning and teaching that move beyond the measurement of simple rote learning tasks or learner satisfaction. Some questions that could guide future research include:

1. What are the effects of online discussions, joint projects, or other course activities on individual and collective thinking processes?
2. What is the nature and effect of teacher and/or student modeling and feedback in online discussions?
3. What elements of design and delivery best scaffold individual and/or collective construction of knowledge in the online environment?
4. How do student-to-student or teacher-to-student interactions propel discussions to deeper or more complex levels of thinking?
5. What does "social negotiation of meaning" look like in the online environment? What best supports it?
6. What are effective ways to evaluate levels of interaction in an online course?
7. What strategies for ongoing support do online instructors need to nurture and sustain a more complex learning environment?
8. What strategies help members of an online learning community (individually and collectively) become more self-aware and self-directed in their learning process?

Designing and teaching online courses that are grounded in social constructivist theories certainly begin to address concerns raised about quality in the online learning environment. However, only as we study our own practices, continually testing the effectiveness of what we do, will we be able to uncover the richness of the online environment and its potential to provide powerful learning opportunities to an ever-expanding audience.

REFERENCES

American Federation of Teachers (2000). AFT proposes standards for online colleges and universities. Retrieved September 25, 2001, from http://www.aft.org/convention/onlinepr.html

Berge, Z. I., & Collins, M. P. (Eds.) (1995). *Computer mediated communication and the online classroom.* Cresskill, NJ: Hampton Press.

Brower, R., & Klay, W. E. (2000). Distance learning: Some fundamental questions for public affairs education. *Journal of Public Administration Education*, 6(4), 215-232.

Brown, J. S., Collins, A., & Duguid, P. (1989). Situated cognition and the culture of learning. *Educational Researcher*, 18(1), 32-42.

Carnevale, D. (2000). U.S. lawmaker questions quality of the online-learning experience. *Chronicle of Higher Education*, 46(38), 51.

Dillon, A., & Gabbard, R. (1998). Hypermedia as an educational technology: A review of the empirical literature on learner comprehension, control and style. *Review of Educational Research*, 63(3), 322-349.

Duffy, T. M., & Cunningham, D. J. (1996). Constructivism: Implications for the design and delivery of instruction. In D.H. Jonassen (Ed.), *Handbook of research for educational communications and technology*. New York: Macmillan.

Eamon, D. B. (1999). Distance education: Has technology become a threat to the academy? *Behavior Research Methods, Instruments, & Computers*, 31, 197-207.

Hantula, D. A. (1998). The virtual industrial/organizational psychology class: Learning and teaching in cyberspace in three iterations. *Behavior Research Methods, Instruments, & Computers*, 30, 205-216.

Hara, N., & Kling, R. (2000). Students' distress with a Web-based distance education course. Retrieved October 6, 2001, from http://www.slis.indiana.edu/CSI/wp00-01.html

Hiltz, R.S. (1998). *Collaborative learning in asynchronous learning networks: Building learning communities*. Paper presented at WebNet 98 World Conference of the WWW, Internet and Intranet, Orlando, FL.

Koch, C., & Gobell, J. (1999). A hypertext-based tutorial with links to the Web for teaching statistics and research methods. *Behavioral Research Methods, Instruments, & Computers*, 31, 7-13.

Koschmann, T. (1996). Paradigm shifts and instructional technology: An introduction. In T. Koschmann (Ed.), *CSCL: Theory and practice of an emerging paradigm* (pp. 1-23). Mahwah, NJ: Erlbaum.

Neuman, W. R. (1995). The psychology of the new media. *Education Review*, 48-54.

Palloff, R. M., & Pratt, K. (1999). Building learning communities in cyberspace: Effective strategies for the online classroom. San Francisco: Jossey-Bass.

Putnam, R. T., & Borko, H. (2000). What do new views of knowledge and thinking have to say about research on teacher learning? *Educational Researcher*, 29(1), 4-15.

Pychyl, T. A., Clarke, D., & Abarbanel, T. (1999). Computer-mediated group projects: Facilitating collaborative learning with the World Wide Web. *Teaching of Psychology*, 26, 138-141.

Robbin, A. (2000). Creating social spaces to facilitate reflective learning on-line. Available at http://www.slis.indiana.edu/csi/wp01-01.html

Rogoff, B. (1990). *Cognitive apprenticeship: Cognitive development in social context*. New York: Oxford University Press.

Salomon, G., & Perkins, D. N. (1998). Individual and social aspects of learning. In P.D. Pearson & A. Iran-Nejad (Eds.), *Review of Research in Education*, 23, 1-24.

Scardamelia, M., & Bereiter, C. (1996). Computer support for knowledge-building communities. In T. Koschmann (Ed.), *CSCL: Theory and practice of an emerging paradigm* (pp. 249-268). Mahwah, NJ: Erlbaum.

U.S. Department of Education, National Center for Education Statistics. (1999). Distance education at postsecondary education institutions: 1997-98. Retrieved September 25, 2001, from http://nces.ed.gov/pubs200/2000013.pdf

Vodanovich, S.J., & Piotrowski, C. (1999). Views of academic I-O psychologists toward Internet-based instruction. *The Industrial Organizational Psychologist, 37*(1), 52-55.

Vygotsky, L. (1978). *Mind in society: The development of higher psychological processes.* Cambridge, MA: Harvard University Press.

Wertsch, J. V., Del Rio, P., & Alvarez, A. (Eds.). (1995). Sociocultural studies of mind. New York: Cambridge University Press.

White, K. W., & Weight, B. H. (2000). *The online teaching guide: A handbook of attitudes, strategies, and techniques for the virtual classroom.* Boston: Allyn & Bacon.

Melodee Landis
Diane Wolfe

Distance Realities: Rural Wisdom

SUMMARY. In the eastern part of Nebraska, schools received a state grant to build a two-way audio-video network for the purpose of improving student skills in technology. A few network teachers were trained and earned Microsoft Office User Specialist (MOUS) and Windows NT certification. These skilled instructors then trained others and developed a team approach to offer computer networking and Microsoft Office courses to students in 8-11 small districts in the region. At the conclusion of the Office courses, a randomly selected group of students took the MOUS exams with favorable results. The distance system's management team has given careful consideration to the complex management issues and appropriate incentives for teachers which has resulted in high performance that may not otherwise have been possible. *[Article copies available for a fee from The Haworth Document Delivery Service: 1-800-HAWORTH. E-mail address: <getinfo@haworthpressinc.com> Website: <http://www.HaworthPress.com> © 2002 by The Haworth Press, Inc. All rights reserved.]*

KEYWORDS. Distance learning, distance education, two-way audio and video, rural distance learning, Microsoft certification, high school distance education, rural network, team teaching

MELODEE LANDIS is Assistant Professor, Teacher Education, University of Nebraska at Omaha, 6001 Dodge Street, Omaha, NE 68182-0163 (E-mail: mlandis@unomaha.edu). DIANE WOLFE is Distance Learning Coordinator/Technology Trainer, Educational Service Unit #2, P.O. Box 649, 2320 North Colorado, Fremont NE 68026 (E-mail: dwolfe@mail.esu2.org).

[Haworth co-indexing entry note]: "Distance Realities: Rural Wisdom." Landis, Melodee, and Diane Wolfe. Co-published simultaneously in *Computers in the Schools* (The Haworth Press, Inc.) Vol. 19, No. 3/4, 2002, pp. 159-169; and: *Distance Education: Issues and Concerns* (ed: Cleborne D. Maddux, Jacque Ewing-Taylor, and D. LaMont Johnson) The Haworth Press, Inc., 2002, pp. 159-169. Single or multiple copies of this article are available for a fee from The Haworth Document Delivery Service [1-800-HAWORTH, 9:00 a.m. - 5:00 p.m. (EST). E-mail address: getinfo@haworthpressinc.com].

In the past 15 years, a plethora of research aimed at evaluating student performance in two-way audio and video classes has affirmed the viability of this form of teaching and learning. In study after study, students taking courses via distance technologies have proven their abilities to perform as well as, or better than, their traditionally taught counterparts (Eiserman & Williams, 1987; Moore & Thompson, 1990; U.S. Congress, 1989).

As the research on distance instruction continues to build, however, findings indicate that, just as in the traditional classroom, there are lessons we are learning about how to manage these systems, what instruction works best, and how different approaches to the implementation of distance learning systems can make a difference. Skeptics point out that rarely are these "wisdoms" actually applied to programs implementing distance education (Young, 2000). Larry Cuban (1993) goes so far as to proclaim that, in the battle between traditional classroom practices and those practices that are best suited for technology, the old strategies win. There is the fear that the traditional patterns of classroom organization are impermeable to change, and that the newer technologies applications may prove ineffective over time due to our inability to use them properly.

The Eastern Nebraska Distance Learning Consortium (ENDLC) may be an exception to these pessimistic views of the future of distance education. Throughout the infancy of this distance learning network, program personnel gathered data of many types to monitor and adjust its activities. Teacher and administrator questionnaires related to satisfaction with the system and the instructional program were unusually positive for a beginning distance program. Teacher responses on surveys of self-efficacy were equally high. Student attitudes were positive, and their achievement of course objectives was comparable to or above that expected in traditional classes. In just three years, this consortium of schools in the northeastern quadrant of Nebraska has installed the equipment to serve 37 districts and has launched classes that are changing the lives of the area high school students.

This article takes a look at the factors that may underlie the success of this program. It seeks to share the successes, challenges, and strategies that have evolved over the course of the first three years of operation in the hopes these experiences may be beneficial to others who undertake their own distance learning programs.

A CLEAR DIRECTION

Nebraska is no newcomer to the distance learning scene. The geography and demographics of the state make it a perfect candidate for distance education. The majority of Nebraska's population resides in the southeastern corner of the state, leaving the vast majority of its land and people to agricultural, rural communities.

The communities involved in the ENDLC understood early on that technology was one of the careers that could best help their students succeed. Project leaders perceived that, if students could receive more training in computer networking and applications, the investment required for distance technologies could be of great benefit. Thus, the districts formed a consortium to underwrite and plan a distance network.

When the consortium applied for a state grant to help fund the project, several of the objectives centered on developing teacher and student skills in technology (see Table 1).

The objectives focused much of the consortium's activities on the training, planning, and support needed to successfully deliver two high school courses–one in computer systems networking management and one in Microsoft Office products. The consortium also focused on higher-level mathematics as a common need among the districts. While the math courses have been successful as well, the instructional elements used in the technology courses have proven to be most unique.

The key to successful management of distance education often lies in planning, organization, leadership, and control of a distance network. The project's instructional objectives would prove to be no easy undertaking, but this common vision among the districts was, without a doubt, one of the strengths of the network.

NETWORKING FOR NETWORKING

With the help of funding from state lottery monies, the consortium assumed a unique approach to provide incentives for the faculty leadership needed to create a computer networking class where there had been none. It was decided early on that professional certification should be a prerequisite for the lead teacher-developers of the computer networking course. In June of 1998, two lead teachers were selected to lead the charge. Both had already passed the Microsoft Certified Professional exams in Windows NT Workstation 4.9. The grant funds enabled them to attend several workshops and seminars in order to pass the Networking Essentials exam as well.

Once the two lead teachers were certified, three more were selected to become networking teachers. The lead teachers met once each week with the three novices to prepare them for the exams and to begin plan-

TABLE 1. Teacher Objectives of the Eastern Nebraska Distance Learning Consortium

Teacher Objectives

Teachers will be effective teachers of computer systems network management courses using fully interactive, two-way distance learning as indicated by:

   a) their certification as Microsoft Certified Professionals in Operating Systems, and

   b) successful teaching of the Computer Systems Network Management course sequence taught through distance learning.

Secondary teachers will be effective teachers of computer office applications courses using fully interactive, two-way distance learning as indicated by:

   a) successful teaching of the distance learning office application sequence, and

   b) their certification as Microsoft Office proficient users of Word and Excel.

Student Objectives

80% of students completing an introductory instructional technology (IT) course will demonstrate:

   a) knowledge of careers in technology,

   b) awareness of skills needed for success in IT careers, and

   c) capacity to assess personal abilities/interest in IT.

80% of students completing the word processing will be able to:

   a) process and format text to create documents, including letters, formal technical reports, and personalized form letters;

   b) create and format charts, tables and graphics;

   c) manage editing of a document by work groups of users;

   d) create addresses and label sets; and

   e) prepare documents for Internet publication and use Internet resources.

80% of students completing the word processing will be able to create and use:

   a) budgets,

   b) marketing and sales reports,

   c) invoices and purchase orders,

   d) accounting and financial statements,

   e) spreadsheet information for electronic networks,

   f) data analysis,

   g) statistical tables, and

   h) forecasts and amortization schedules

ning the network management course. Through product research and careful strategizing, the group decided that the best possible curriculum for students would be a combination of teacher-created materials and the Net Prep program from 3COM. The teachers were confident that work on A+ Certification, the 3COM materials and the Microsoft materials would provide a firmer networking foundation than limiting the course to Microsoft NT.

At the end of the second project year (April 2000), the first networking courses were posted to the consortium's roster of class listings. In the fall of 2000, four networking teachers offered networking courses. Two of these offerings were taken by districts; one site delivered to three receiving districts, another to one other district. The third and fourth offerings, however, didn't get takers so the two distance teachers decided to share the delivery of the course using the distance system. Because of this unusual opportunity to team-teach the networking course in Tekamah-Herman and Logan View, both the teachers and the students were enthusiastic about it being a very valuable experience.

At the close of the three-year project period, the educators and students reported that the objectives of the project were accomplished. Of the 25 students who enrolled in the courses, 24 completed the course requirements. Some students who took the course reported a change in career plans because of the networking management course: at least three students decided to pursue careers in network-related fields because of the courses; another decided *not* to pursue that specific route because of the course. These responses are positive since they result from a raised awareness about tech-based careers. All participants expressed gratitude for the opportunity to attain skills that they would not otherwise have been able to access. Network schools also reported an increased interest in the courses, and students who have taken the course have expressed interest in a second or follow-up course.

QUALITY STANDARDS

Though traditional subject areas have recently established strict standards for teacher training, the technology field has not yet "come of age" in this respect. Though many national organizations have developed such standards, they are not considered mandatory; therefore, finding people with technology expertise in rural areas can be very difficult. The ENDLC, however, dared to require a high level of competence in technology of the teachers working with its distance courses.

Just as the teachers who taught the networking management classes were required to obtain certification, so, too, were the teachers who were to teach the Microsoft Office classes. Although Microsoft certification is frequently required by trainers in an industrial setting, this is a relatively rare occurrence in PK-12 schools. Some educators argue that the levels of performance required to obtain certification are much higher than necessary to instruct students who are young and may have relatively simplistic needs for applications. Nonetheless, the ENDLC project stipulated that their teachers of office applications were to obtain their Microsoft Office Proficient Users (MOUS) certification as a prerequisite to teaching the Microsoft Office course.

Again, two lead teachers trained additional teachers. One of the lead teachers passed the MOUS exams in Word, Excel, PowerPoint, and Access at the expert level. The other attained the proficient level in Word and Excel and the expert level in PowerPoint. During the training period, the group had two meetings at which they were provided an interactive CD. Thus, the bulk of the learning was done independently by the teachers, with support from the lead teachers. Amazingly, all participating teachers earned proficiency level certification on Word and Excel.

While the school-based lead teachers were awarded a stipend from the grant, it was left up to each district to provide incentives/rewards for their own teachers. A couple of districts provided a release period for planning, but some did not. This brought a common problem to the foreground–how to provide incentives for distance teachers. The consortium has not reached consensus on this problem, and research indicates that this can be a real sticking point (U.S. Congress, 1989; Cyrs & Smith, 1990; Graf, 1993; Moore & Thompson, 1990).

In the third year of the project, Microsoft Office classes were offered in nine distance classrooms. Sixty-one students completed the courses via the distance learning network. Of those sixty-one, seven students were selected at random to take one of the MOUS exams. Three of the four students who took the Word exam passed. The three students who took the Excel exam all passed. All students who took the course by distance received satisfactory grades for the course.

At least one district did something that is fairly common among distance schools. The district received the Microsoft Office course from a remote district for a year, during which one of the receive-site teachers monitored the course. After the initial year, the receive-site then offered the course onsite. This model of dissemination of new course offerings is often overlooked in the literature, particularly when researchers are lamenting decreasing numbers of distance offerings and students.

As is the case with many districts that share courses via distance technologies, both teachers and students often mentioned getting to know students and teachers from other districts as one of the significant benefits of the new form of teaching and learning. Because of the number of schools that partnered to share Microsoft Office courses, the social impact was considerable.

It would be difficult to overstate the complexity involved in undertaking this type of course as a distance learning offering. Since the courses were hands-on, computers at all of the sites had to be equipped and set up in a fairly standard manner to facilitate communication. Being in charge of such a class was no day at the beach, as one teacher put it:

> It was really hard sometimes because we don't have the technology so that I can see the screens of my students. This means that, if a student is having a problem, they have to tell me and then we also have to talk through what's on his screen to work it out. It's a real challenge some days but we get along.

The teachers who taught the Microsoft courses felt that the MOUS certification process greatly enhanced their credibility as business educators. As a result, many plan to work to attain certification in Office 2000 and Office XP. The teachers also indicated on a questionnaire that they felt extremely competent in their computer skills. Thus the combination of teacher collaboration and the MOUS standards of excellence appeared to improve their feelings of efficacy about their computer skills.

MANAGEMENT AND SUPPORT

Too many times distance learning projects are originated by well-intended administrators who vaguely recognize weaknesses in their course offerings and see distance technologies as a panacea (Brigham, 1992). The ENDLC project was not without its difficulties, and the management was the central variable when the consortium was faced with problems. Moore and Thompson (1990) describe the importance of capable management for distance learning activities:

> Distance education enterprises are highly complex organizations. The issues concerning them are as complex as the enterprises

themselves. In order to be successful, distance education enterprises require a high degree of planning, management control, and communication. (p. 34)

To facilitate operations, the ENDLC developed an Inter-local Agreement that required a level of commitment by all participating districts. This compact was a budgetary necessity so that project leaders had the authority to negotiate on behalf of all member schools. It was also important to implementation activities as the network was established. The management team for the network, consisting of a group of representative administrators and staff, also had to tackle one of the stickiest wickets in the distance learning field–scheduling.

When courses are shared among several sites, the problems associated with scheduling multiply. Because this consortium was so large, it had special difficulty bringing all member districts to consensus on one daily schedule. As a result, the consortium agreed to operate with two daily class schedules. One schedule started early in the morning and ended each class after 47 minutes, thus allowing for a three-minute passing period. The other schedule started at the same time but class ran for 50 full minutes and eliminated the three-minute passing period. This was done to accommodate the differing needs of the districts. Each district could select the time schedule that was most appropriate to their setting.

Another key element in the management of the network was the regional service agency, Educational Service Unit #2 (ESU#2) in Fremont, Nebraska. The project director was selected from ESU#2 staff and other ESU consultants supported the instructional development of the two courses. The agency served as fiscal agent and project coordinator throughout the grant period, and it is anticipated that this will continue. ESU#2 personnel also served as the point of contact for technical difficulties with the system. This project had an exceptional record related to dealing with technical problems. While there were a few technical difficulties at the outset of the project, the remainder of the three years had an amazingly low incidence of technical errors.

Other difficult management issues yet to be tackled by consortium management include:

a. how to provide an incentive for districts to offer courses over the network,
b. how to establish consensus on follow-up offerings so that they reflect common needs among the districts,
c. how to hire additional teachers to teach over the network.

CONCLUSIONS

The success of the Eastern Nebraska Distance Learning Consortium is partially the result of the rich heritage of the distance learning networks in Nebraska, but mostly it is due to the wisdom of a group of savvy administrative, consultative, and instructional personnel who have capitalized on their collective knowledge. Without the vision and consensus agreements of the management team, the project would have lacked direction and support. Likewise, without the careful attention to strategies that would be most successful in creating and delivering the courses, most of these students would not have gained access to the valuable training they have received in computer networking and applications courses. The data from the Eastern Nebraska Distance Learning Consortium project are in line with the data from many distance learning projects across the nation. The success of the project is commensurate with the amount of support given the teachers who plan, develop, and deliver courses over the network.

Thus, this project takes its place alongside other projects that have proven that technology projects can be effective in diverse settings (Warschauer, 2000). The collaboration and quality standards upheld by the consortium's distance leaders resulted in benefits that reached beyond the intended outcomes of the project:

1. Consortium leaders recognized the value of group needs assessment and consensus.
2. The team of teachers produced courses beyond the scope originally planned.
3. Teachers who team taught using the distance network reported the most positive experience of all teachers in the project (as did their students). This discovery may be especially valuable to projects seeking ways to provide an incentive for teacher involvement in distance education.
4. Teachers of the courses have continued to work together in delivering the courses, forming a camaraderie that is rare between schools.
5. Teachers jointly worked to solve problems they all experienced when teaching the course. (One such problem arose with the network equipment. While the distance video was excellent, sometimes the wall-mounted cameras did not provide the close-ups needed. The group discovered that using a video camera attached to the system through the Elmo was of sufficient quality to address the problem.)

6. The cohesiveness of this group of teachers has provided a positive momentum to distance learning that should have important ramifications for the future of this mode of teaching and learning in the region.
7. The peer pressure/camaraderie among the teachers inspired each to seek higher standards of excellence than perhaps they would have on their own.
8. The requirement that participating teachers pass certification exams established a standard of excellence that was in turn reflected in the achievements of their students.
9. New administrative agreements and policies were put in place that facilitated the functioning of the project and will pave the way for future activities.
10. Scheduling conflicts were accommodated with two separate schedules from which districts could choose.

Any consortium of schools planning a distance learning partnership must give careful consideration to the complex management issues as well as to incentives for teachers who take on this new form of teaching and learning. As a result of attention to both of these elements, the ENDLC finds itself in a position where high performance is the status quo for course delivery on their distance network. If distance learning is to survive, the sum total of most applications must add up to quality that surpasses the traditional classroom. Due to the investment of its leaders, the ENDLC has a good chance of attaining that goal.

REFERENCES

Brigham, D. E. (1992). Factors affecting the development of distance education courses. *Distance Education, 13*(2), 169-192.

Cuban, L. (1993). Computer meets classroom: Classroom wins. *Teachers College Record, 95*(2), 185-210.

Cyrs, T. E., & Smith, F. A. (1990). *Teleclass teaching: A resource guide.* Las Cruces, NM: New Mexico State University.

Eiserman, W. D., & Williams, D. D. (1987) *Statewide evaluation report on productivity studies related to improved use of technology to extend educational programs. Sub-report Two: Distance education in elementary and secondary schools. A review of the literature.* Logan, UT: Wasatch Institute for Research and Evaluation. ERIC Document Service ED 291 350.

Graf, D. (1993). *Teleteaching: Distance education planning, techniques, & tips.* Ames, IA: Media Resources Center, Iowa State University.

Moore, M. G., & Thompson, M. M. (1990). *Effects of distance learning: A summary of literature.* University Park, PA: The American Center for the Study of Distance Education.

U.S. Congress, Office of Technology Assessment. (1989). *Linking for learning: A new course for education.* (OTA-SET-430). Washington, DC: U.S. Government Printing Office.

Warschauer, M. (2000, January 7). Technology and school reform: A view from both sides of the tracks. *Education Policy Analysis Archives, 8*(4).

Young, J. R. (2000, January 14) Faculty report at University of Illinois casts skeptical eye on distance education. *The Chronicle of Higher Education, 46*(9), A48.

Mohammad Khalid Hamza
Bassem Alhalabi
Sam Hsu
Maria M. Larrondo-Petrie
David M. Marcovitz

Remote Labs:
The Next High-Tech Step
Beyond Simulation for Distance Education

SUMMARY. As computer and networking technology has improved, computer-mediated communication and distance learning (DL) have become more prevalent. Software is used in a DL environment to replace traditional laboratory exercises. Software simulation provides wide-scale access to laboratory exercises at a low cost. However, simulations do not

MOHAMMAD KHALID HAMZA is Assistant Professor, Department of Educational, Technology & Research, Florida Atlantic University, 2912 College Avenue, Davie, FL 33314 (E-mail: khamza@fau.edu).
BASSEM ALHALABI is Assistant Professor, Department of Computer Science and Engineering, Florida Atlantic University, 777 Glades Road, Boca Raton, FL 33431 (E-mail: bassem@cse.fau.edu).
SAM HSU is Associate Professor, Department of Computer Science and Engineering, Florida Atlantic University, 777 Glades Road, Boca Raton, FL 33431 (E-mail: sam@cse.fau.edu).
MARIA M. LARRONDO-PETRIE is Associate Professor, Department of Computer Science and Engineering, Florida Atlantic University, 777 Glades Road, Boca Raton, FL 33431 (E-mail: maria@cse.fau.edu).
DAVID M. MARCOVITZ is Assistant Professor, Education Department, Loyola College in Maryland, 4501 N. Charles Street, Baltimore, MD 21210 (E-mail: marco@loyola.edu).

[Haworth co-indexing entry note]: "Remote Labs: The Next High-Tech Step Beyond Simulation for Distance Education." Hamza, Mohammad Khalid et al. Co-published simultaneously in *Computers in the Schools* (The Haworth Press, Inc.) Vol. 19, No. 3/4, 2002, pp. 171-190; and: *Distance Education: Issues and Concerns* (ed: Cleborne D. Maddux, Jacque Ewing-Taylor, and D. LaMont Johnson) The Haworth Press, Inc., 2002, pp. 171-190. Single or multiple copies of this article are available for a fee from The Haworth Document Delivery Service [1-800-HAWORTH, 9:00 a.m. - 5:00 p.m. (EST). E-mail address: getinfo@haworthpressinc.com].

adequately replace all aspects of the real laboratory environment. This paper reviews DL alternatives to real laboratories and discusses whether the present alternatives successfully give students the experience of real laboratory experiments without physically attending a laboratory. The review found that present alternatives to real laboratories use software simulation, which do not accomplish the desired exposure to real lab environments in some disciplines, such as engineering. The paper presents an alternative to simulation, presently under development by the authors, in which real laboratory facilities can be accessed remotely via the Internet. These real physical laboratories provide the one dimension that simulation cannot: real response of real physical elements to real inputs. *[Article copies available for a fee from The Haworth Document Delivery Service: 1-800-HAWORTH. E-mail address: <getinfo@haworthpressinc.com> Website: <http://www.HaworthPress.com> © 2002 by The Haworth Press, Inc. All rights reserved.]*

KEYWORDS. Remote labs, simulation, laboratory, distance learning

Distance learning (DL) has become a powerful educational tool to reach students at times and places that are not strictly dictated by the educational institution. In some cases, this is merely a matter of convenience; in others, DL makes education possible for people whose schedules or locations do not permit other alternatives. New technology has made it possible to overcome many of the obstacles of distance in the educational process. Electronic mail, chat rooms, and live interactive video conferencing, for example, help to bring together the people involved in the educational process. The World Wide Web has made available many of the resources that used to be reserved for use on an educational campus. Some resources, such as hands-on laboratories, are difficult to transfer electronically to students.

Four options that are currently used for laboratories in DL are

a. videotapes of laboratory experiments, reducing the lab to a passive experience;
b. regular laboratory settings, providing students with a complete laboratory experience but eliminating the DL course for students who cannot physically attend;
c. portable laboratory kits, meeting all DL needs, but eliminating DL for laboratories that are expensive or dangerous, requiring a controlled environment;
d. software simulations.

This article investigates current simulation environments used to replace laboratories in DL settings and offers a fifth possibility to be used in situations where simulations do not meet the students' needs. While simulation served important purposes, we found that, in some cases, it was not an adequate substitute for real laboratories. Simulation serves well the purpose of initial experimentation, but it does not provide the same range of possibilities of manipulating real physical material. In some fields, such as engineering, the real response of real physical elements is crucial.

The authors propose the concept of remote laboratories as an alternative to simulations in a DL environment. In remote laboratories, students will be able to access and manipulate real physical material at a distance. The range of possible inputs and outputs will be limited, not by the limitations of the software, but by the physical constraints of the laboratory.

THE INTERNET: A WORLD OF INFORMATION

With the arrival of the Internet and its accelerating popularity, institutions of higher education have a golden opportunity to expand their educational resources via diverse distance modalities. During the pioneering of the Internet, its potential was recognized as the most dynamic tool in distance learning (Turoff, 1994). The wealth of information that the Internet holds, the constant updates, the ease of transmitting information instantaneously, and its cost-effective methods of reproduction make distance education a viable mode of education (Gaines, 1996; Hirumi & Bermudez, 1996). However, many educators are concerned only with providing their students access to materials over the Internet without regard to the pedagogical repercussions of using this new medium. Some questions that need to be considered: What instructional strategies and objectives underlie the use of this newly implemented technology? Is the technology going to aid the teacher in enhancing or promoting learning? What learning are educators seeking to foster in students? Put more simply, does the new technology enable students to do something they could not already do, or does it enable students to do something they could do, but better (Harris, 1998)?

Virtual universities have emerged as acceptable alternatives to conventional universities. Barba (1993) and Beaudoin (1997) contend that virtual campuses will be successful if students and teachers sustain a level of interactivity commensurate with their traditional counterparts. This can only be true if quality is regarded with the same importance as quantity.

In the rush to embrace distance education, some specialized fields have been forced to either remain on the sideline or sacrifice quality. Laboratory sessions, for instance, are vital to engineering programs. Albeit sophisticated by contemporary guidelines, today's distance technologies are insufficient in allowing students to complete degree requirements without attending the academic campus to use tangible laboratory facilities. Software simulations have become the leading solution to this challenge. Harasim, Hiltz, Teles, and Turoff (1995) argue that software simulations are not satisfactory for achieving learning comprehension in many laboratory experiments. Software simulation used in "performing" engineering laboratory experiments, for example, fostered the establishment of Web-based engineering curricula, but the quality of education does not compare to that of the traditional campus. The challenge is to find ways to access real labs remotely via the Internet, a creative exploration that the authors refer to as *remote labs*.

The Research Questions

This ongoing research project seeks to answer several important questions about DL and the use of laboratory exercises in DL:

1. How do current DL programs allow students to perform real or virtual laboratory exercises?
2. Are these real or virtual laboratory exercises educationally appropriate for the students?
3. Is there a need for real laboratory exercises that can be accessed from a distance (i.e., remote labs)?
4. Under what circumstances are remote labs more educationally appropriate than the alternatives?

This paper reviews current DL programs to begin to answer question 1. After the review, this paper lays the theoretical groundwork to answer questions 2 through 4. With the theoretical need established, future research will be needed to establish the circumstances under which remote labs will have greater benefits than the alternatives.

REVIEW OF EXISTING VIRTUAL LABORATORIES
ON THE INTERNET

The review of existing virtual laboratories on the Internet was achieved by examining the course content offered by prominent public and private universities in North America and the United Kingdom that offer full- or part-time programs via the Internet (Hutchison, 1999). A small number of these institutions are virtual universities that have no established campus structure. The organizations reviewed are listed in Table 1. Multiple search engines (e.g., *http://www.dogpile.com/*) were used to search for materials from these universities. Their Web sites were accessed and carefully examined for information leading to real lab experiments and/or virtual lab experimentation. Access to various universities' virtual sessions under a guest account was attempted to carefully examine the virtual or real lab-like environment provided.

The search for "Internet University" on the World Wide Web produced an index of 83 accredited universities that offer 2,738 distance education courses; however, not all of these universities offer laboratory-oriented courses. In fact, more than 95% of all providers listed offer virtual classrooms only. The remaining 5% offer online laboratory courses such as those listed in Table 1. Of this fraction of institutions, the Open University in Great Britain (http://www.open.ac.uk/) (Van Gorp & Boysen, 1997) recognized the challenge of providing lab courses on the Internet and employed significant efforts to eliminate shortcomings.

Our review revealed that most of the tools employed to train students over the Internet are primarily simulation software, also known as *virtual labs*. In such environments, knowledge gained by the student is limited by the constraints, boundaries, and other capabilities offered by the simulation software of the manufacturer. Examination of literature and existing distance education Web sites indicated that students are only free to perform experiments in a limited environment.

A dearth of laboratory courses was noted in some specialized, practically oriented courses (e.g., logic design, microprocessors, and electronic circuits). In these courses the hands-on experience of laboratory experiments is crucial to understand the basic concepts. Extra reading or even watching the experiment performed by others falls short of the requirements necessary for proper education (Harasim et al., 1995). Four alternative methods are currently used to provide labs to DL students: videotapes, home experiment kits, student site facilities, and simulation software (Harasim et al., 1995). Among these four schemes, simulation software has been identified in field literature as the best alternative because it is easily transportable and cost-effective (Gorrell, 1992; Thomas & Hooper, 1991).

Very few universities offer full-fledged laboratory courses over the Internet, although the Open University at Great Britain has made tremendous progress in trying to establish virtual laboratories. Michigan

TABLE 1. List of Universities Reviewed in This Study with Online Laboratories

Purely Virtual Universities with No Physical Campus		
California Virtual University	http://www.california.edu/	Not Accredited
Virtual Online University	http://www.athena.edu/	Not Accredited
The Global Network Academy	http://www.gea-college.si/	Not Accredited
On Line Education	http://otto.cmr.fsu.edu/	Not Accredited
ME/U Knowledge On Line	http://www.jec.edu/	Not Accredited
On Line University	http://www.lolu.org/	Not Accredited
Chemekata On Line	http://statewide.orst.edu/	Accredited
NetMath	http://www-cm.math.uiuc.edu/dep/	Accredited
The World Lecture Hall	http://www.vlh.com/	Not Accredited
CCU's World OnLine	http://www.bidmc.harvard.edu/	Accredited
ZDNet University	http://www.zdnet.com/	Not Accredited
Universities with an Established Physical Campus		
Harvard University	http://www.harvard.edu/	Accredited
University of Oregon	http://www.uoregon.edu/	Accredited
Open University at Great Britain	http://www.open.ac.uk/	Accredited

State University (Online Instrumentation Lab, *http://vu.msu.edu/preview/tc891/*) and Harvard University (Psychology Laboratory, *http://www.courses.fas.harvard.edu/~psy17/*) offer their students introductory simulation-based virtual lab facilities (Alhalabi, Hamza, & Anandapuram, 1998; Alhalabi, Hamza, & Anandapuram, 1999).

Given the popularity of virtual labs, it is important to question the educational value of software simulation. The next section will examine times when we believe software simulation is an appropriate alternative to real laboratory exercises.

SOFTWARE SIMULATION: ADVANTAGES AND SHORTCOMINGS

Improvements in software simulation have, in some cases, made it a viable alternative to real labs. For example, in the past few years, the Multiverse Project (Institute for Computer Based Learning, 1999) developed student-friendly software that provides step-by-step explanations of lab assignments and expected results of the experiments. The software available in WEB/JAVA has, to some extent, met laboratory requirements but is not devoid of shortcomings.

Advantages

The literature is replete with examples of circumstances where simulation is better than real laboratory experiments (Hensgens, van Rosmalen, & van der Baaren, 1995; Khoo & Koh, 1998; May, 1997; Stratford, 1997; Veenman & Elshout, 1995; Zirkel & Zirkel, 1997). In these cases, it is claimed that simulations are better regardless of whether they are to be used in a distance or traditional setting. However, simulation is not always the best mode of instruction.

Khoo and Koh (1998) and Hensgens et al. (1995) classify circumstances when simulation is more effective than real laboratories or real practice:

1. Cases when the real situation is dangerous, such as nuclear power stations, or too costly, such as astronaut training
2. Cases where real phenomena are not accessible experimentally, such as where simulation could be used to speed up or slow down reaction times
3. Cases where visualization can enhance (or make possible) the observation of certain phenomena

Veenman and Elshout (1995) found that students with low intelligence and low metacognitive (managing their own learning) skills did better in the more structured environment of a simulation. In essence, these students needed structure and guidance to master the basic lessons of the simulation or laboratory.

In a review of simulation research, Stratford (1997) found that simulations are "useful in confronting students with their misconceptions in order to promote conceptual change" (p. 16). However, he felt that modeling exercises in which students developed their own simulations were even more useful.

Zirkel and Zirkel (1997) discussed the use of simulation environments to alleviate ethical and environmental objections to live dissections. While their review of research indicated that high-tech simulations were as effective as live dissections, they noted, "The high-tech packages to date may not have fulfilled their interactive potential in terms of instructional efficacy, thus tempering the advocacy of the developer-researchers" (pp. 55-56).

In studies of social studies and science simulations for K-12 students, May (1997) found that "when implemented effectively, simulations provide an authentic yet controlled learning experience" (p. 28), while Frye and Frager (1996) criticized many simulations, such as Oregon Trail, because responses are predetermined.

Shortcomings

Predetermined responses are the most obvious shortcoming of simulations. While this shortcoming is most obvious in simple simulations like Oregon Trail in which students choose from a limited menu of choices at each decision point and the simulation responds with a predetermined response, it is equally true for sophisticated simulations. Student input and system response are limited by the software capabilities and not by the creativity of the student.

Therefore, we believe that simulation is inappropriate as a substitute for a real laboratory and is not the best possible laboratory model for the distance environment, except in cases, such as those previously discussed, in which simulation is better than real laboratories and would be used regardless of distance. Our reasons for this conclusion follow:

1. The design of a simulation depends largely on the student's perception as anticipated by the designer. Potentially, the various procedures that the student must perform might be more advanced than what the student can capably perform. One step out of sequence renders the entire exercise a futile attempt. The knowledge gained by a simulated experiment largely depends on the design, authenticity, limitations, and cost of the software.
2. Simulation software at its best might only produce an approximation that can yield erroneous results. Under these conditions, student understanding will depend on the quality of the software more than the capability of the student.
3. The results of experiments conducted through simulation software must be programmed for use within the scope of distance learning parameters. This learning scenario places the student in an environment where he or she must adhere to prescribed inputs that deny the freedom to experiment with disparate criteria that accompany a real laboratory setting.
4. The thrill of spontaneity from autonomous experimentation vanishes under such orchestrated conditions as simulations. Interest ebbs, directly affecting the student's ability to absorb new information.

5. Generally, throughout most institutions, the number and type of experiments change from semester to semester. The addition of new experiments that accompany each semester's revised syllabus also requires a revision of the package contents. Whenever such changes take place, revising the software is not an attractive proposition because it becomes expensive and time consuming.

6. Using software to produce the best results depends on the student's understanding of its use. A student who clearly understands the software is likely to achieve better results than the student whose understanding falls short. Hence, the proficiency of the software becomes more significant than the proficiency of the student.

7. The excitement and interest that accompany remote lab experimentation may become all but absent in simulated environments because these antiseptic conditions may fail to generate expectations and curiosity in the student conducting the experiment. Curiosity kindles interest, which helps the student more clearly understand the learning concepts.

8. When curiosity ebbs, the meaningful components of care, caution, and observation are limited. This behavior causes the student to rush through prescribed steps to arrive at the ultimate results. Such behavior deprives the student the opportunity to understand and appreciate the various concepts contained in the act of experimentation.

9. Simulations introduce an element of fiction. The knowledge gained is narrow and the freedom to study various possibilities is wanting. There are no answers to "what if," because the student simply cannot attempt "what-if" experimentation. The necessity of the student to produce genuine thinking or to try different approaches to the experiment is totally lacking.

For these reasons, we believe that while simulation has its place, it is not as a substitute for the real laboratory. In those cases when the real laboratory is best, an alternative to simulation is needed. The following section describes our experiences with and prototypes of remote labs: real laboratories than can be accessed from a distance.

EXAMPLES OF REMOTE LABS

We have designed several examples of remote labs. The microelectronics lab has real benefits over simulation, and it was developed as a proof of concept. The other examples described in this section demonstrate the range of applications of remote labs over a wide area of science and engineering disciplines.

The remote lab design is based on the principles of instructional systems design (ISD) and the use of computers as cognitive tools, vital keys that make this type of learning environment both effective and creative. ISD refers to the systematic and reflective process of translating the principles of distance education, learning, and instruction into remote lab instructional materials, activities, information resources, presentations, process evaluation, and revision (Smith & Ragan, 1999). The ISD process is essential in remote distance education and for effective remote lab instruction where students have minimal face-to-face contact with the teacher and may never physically step into a classroom or lab. The general architecture of a remote lab is depicted in Figure 1. The following are examples of some areas in which real labs, and thus in DL, remote labs, are instructionally superior to simulations. In some of these areas, the researchers have developed working prototypes.

Microelectronics Lab in Electrical Engineering

In microelectronics, circuits are designed and behaviorally verified by theoretical and conceptual computations. This complex computation that involves thousands of different parameters of the various components used in the circuit design is known as *circuit simulation*. This simulation facilitates building quality complex circuits. The problem with circuit simulation is that it uses suggested programmable values for components that are believed to resemble actual working electrical components. For example, if the student is using a capacitor in the design with a value of 10 microfarads, the simulator will compute the circuit response based on this value, and the performance of the resulting circuit may be satisfactory. When the circuit is actually constructed using the same value capacitor, however, the circuit may not work as desired. The reason is that when you buy a 10 microfarads capacitor, it is never exactly 10; it is 10 plus/minus some tolerance, which is normally 20%. Simulation with all but the most expensive simulators will miss the variability of real components. Additionally, computing time can be prohibitive to simulate complex circuits hundreds of times to account for a range of possible component parameters.

Companies use simulation with fixed values to verify the correctness of the design in theory and to assure proper circuit behavior. However, before putting the circuit in mass production, the companies always

FIGURE 1. General Remote Labs Architecture

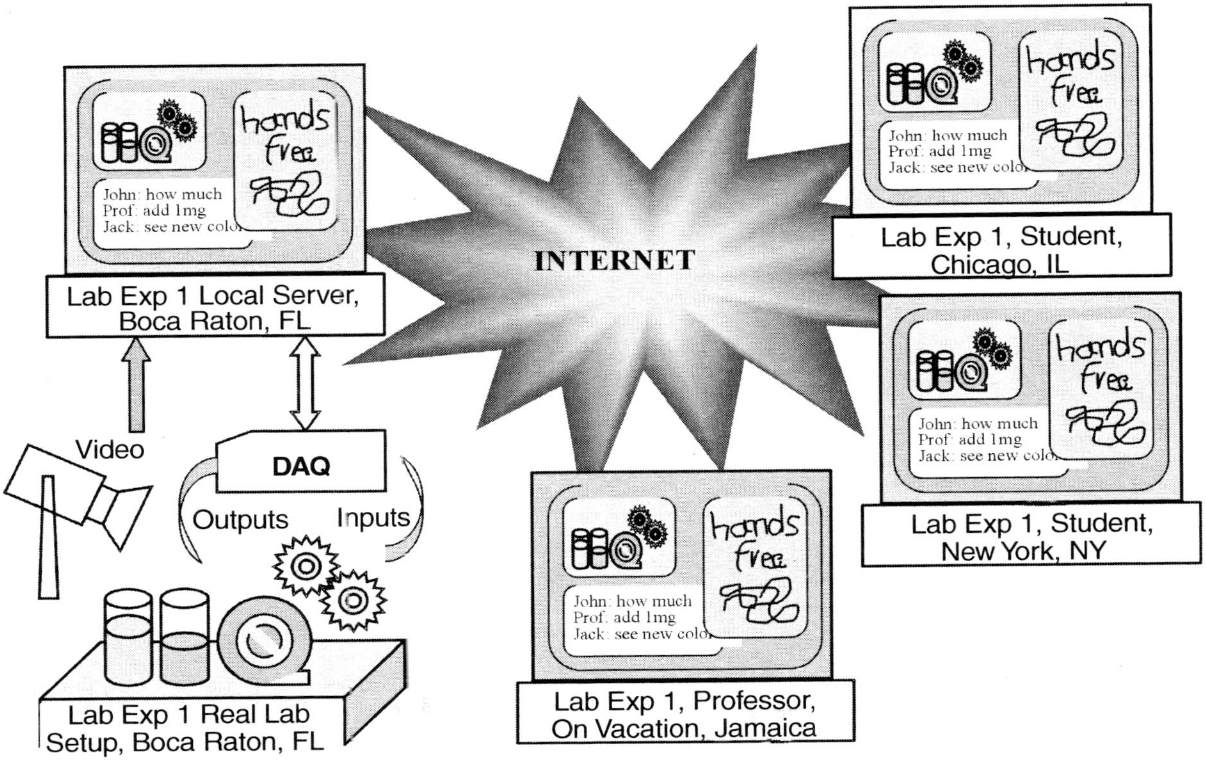

prototype the circuit on a printed circuit board (build it with actual components and turn it on to see if it actually works).

The solution to this problem for remote labs emerged from recent advances in fast prototyping technologies, where circuits are built on programmable breadboards and all circuit connections are assigned by computer interface. The authors took the prototyping technologies one step further and brought real laboratories to DL. They developed a simple system (as proof of concept), which students can access remotely from any computer on the Internet and experiment with electronic components as shown in Figure 2. (Try this simple electric element characterization at *http://jupiter.cse.fau.edu/directory.html*. Use guest/guest for user ID/password.) Students can choose an element, apply a sequence of currents, and read the actual voltage drops on the elements. These actual values are always different from the theoretically computed ones using the assumed known values for the elements. The reason for the difference is that the true values of the electric elements are not guaranteed.

Logic Design Lab in Computer Engineering

In a real logic design (LD) lab, students use breadboards and kits to iterate three basic steps:

1. Mount a few logic design chips (e.g., NAND and NOR gates) and connect the chips with wires.
2. Connect the board to the power supply.
3. Verify by observation whether the circuit is functional. If it is not, which is almost always the case for the first few trials, the students will rewire the board and run it again.

During their physical presence in the lab, students are merely rewiring the breadboard, staging certain inputs, and observing the resulting output. If these three actions are performed remotely, the online LD remote lab is born. The first and third actions are simply the input and output (I/O) part of the experiment, which could be replaced by a standard computer interface with the proper instrumentation device. Any computer on the Internet can perform these I/O operations when connected to a server/host that is running the necessary software and hardware interfaces and is connected to the experiment. The second action of wiring and rewiring offers the true challenge. Standard breadboards are replaced by special interactive breadboards whose pins are connected to a programmable interconnect network controlled by a host computer with

FIGURE 2. The Electric Element IV Characterization Experiment

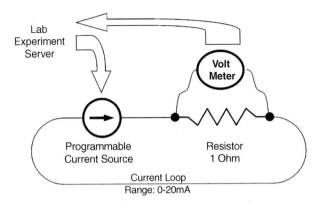

Lab Experiment Server

Volt Meter

Programmable Current Source

Resistor 1 Ohm

Current Loop
Range: 0-20mA

a proper software interface. A connection between any pin to any pin is accomplished by a click of a mouse on the software interface. If all necessary logic design components (NANDs, NORs, etc.) are placed on the interactive breadboard whose interconnect network is interfaced to a computer, a full experiment is conducted through the computer software interface without ever touching the breadboard. Anything that can be performed on a local computer can be done on any computer on the Internet, allowing real engineering experiments to take place at a distance.

The use of a host computer should not be confused with software simulation because students are still manipulating physically working electronic parts and still have the freedom to make any connections they choose. The computer simply acts as a front-end interface to lay out connections on-screen and download the information to the interactive breadboard.

Microprocessor Lab in Computer Engineering

In a microprocessor lab, students write assembly language programs, compile them, download the assembled program (machine code) to a microprocessor kit, run the program, and observe the outputs. In a typical scenario, the microprocessor lab is equipped with 20 stations and it services about 100 students per semester. The lab is normally too busy, sometimes students have to come to the lab at inconvenient times, and the number of students allowed to take the course is limited by the total number of seats in the laboratory. Students still prefer to perform their experiments in the lab even though simulators/emulators are available, which could be used at home. The reason is that they need to see the actual compiled computer code being run on the actual microprocessor kit. Many programs involve real-time computation that could not be mastered through simulation. Allowing remote access to the real microprocessor kit attached to a host computer increases the efficient use of available lab space.

Thermal Effects on Solutions in Chemical Engineering

In a chemical reaction, the environment temperature may severely affect the reaction of chemical solutions, especially if it changes dynamically in response to the reaction itself. Some advanced simulators allow the experimenter to input temperature factors to the simulation, but these factors are either fixed or linear and never match the actual unpredictable temperature.

For distance education, Internet accessible labs could be automated with proper computer interfaces and real data acquisition and control systems. The thermal sensors measure the room and liquid temperatures. Relays control the liquid heating and cooling elements. Precision pipettes handle the liquid injection and dispensing. Real color and smoke are observed via real video streaming. A special flushing system is provided for emergencies. All activities are automated by a data acquisition and control system and automated by a screen software interface.

Material Strength in Mechanical Engineering

In a typical mechanical engineering experiment, students test material strength by applying progressive force on a representative material bar and observe the break point. When material comes with different grades from different manufacturers, there is no way of simulating the actual response of the material. The experiment setup tests the elasticity of a metallic beam. The metallic beam is firmly mounted at one side in a horizontal position as shown in Figure 3.

Students apply a sequence of known forces on the free edge of the beam and measure the amount of displacement that is proportionally due to the force. For every temperature reading, the various readings of force and displacement are plotted on a graph, as shown in Figure 4. For every force value, after displacement is measured, the force is removed to allow the beam to restore its original straight shape. Once the force (F) reaches a maximum value at which the beam does not restore to its straight form (permanently bent), this last force reading is considered the break point. After each break point, the beam is automatically straightened by applying the same force backwards. From the graph, students can visually observe the elastic behavior of a metallic beam to determine if it is linear or nonlinear. Also they learn how fast elasticity is lost due to temperature increase.

All quantities in this experiment are controlled by a data acquisition system–via the use of Lab View programming, which is connected to the serial port of the computer. A software interface is written to control and automate all experiment activities without any direct human inter-action with the physical setup. Then the computer is set up as a Web server so that student can invoke the software interface from any ma-chine on the Internet. A real-time video streaming camera is also mounted to allow live viewing of the experiment.

River Pollution in Environmental Engineering

Our final example of experiments where real labs, and consequently remote labs, cannot be replaced by mere simulation is related to envi-ronmental engineering. Suppose students are required to perform an ex-periment on the water of a river, measuring the atmosphere temperature

FIGURE 3. Mechanical Engineering Remote Lab Setup

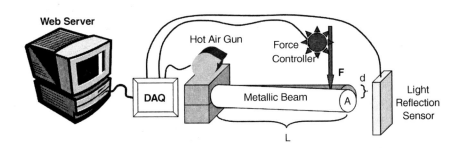

FIGURE 4. Breakpoint Graph from Mechnical Engineering Remote Lab

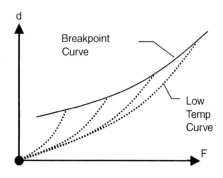

and water temperatures at different depths. Also, suppose they need to measure pH, conductivity, pollution, and the flow of the water. The difficulty is not merely the inconvenience of getting to those remote areas, but to stay there for days or weeks to collect information.

With the powerful idea of remote labs, such environmental stations can be mounted on various places on rivers, mountains, jungles, etc., and students can simply access them from anywhere and perform the experiments. Additionally, institutions can share the same setups.

INTERACTIVE WHITEBOARD TO SUPPORT REMOTE LABS

Due to the nature of science and engineering laboratories and their requirement of complex explanations, professors must be equipped with interactive tools that enable them to teach students while conducting experiments online. A whiteboard interface, known as *Softboard* (Hsu & Adusumilli, 1998), is being developed. *Softboard* allows the user to write freehand on a normal computer screen using a light pen.

A light pen has the capability of detecting the active pixel position on the screen. Using this coordinate information, *Softboard* enables a teacher to "draw" directly on the computer screen. As users move the light pen around the screen by pressing the button on the pen, they can draw or write freehand on their local screens, and the writing will be displayed on the remote student computer screen. The handwriting or drawing on *Softboard* will thus be displayed both on the user's and all remote participants' screens. With the freedom to write freehand, a teacher can explain and illustrate an idea more effectively to the audience. This effect is similar to writing on a blackboard in a conventional classroom setting. *Softboard* will be of great value in enhancing a teacher's capability to convey ideas to the students while teaching an online course.

REMOTE LABS: A STEP BEYOND REAL LABS

Remote labs naturally possess advantages that are not available at real laboratories, including time sharing, allowing many students to share one lab setup at the same time; resource sharing, allowing several institutions to share one lab setup; temporary allocation, allowing an institution to rent a lab setup on a temporary basis; electronic lab reporting, allowing students to submit labs and instructors to grade labs electronically; volume broadcasting, allowing an instructor to perform an experiment and broadcast it to a large number of remote students; experiment archiving, allowing experiments to be recorded and archived for future review or distribution; performing automated repetitive procedures, allowing students to set up experiments and adjust the parameters to repeat similar experiments over and over; accessibility, allowing students with disabilities equal access to laboratory facilities using their own computers which are already configured for their special needs; and accessing impractical locations, allowing experimental stations to be set up in difficult and remote locations, such as mountaintops and ocean bottoms, for access by all.

Combining the advantages of real laboratory access over a distance with the advantages of a computer-controlled interface extends the power of remote labs. This makes them a viable alternative for institutions whose students are not attending classes via distance technology.

CONCLUSION

As the digital world deepens in complexity and advances at an accelerating rate, funding and cost-effectiveness for DL technologies become important to most educational institutions that are attempting to keep up with tough global competition. With remote labs, learning institutions will be able to afford high-tech tools. Remote labs allow large numbers of students, at lower costs, to perform real experiments any time, any place.

Remote labs allow real time interaction with real materials. Unlike time-shift instruction (experiencing instruction following the live lesson through videotape or software simulation), the real-time instruction of remote labs is more effective, while providing students the ability to receive instruction without the teacher's direct presence. Students in remote lab environments have the freedom to analyze their experiments at a distance and compare them with the real settings that produced the results. Students are able to conduct experiments, collect information, synthesize the information, and create their own conclusions based on data collected, from input and output, without physically attending a lab.

Students are able to attend remote labs at different hours without disruption to the classroom or to the actual lab's conventional hours and without creating extra work for lab operators or teachers. Students have the unlimited freedom to experiment at a time that is convenient to them.

Software simulation remains an important tool in situations when real labs are not as appropriate or effective. Simulations are appropriate for teaching in a controlled environment, such as teaching theoretical concepts, confronting students with their misconceptions, and teaching students with limited metacognitive skills. When the concepts accentuate theory, a well-designed simulation package will meet instructional objectives. However, simulation software should be used for a limited set of experiments.

Many real laboratories are designed to allow for student experimentation. It is the act of experimenting that reveals the various concepts involved. The flexibility of the real lab environment–and in distance settings, the flexibility of remote labs–is necessary for fostering cognitive and intellectual skills in students (Barba, 1993). Hence, experiments conducted in real laboratories tend to stimulate and intensify all types of learning skills in students.

While simulation packages have a significant place in distance education, they can never replace the need for real labs where students are able to construct their own knowledge and put their theory and practice to a real test. Hence, we believe remote labs will expand the efficacy of distance education by making available laboratory courses that were unavailable via distance education and by making available effective instructional strategies for those distance courses that were otherwise forced to rely on inferior replacements for real labs.

REFERENCES

Alhalabi, B.A., Hamza, M.K., & Anandapuram, S. (1998). Real laboratories: An innovative rejoinder to the complexities of distance learning. *Open Praxis, 2,* 24-30.

Alhalabi, B.A., Hamza, M.K., & Anandapuram, S. (1999). Virtual education: Reality or virtuality. *Technology and Teacher Education Annual, 10,* 1523-1528.

Barba, R.H. (1993). The effects of embedding an instructional map in hypermedia courseware. *Journal of Research on Computing in Education, 25*(4), 405-412.

Beaudoin, M. (1997, June). *Interaction–the critical element in distance education.* Paper presented at the Wold ICDE Conference, State College, PA.

Frye, B., & Frager, A.M. (1996). Civilization, colonization, SimCity: Simulations for the social studies classroom. *Learning & Leading With Technology, 24,* 21-23.

Gaines, B.R. (1996). Convergence to the information highway. *Proceedings of the WebNet Conference, San Francisco.* Retrieved September 1, 2001, from http://aace.virginia.edu/aace/conf/webnet/html/KGaines/gaines.htm

Gorrell, J. (1992). Outcomes of using computer simulations. *Journal of Research on Computing in Education, 24*(3), 359-366.

Harasim, L., Hiltz, S.R., Teles, L., & Turoff, M. (1995). *Learning networks: A field guide to teaching and learning online.* Cambridge: MIT Press.

Harris, J. (1998). *Virtual architecture: Designing and directing curriculum-based telecomputing.* Eugene, OR: International Society for Technology in Education.

Hensgens, J., van Rosmalen, P., & van der Baaren, J. (1995). Authoring for simulation-based learning. *Instructional Science, 23,* 269-296.

Hirumi, A., & Bermudez, A. (1996). Interactivity, distance education, and instructional systems design converge on the information superhighway. *Journal of Research on Computing in Education, 29*(1), 1-16.

Hsu, S., & Adusumilli, K.K. (1998, November). *Softboard: An online blackboard.* Paper presented at WebNet '98, Orlando, FL.

Hutchison, C. (1999). *Distance learning on the Internet.* Retrieved April 2, 2002, from http://www.ascusc.org/jcmc/vol1/issue1/hutchison/vunivs.html

Institute for Computer Based Learning (1999). *Software engineers: Multiverse project.* Retrieved September 1, 2001, from http://www.icbl.hw.ac.uk/jobs/mverse.html

Khoo, G., & Koh, T. (1998). Using visualization and simulation tools in tertiary science education. *The Journal of Computers in Mathematics and Science Teaching, 17*(1), 5-20.

May, D.G. (1997). Simulations: Active learning for gifted students. *Gifted Child Today Magazine, 20,* 28-30.

Smith, P., & Ragan, T.J. (1999). *Instructional design* (2nd ed.). Upper Saddle River, NJ: Prentice-Hall.

Stratford, S.J. (1997). A review of computer-based model research in precollege science classrooms. *Journal of Computers in Mathematics and Science Teaching, 16*(1), 3-23.

Thomas, R., & Hooper, E. (1991). Simulations: An opportunity we are missing. *Journal of Research on Computing in Education, 23*(4), 497-513.

Turoff, M. (1994). The marketplace road to the information highway. *Boardwatch Magazine.* Retrieved April 2, 2002, from http://www.njit.edu/njIT/Department/CCCC/VC/Papers/Market.html

Van Gorp, M. J., & Boysen, P. (1997). ClassNet: Managing the virtual classroom. *International Journal of Educational Telecommunications, 3*(2/3), 279-292.

Veenman, M.V.J., & Elshout, J.J. (1995). Differential effects of instructional support on learning in simulation environments. *Instructional Science, 22*, 363-383.

Zirkel, J.B., & Zirkel, P.A. (1997). Technological alternatives to actual dissection in anatomy instruction: A review of the research. *Educational Technology, 37*(6), 52-56.

Sally R. Beisser
Peggy Steinbronn

Hybrid Online Coursework to Enhance Technology Competencies of School Principals

SUMMARY. This paper describes a hybrid online graduate-level course designed for future administrators to examine programs and principles of school curriculum. The course was designed and taught at a medium-sized private university in the Midwest. The hybrid course involved both face-to-face, on-campus meetings and use of Web-based courseware. While administrators do not necessarily perceive themselves as leaders in technology in schools, participants in this study acknowledged that the completion of a hybrid online course increased their willingness to engage in technology, to encourage technology initiatives, and to support teachers in integrating technology in the teaching and learning process. *[Article copies available for a fee from The Haworth Document Delivery Service: 1-800-HAWORTH. E-mail address: <getinfo@haworthpressinc.com> Website: <http://www.HaworthPress.com> © 2002 by The Haworth Press, Inc. All rights reserved.]*

KEYWORDS. Computer uses in education, distance education, educational technology, hybrid online course, online learning, technology and the school principal, technology leadership, technical support, technol-

SALLY R. BEISSER is Assistant Professor, 3206 University Avenue, Drake University, Des Moines, IA 50311 (E-mail: sally.beisser@drake.edu).
PEGGY STEINBRONN is Internet Systems Manager, Drake University, Carnegie Hall, Des Moines, IA 50311 (E-mail: peggy.steinbronn@drake.edu).

[Haworth co-indexing entry note]: "Hybrid Online Coursework to Enhance Technology Competencies of School Principals." Beisser, Sally R., and Peggy Steinbronn. Co-published simultaneously in *Computers in the Schools* (The Haworth Press, Inc.) Vol. 19, No. 3/4, 2002, pp. 191-205; and: *Distance Education: Issues and Concerns* (ed: Cleborne D. Maddux, Jacque Ewing-Taylor, and D. LaMont Johnson) The Haworth Press, Inc., 2002, pp.191-205. Single or multiple copies of this article are available for a fee from The Haworth Document Delivery Service [1-800-HAWORTH, 9:00 a.m. - 5:00 p.m. (EST). E-mail address: getinfo@haworthpressinc.com].

191

ogy-using administrators, Web-based courses, Web-based learning environment

LACK OF ADMINISTRATIVE LEADERSHIP
IN TECHNOLOGY

Exemplary computer-using teachers differ from other teachers in a variety of ways. They teach in an exemplary instructional environment of collegiality and social networking where there is school support for technology. They have strong academic backgrounds and are employed in schools with adequate financial resources and relatively small class sizes (Becker, 1994). In addition, other factors encouraging technology expertise among teachers include relevant staff development, on-site computer coordination, and technical assistance. A key participant in making technology decisions is the school principal. However, administrative leaders do not necessarily perceive themselves as leaders in technology in the schools. Educational administration graduate students in this university survey research study acknowledged that their own faculty, staff, or students often surpassed their computer skills.

Prevailing views of leadership suggest that the principal's role should not be to direct others but to create a school culture in which decisions are made collaboratively. Thus, "facilitative" leadership exercises power through others, not over them (Conley & Goldman, 1994). James Weber (1989) identified five main functions of effective instructional leadership, including defining school mission, promoting a positive learning climate, observing and giving feedback to teachers, managing curriculum and instruction, and assessing the instructional program.

However, facilitative leadership emphasizes organizational culture, thus creating a dilemma for school leaders who wish to promote and support technology-using teachers in their schools. On the one hand, school administrators have long realized that quality schools use technology effectively (Bialo & Sivin-Kachala, 1996; Dwyer, 1994; Kosakowski, 1998; Zehr, 1998). They know that technology-using teachers need technology training and support (Becker, 1994). On the other hand, building principals often lack the necessary technological skills to provide facilitative leadership in making decisions to support staff development, computer coordination, and technical assistance.

Research (*Education Week*, 1998; Glenna, & Melmed, 1996) concludes that a number of factors influence the success of technology-rich schools. Administrative support may include funding, restructuring schedules, providing physical space, and making curricular decisions to reflect a new learning environment. However, the administrators in our study reported that they need adequate skill development themselves in order to provide facilitative leadership in funding efforts, finding adequate space, and scheduling and designing curriculum to build or lead a technology-rich school.

Teacher training institutions have clearly recognized the need to prepare pre-service and in-service teachers to make technology an integral part of their teaching and learning environments (Davis, 1998; Davis, Kirkman, Tearle, Taylor, & Wright, 1996; Pelligrino & Altman, 1997; Strudler & Wetzel, 1999; Stuhlman, 1998; Thompson, Schmidt, & Hadjiyianni, 1995). Yet many school administrators lag in their competencies and confidence in using computer technology for things other than e-mail communication and word-processing. Educational administration preparation coursework typically focuses on school finance, administrative leadership, school law, contract negotiations, strategic planning, and similar classes, leaving few, if any, elective options for basic or advanced technology training as administrative leaders in the school setting.

Therefore, our "hybrid online course," Principles of Curriculum, was especially designed for educational administration graduate students, with initial face-to-face meetings followed by online learning. This course provided future principals with an opportunity to develop essential technology skills by completing one-third of the course online. In addition, students were exposed to Technology Standards for School Administrators (ISTE, 2002) to support effective use of technology in their leadership roles as school administrators.

WEB COURSE DEVELOPMENT

At this Midwest university, a faculty-driven Web program began in 1997 with no operating budget, enrolling 149 students in 12 online courses. Faculty participated because they were professionally interested in creating a Web presence for the university in order to engage students in online learning. In January 2000, an Internet system's manager position was created to provide technical, pedagogical, and other training support for faculty. Workshops provided hands-on training to learn Web software, principles of Web design, and elements of effective online teaching and learning. Faculty workshops provided instruction for interested participants about the use of WebCourse in a Box™ or Blackboard™, commercial software for developing online courses.

Academic Computing Fellows assisted in this effort and provided one-on-one mentoring for faculty new to the online teaching environment. Students enrolled in Web courses receive technical support from the Internet system manager when necessary. Enrollment in the Web program continues to increase. Currently the university offers 65 Web-based courses for a population of 5,200 undergraduate and graduate students. In 2001, 624 students took advantage of Web-based learning opportunities.

ELEMENTS OF A QUALITY ONLINE EDUCATION COURSE

Research studies in support of online course development substantiate that Web-based learning environments constitute additional space in which people can learn, teach, communicate, work, trade, and spend leisure time (Harris, 1998; Picciano, 2001; Somekh & Davis, 1999).

Educators in particular, who are well aware of the potential of distance education, have adopted it for creating new learning environments, and have harnessed its power for relevant educational uses (Martinez & Bunderson, 2000; Mioduser, Nachmias, Lahav, & Oren, 2000). For example, key features of Web-supported courses include sophisticated *information manipulation*. Students generate, transmit, store, process, and retrieve information from online libraries, databases, journals, virtual museums, and other Internet repositories of information.

Courses on the Web serve as a *communication facilitator* for e-mail, group conferencing, and threaded discussions, enabling peers, instructors, and experts to collaborate. Online learning invites a *creative environment* to allow students to generate and publish their own research or Web sites with minimal technical assistance. Finally, the Web serves as an *instructional delivery medium* to disperse pertinent material, connect to relevant URLs, and assess student understanding through quizzes and feedback analysis.

CREATING QUALITY ONLINE CURRICULA

A hybrid course design (Ko & Rossen, 2001) may be described as one in which students interact face-to-face, as well as through a Web-based component during the course of study. Specifically, our hybrid, course, Principles of Curriculum, invited *information manipula-*

tion as students used hotlinks in their WebCourse in a Box™ Web site. They searched ERIC databases, ERIC digests, and OERI research syntheses, and used selected Web sites to write a required research paper. Students read about an educational issue or topic of interest, and then critiqued the ways in which the author's work or point of view impacts the role of a school administrator.

The online Web site served as a *communication facilitator* as students e-mailed one another and their professor. Each student communicated online with each of three other class members to provide critical feedback on his or her research papers. Asynchronous threaded discussions were available to all class members, as were all other research papers. One graduate student remarked, "I had three times the feedback on my work. Comments were very insightful." Another student in the class stated, "In three years of graduate school, I have never had an opportunity to read someone's research, thus being able to learn from someone else's thinking and writing."

The online course helped to encourage a *creative environment*, as educational administration students wrote and published their research papers online, following face-to-face instruction on campus. Students were pleased to electronically publish their own research and have access to one another's papers. Some members constructed dissemination Web sites and were able to share their research with a larger audience. Others added their resumes to their electronic portfolios for future job searches.

In order to promote the online *delivery medium* of the course, students connected to relevant curriculum URLs, responded to the textbook author's interactive Web site, completed quiz questions online, checked assignments and grades, and provided electronic feedback to the professor. Student responses were favorable and encouraging. One student said, "I am a computer dinosaur. This course helped increase my skills and decrease my anxieties."

The hybrid design of this course utilized the online component as more than just an electronic syllabus. In addition to initial face-to-face discussions and technology orientation, the Web-based courseware was used to provide students with encouragement, reminders of due dates, and troubleshooting suggestions on how other students had solved specific technology problems.

While initial planning resulted in designing an online component of the Principles of Curriculum course, it is crucial to note that the decision to actually implement the online alternative was a democratic one. After demonstrating the online option in class, students indicated, through a class vote, their preference to complete the last third of the course online. A majority agreed to this option. One student said, "At first, I was not thrilled to take the last block of instruction through the Internet. But, now I am sold on it."

Online learning met the needs of adult learners (Collis, Winnips, & Moonen, 2000; Imel, 1998; Johnson, Aragon, Shaik, & Palma-Rivas, 2000). Distance learning was not only an approach for integrating technology into adult learning, but it helped students consider how technology could be used to support and expand learning in their role as future school administrators. Not only did the adults learn content through technology, they learned about the technology itself.

Because most students did not have prior online course experience, class was held in a computer lab during the face-to-face sessions. Working together initially helped build skills in a sequential, developmental process. Skills and strategies for solving problems were acquired gradually and in stages that were more or less predictable (Hilgard & Bower, 1974). Effective teaching must involve a sensitive assessment of the individual's status in the learning process, as well as a presentation of problems that slightly exceed the level already mastered. Tasks must be neither too easy nor too difficult to understand. Hunt (1961) describes this as the "problem of the match," based on the principle that learning occurs only when there is an appropriate match between the circumstances that the learner encounters and the schemata already assimilated into his or her repertoire. Technical assistance, provided by the Internet systems manager, was critical in teaching appropriate skills and troubleshooting.

Technical support issues impact the success of an online experience. Learner competence and comfort level with the technology were enhanced when direct online instruction occurred prior to the online portion of the course. Besides direct instruction by the Internet systems manager, hard copies of directions that included screen shots taken directly from the Web course software were provided to the students. Students were given time to practice the various components of online interaction during the instructional time. This included posting to the forum, replying to someone else's post, uploading files, submitting assignments, and adding information to an online portfolio. Students were encouraged to log onto the course to ensure that technical difficulties could and would be kept to a minimum and/or eliminated prior to the online weekend. They were encouraged to contact the Internet systems manager to sort out any technical difficulties. Technical online support was demonstrated in class, including how to use the online Request for

Technical Support form. Telephone and e-mail requests for technical support were available for students during the final online weekend of the course.

COURSE PARTICIPANT DEMOGRAPHIC INFORMATION

Of the 100 course participants who enrolled in four sections of this course, there was a 61% response rate to the four-page Likert-scale survey. More males (60%) than females (40%) completed the survey. Females tended to be in the mid-career category while most males were in the early career stage. Nearly half of the respondents (48%) were in the 35-44 year age range, while one-third (33%) were in the 22-34 range, with 18% in the later career range of 45-54 years of age. Most participants (44%) worked in small Midwest school districts of fewer than 1,000 students, while 28% were from medium-sized districts of 1,000 to 2,500 students. Ten percent were from large districts of 2,500 to 4,000 students, and 18% were from very large districts of over 4,000 students.

Respondents reported little or no training in using computer technology in their preparatory coursework to become school administrators. They reported receiving some technology training through summer workshops, school in-service sessions, or as part of a college-level course. Unfortunately, 30% reported no formal training and 1% reported no use of computers whatsoever.

There is discrepancy in the type of computers used at work and for personal use. While respondents used primarily Macintosh computers (65%) for work, most had PCs at home for personal use (63%). While 13% did not use a computer at all for personal use, only 2% reported not using a computer at work. Because computer skills were necessary to complete the online portion of this course, students were asked if they felt prepared. Over half (56%) reported both the lack of sufficient background and the lack of confidence to complete the online course requirement. In addition, they acknowledged limited use of software (see Table 1). Respondents used the Internet and desktop publishing to some extent but had low-level use of databases and multimedia programs, and limited experience in Web page development.

Respondents reported moderate to high skill levels using desktop or laptop computers, CD-ROMs, and printers, but low-level use of projection devices, digital cameras, and nearly no use, whatsoever, of graphing calculators (see Table 2).

TABLE 1. Proficiency Using Computer Software Applications

| | Percentage of Skill | |
Computer Applications	Little or None	Moderate to High
1. Databases	77	39
2. Desktop Publishing (e.g., Pagemaker or Claris Works)	28	72
3. Electronic Communication (e.g., E-mail, chat-lines)	7	93
4. Graphics/Drawing Programs (e.g., Kid Pix, Color It!)	62	38
5. Instructional Software Programs	39	61
6. Internet, World Wide Web (WWW)	15	85
7. Multimedia Authorware (e.g., Hyperstudio)	79	21
8. Presentation Software (e.g., PowerPoint)	54	46
9. Simulations or Tutorials (e.g., self-instructional software)	74	26
10. Spreadsheets (e.g., Microsoft Excel)	49	51
11. Teacher Utilities (e.g., grading programs, electronic portfolios)	34	66
12. Word Processing/Desktop Publishing	7	93
13. Web Page Development	82	18

Interestingly, respondents said they were "comfortable" using technology for their own educational work and learning (see Table 3). They also indicated that their greatest proficiencies were in using e-mail and word processing (Table 1). The comfort level of the respondents did not include more complex software applications.

In fact, as future administrators, they perceive that classroom teachers and students possess greater technology competencies and skill attainment than that of the administrator. They overwhelmingly (100%) expressed that technology is important for teachers, as well as principals (97%), in order to improve learning. They did not agree that computer technology made life more difficult (97%), nor did they feel uncomfortable promoting it (90%). However, most (90%) recognized that administrators should use computer technology more than they do, that they should improve their skills (95%), and that they need more training to lead teachers (92%). If administrative leaders are to promote online learning for teachers and students, they need to develop greater proficiencies themselves. Fortunately, this research indicated that they wish to do so (see Table 4).

For most respondents, the Principles of Curriculum course was their first online experience. As shown in Table 4, 74% responded that online

TABLE 2. Proficiency Using Computer Hardware

	Percentage of Skill	
Computer Hardware	Little or None	Moderate to High
1. Computer (Desktop or Laptop models)	15	85
2. Computer Projection Device (e.g., Proxima, NoteVision, LCD panel)	67	33
3. CD-ROM	30	70
4. DVD	75	25
5. Digital Camera (e.g., Sony Mavika or QuickTake)	67	33
6. Distance Education (e.g., ICN room)	66	34
7. Graphing Calculator	95	5
8. Printer	11	89
9. Scanner	57	43
10. Video Camera	33	67

coursework was a valuable way to learn content knowledge and skills, as well as an efficient and convenient way of learning (80%) for adult learners.

Most respondents thought online coursework facilitated access to library research resources, allowed interaction and communication with classmates, incorporated threaded discussions, and provided feedback from the professor. Although most technical assistance was successfully provided when needed (68%), participants indicated a preference for face-to-face courses over online courses (75%). However, without the hybrid course design, most of these students would have had no online course experience. As a result of this course, they reported a willingness to encourage Web-based learning for teachers and students, as well as their own continued interest in online coursework. Finally, they suggested that completing an online course increased their willingness to promote technology in future teaching and learning leadership experiences.

LEARNING STORIES IN RESPONSE TO THE HYBRID ONLINE COURSE

The survey included qualitative comments called *learning stories* to gather data on the respondents' "technology success stories," their "discouraging experiences using technology," and "technology leadership of other administrators."

TABLE 3. Attitudes Toward Technology Use

	Statements	Percentage of Disagree/Agreement	
		Disagree/ Strongly Disagree	Agree/ Strongly Agree
1.	I am comfortable using technology for my own educational work and learning.	8	92
2.	Computers are valuable tools to improve thinking and learning in education.	2	98
3.	It has been a struggle for me to use a computer successfully.	79	21
4.	Computer-related technologies should be used by teachers more than they are now.	8	92
5.	Computer-related technologies should be used by administrators more than now.	10	90
6.	Teachers in my district seem to have greater skill levels in using technology than most of their administrators.	30	70
7.	Students seem to demonstrate greater skill levels in technology than most teachers in my district.	44	56
8.	I feel it is important for teachers to use technology in teaching and learning.	0	100
9.	I feel it is important for principals to use technology in administrational leadership.	3	97
10.	I do not feel comfortable promoting technology use in my role as an administrator.	90	10
11.	Technology should be used throughout the curriculum to improve learning.	2	98
12.	Administrators need more training in order to use technology effectively.	5	95
13.	I think computers make educators' and students' work more difficult.	97	3
14.	I would like to improve my computer-related technology skills as an administrator.	5	95
15.	I need more training and experience in order to lead teachers in using technology.	8	92

Respondents reported *technology success* stories in developing technology skills and completing Web-based tasks through the following activities:

1. Building electronic portfolios.
2. Participating in threaded discussions regarding research papers.
3. Strengthening required research skills.

TABLE 4. Online Learning Experiences

Statements	Percentage of Disagree/Agreement	
	Disagree/ Strongly Disagree	Agree/ Strongly Agree
1. Online coursework is a valuable way to learn content knowledge and skills.	26	74
2. I think online courses are efficient and convenient for adult learners.	20	80
3. I had sufficient background and confidence before completing Web coursework.	56	44
4. Web courses motivate me because I am in command of my own learning activities.	40	60
5. Online courses facilitated access to library research or electronic resources.	26	74
6. Web-based instruction allows interaction and communication with others in class.	24	76
7. Online learning successfully incorporates threaded discussions or case studies.	21	79
8. I felt I had effective feedback from the instructor/professor in a Web-based course.	27	73
9. I had technical support when I needed it during my Web course experience.	32	68
10. I prefer face-to-face courses rather than Web-based courses using my computer.	25	75
11. I prefer hybrid online courses with partial face-to-face and part Web-based meetings.	38	62
12. I prefer online classes that are offered entirely as a Web instruction.	88	12
13. I would encourage teachers to learn through online educational experiences.	27	73
14. I would encourage students to explore and learn through online classes.	22	78
15. Given a chance, I would take an online course myself (entirely online or hybrid).	31	69
16. Completing an online course makes me more willing to promote technology in future teaching and learning experiences as an administrative leader.	29	71

Note: The 4-page survey, "Administrators' Use of Computers and Information Technologies to Improve their Roles in the Educational Process," is available upon request from the authors.

4. Completing one-third of the course at a time and at a pace that was convenient for adult learners.
5. Exploring technological resources and representing information in electronic format.
6. Becoming more confident and aware of what computers can do in teaching and learning.
7. Communicating effectively about complex processes (research and troubleshooting).
8. Increasing research and writing skills from exposure to quality work of others.

9. Developing better problem-solving and critical-thinking skills utilizing technology.
10. Becoming independent learners through their online experience, yet helping each other spontaneously and willingly in collaborative ways.

Discouraging experiences were frequently a frustration with the technology itself:

1. Slow Internet connection using a dial-up modem.
2. Inability to figure out how to upload the research paper during the Web-based course.
3. Having to use antiquated technology.
4. Having the school server down for several days (with no notice) when needing to get work done.
5. Problems receiving papers from other students.
6. Trying to keep up with the new postings and threaded discussion comments.
7. Getting a Web page reformatted for the university server (time consuming).
8. Trying to access someone else's paper.

Observations of *technology leadership of other administrators* were fairly typical in nature. These examples reflect managerial or organizational tasks rather than exemplary uses of technology. Most responses do not represent visionary or high-level use of the capabilities of new technologies in their school settings. Observations by respondents included:

1. Substantially increasing communication with staff via e-mail (fewer meetings).
2. Using e-mail to communicate with parents about school-related issues.
3. Providing feedback to teachers via e-mail on the quality of instruction.
4. Develop new grading software to automate the old report card process.
5. Obtaining forms via e-mail for student reports that need to be submitted.
6. Pursuing use of an accelerated reading program (a computer-based reading program).
7. Scheduling the Iowa Communications Network (ICN) room for daily use (virtually unused for the previous three years).

8. Providing PowerPoint® presentations for the school board on standardized test results.
9. Developing a listserv to improve communication among all professionals involved with specific students needing "care."
10. Searching the Internet for new ideas to pass along to staff and putting together various products for newsletters, etc.

In summary, students studying to become school administrators not only enter the profession with limited levels of technological expertise, but also learn from role models who predominantly display low skill levels such as using e-mail, word processing, or PowerPoint. While their university educational administration courses may not require a stand-alone technology course, one successful method to incorporate a variety of communication and information technology skills, according to this study, is through a hybrid online component as part of a required curriculum course of study.

CONCLUSIONS

In reality, most educational administrative preparation programs lack sufficient technology instruction or support for using technology to assist administrators in assuming new leadership roles. Even newly trained principals lack the necessary proficiencies to provide technology leadership and support to their faculty and staff members. Encouraging principals to use technology in teaching and learning is possible using effective strategies and shared experiences such as through a hybrid online course designed to enhance technological competencies. As Harrington (1991) suggests, there is a difference between preparing teachers to use technology and using technology to prepare teachers. If we only prepare teachers to use technology, we limit the conception of the role of technology in education. Administrators, too, need to be prepared to use technology in their leadership roles in the schools. They must be empowered to acquire the necessary technological competencies and be able to facilitate the use of technology through effective administrative leadership.

REFERENCES

Becker, H.J. (1994). How exemplary computer-using teachers differ from other teachers: Implications for realizing the potential of computers in schools. *Journal of Research on Computing in Education, 26*(3), 291-321.

Bialo, E.R., & Sivin-Kachala, J. (1996). *The effectiveness of technology in schools: A summary of recent research.* Washington, DC: Software Publishers Association.

Collis, B., Winnips, K., & Moonen, J. (2000). Structured support verses learner choice via the WWW: Where is the payoff? *Journal of Interactive Learning Research*, *11*(2), 131-162.

Conley, D., & Goldman, P. (1994). *Facilitative leadership: How principals lead without dominating*. Eugene: Oregon School Study Council.

Davis, N. (1998). *Images for teacher education*. Retrieved September 25, 2001, from http://telematics.ex.ac.uk/TLTP/

Davis, N., Kirkman, C., Tearle, P., Taylor, C., & Wright, B. (1996). Developing teachers and their institutions for IT in education: An integrated approach. *Journal of Technology and Teacher Education*, *4*(1), 3-18.

Dwyer, D. (1994, April). Apple classrooms of tomorrow: What we've learned. *Educational Leadership*, *51*(7), 4-10.

Education week on the Web. (1998, October 1). *Technology counts: Schools and reform in the information age. A special report*. Retrieved September 25, 2001, from http://www.edweek.org/sreports/tc/

Glenna, T. K., & Melmed, A. (1996, April). Fostering the use of educational technology: Elements of a national strategy. *A Rand report*. Santa Monica, CA: Rand. Retrieved September 25, 2001, from http://www.rand.org/publications/MR/MR682/contents.html

Harrington, H. (1991). Normal style technology in teacher education: Technology and the education of teachers. *Computers in the Schools*, *8*(1/2/3), 49-57.

Harris, J. (1998). *Virtual architecture: Designing and directing curriculum-based telecomputing*. Eugene, OR: International Society for Technology in Education.

Hilgard, E.R., & Bower, G.H. (1974). *Theories of learning* (4th ed.). Englewood Cliffs, NJ: Prentice-Hall.

Hunt, J.M. (1961). *Intelligence and experience*. New York: Ronald Press.

Imel, S. (1998). Technology and adult learning: Current perspectives. (ERIC Document Reproduction Service No. ED421639).

International Society for Technology in Education. (2002). *Technology Standards for School Administrators* (TSSA Draft v4.0). Retrieved April 7, 2002, from http://cnets. iste.org/tssa/view_standards.html

Johnson, S.D., Aragon, S.R., Shaik, N., & Palma-Rivas, N. (2000). Comparative analysis of learner satisfaction and learning outcomes in online and face-to-face learning environments. *Journal of Interactive Learning Research*, *11*(1), 29-49.

Ko, S., & Rossen, S. (2001). *Teaching online: A practical guide*. Boston: Houghton Mifflin, 10-14.

Kosakowski, J. (1998, June). *The benefits of information technology*. Syracuse, NY: (ERIC Document Reproduction Service No. ED420302).

Martinez, M., & Bunderson, C.V. (2000). Building interactive World Wide Web learning environments to match and support individual learning, *Journal of Interactive Learning Research*, *11*(2), 163-195.

Mioduser, D., Nachmias, R., Lahav, L., & Oren, A. (2000). Web-based learning environments: Current pedagogical and technical state. *Journal of Research on Computing in Education*, *33*(1), 55-76.

Pelligrino, J., & Altman, J. (1997). Information technology and teacher preparation: Some critical issues and illustrative solutions. *Peabody Journal of Education*, *72*(1), 89-121.

Picciano, A.G. (2001). *Distance learning: Making connections across virtual space and time*. Upper Saddle River, NJ: Merrill/Prentice Hall.

Somekh, B., & Davis, N. (1999). *Using information technology effectively in teaching and learning: Studies in pre-service and in-service teacher education*. London: Routledge.

Strudler, N., & Wetzel, K. (1999). Lessons from exemplary colleges of education: Factors affecting technology integration in pre-service programs. *Educational Technology Research and Development, 47*(4), 63-81.

Stuhlman, J. (1998). A model for infusing technology in teacher education programs. *Journal of Technology and Teacher Education, 6*(2/3), 1125-1140.

Thompson, A.E., Schmidt, D., & Hadjiyianni, E. (1995). A three-year program to infuse technology throughout a teacher education program. *Journal of Technology and Teacher Education, 3*(1), 13-24.

Weber, J. (1989). Leading the instructional program. In S. C. Smith & P. K. Piele (Eds.), *School leadership: Handbook for excellence* (2nd Ed.). Eugene, Oregon: (ERIC Document Reproduction Service No. ED 309504).

Zehr, M.A. (1998, October 1). Changing the way teachers teach: Away from the chalkboard. *Education Week, XVIII*(5), 41-43.

Betty Collis
Jef Moonen

The Contributing Student:
A Pedagogy for Flexible Learning

SUMMARY. At the Faculty of Educational Science and Technology in The Netherlands, we do not talk about distance education but rather "flexible learning," where distance is only one of the dimensions for which students have different options. In this article we briefly describe our approach to flexible learning and then focus on the pedagogical model of the "contributing student," which motivates our didactics. The "before-during-after" cycle is presented as a way to involve all students, regardless of their locations, in various contribution-oriented activities. The implications for the teacher are considerable, but the results are seen as positive by students and teachers alike. *[Article copies available for a fee from The Haworth Document Delivery Service: 1-800-HAWORTH. E-mail address: <getinfo@haworthpressinc.com> Website: <http://www.HaworthPress.com> © 2002 by The Haworth Press, Inc. All rights reserved.]*

KEYWORDS. Pedagogy, learning activities, active learning, flexible learning, Web tools

BETTY COLLIS is Shell Professor of Networked Learning, Faculty of Educational Science and Technology, P.O. Box 217, University of Twente, 7500 AE Enschede, The Netherlands (E-mail: collis@edte.utwente.nl).
JEF MOONEN is Professor, Educational Instrumentation, Faculty of Educational Science and Technology, P.O. Box 217, University of Twente, 7500 AE Enschede, The Netherlands (E-mail: moonen@edte.utwente.nl).

[Haworth co-indexing entry note]: "The Contributing Student: A Pedagogy for Flexible Learning." Collis, Betty, and Jef Moonen. Co-published simultaneously in *Computers in the Schools* (The Haworth Press, Inc.) Vol. 19, No. 3/4, 2002, pp. 207-220; and: *Distance Education: Issues and Concerns* (ed: Cleborne D. Maddux, Jacque Ewing-Taylor, and D. LaMont Johnson) The Haworth Press, Inc., 2002, pp. 207-220. Single or multiple copies of this article are available for a fee from The Haworth Document Delivery Service [1-800-HAWORTH, 9:00 a.m. - 5:00 p.m. (EST). E-mail address: getinfo@haworthpressinc.com].

FLEXIBLE LEARNING:
DISTANCE IS ONLY ONE OF THE DIMENSIONS

Flexible learning is not a new phenomenon. Students have for a long time studied their textbooks and worked on their homework in a variety of locations and times, and selected from a variety of resources in the library. It has currently become commonplace for learners to search the Web for resources to use in class projects. Learning also takes place outside of explicit course settings, as students interact with others or take part in events such as fieldtrips or practical experiences outside the classroom. But the term *flexible learning* is the focus of a new wave of interest. To begin, what is flexible learning?

Flexible learning is often taken as synonymous with distance education. This is not necessarily so. As we will illustrate, there are many ways to make education more flexible that can benefit students who are in full-time attendance in an educational institution and even benefit those who are in the same room together. Flexibility can involve options in course resources, in types of learning activities, in media to support learning, and many other possibilities. There is more than distance that can vary (see Collis & Moonen, 2001, Chapter 1 for an analysis of 19 dimensions of flexible learning, of which distance is only one). In particular, for this article, we will focus on the approach to flexible learning in place in the Faculty of Educational Science and Technology at the University of Twente. Within this approach, students who are always at a distance, students who are sometimes at a distance, and students who are always physically present for contact sessions all are active members of the same learning community. The keys to this approach are a pedagogy based on the "contributing student" model, a Web-based learning support system designed to optimize the contributing student approach, and an institutional policy that made it possible to implement the approach in less than a year throughout the faculty. We begin with the last point, as it provided the context for the new approach to distance education.

Initiating a New Form of Distance Education

In mid-1997 the management of the Faculty of Educational Science and Technology made the decision to make its program more flexible so that a new cohort of students could participate. This cohort consisted of working persons who already had a first degree but whose work had now led them to the point that additional training in educational science and technology would be valuable. Typically this sort of cohort is served by a dual-mode approach: The regular students continue as usual, and some form of distance education is made available for the working students. However, we did not feel this approach was desirable, for several reasons. First, we were well aware of difficulties in persistence for working students at a distance, even when extensive support networks (i.e., study centers, online moderators) were available. In our situation, we would not have these extensive support networks; our instructors would simply have to expand themselves to deal with the flexibility requirements of this new cohort of students. Second, in our analyses of how students actually spend their time in a course, we were aware that the face-to-face sessions, which were typically lectures, were only about 10-15% of the actual time spent in the course, with the rest already occurring in flexible and even distance-flexible ways. Students study and work on assignments at locations of their own choice, increasingly using the Web to search for resources and e-mail to communicate with each other and with instructors. The lectures themselves were sometimes appreciated, but most often only a portion of the students were in attendance (in general, in The Netherlands students cannot be forced to attend lectures). Lecturers typically covered the material to be studied in the textbook, point by point. Most importantly, our vision for a new didactic for all of our students, regular or working, was focused on students being active, contributing to their own learning experiences and those of their peers. Such a didactic was not occurring in the traditional lecture setting.

The faculty thus made a bold decision. We would begin in the following academic year offering our program in a new way: with no more than three one-hour contact sessions per course (a course is typically defined as 120 hours of work) and instead of students missing lectures, an instructional approach in which students contribute work regularly, via a Web environment, and build on that work as a basis of their learning experience. The instructor must move from being a giver of lectures to being a designer and manager of learning activities, usually involving groups, where the contact occurs via the specially designed Web environment. The faculty approach evolved around the following principles (Carleer & Collis, 1998):

1. Learning arises from the active *engagement* of the learner, and a *communication-oriented* pedagogy. The active student is our base.
2. Because of changes in society, students are increasingly diverse. Therefore, our courses must become more flexible, not only in

location but also in program, types of interactions, types of communication, and learning materials. A combination of new pedagogies and the use of a well-designed Web system would make these flexibilities, as well as the active-student principle, concrete.

3. We will use technology to extend good teaching, not replace the instructor. We will amplify what he/she does well. "Extending the good instructor" will be one of our mottoes.

4. We will use a "teach once, adapt within" approach whereby the general timetabling of all courses is the same for both cohorts of students, in terms of when the course begins and ends and when certain key events occur such as the final examinations.

5. There will be a "common day" approximately every second Friday, when all students who can come together physically on our campus. Each course begins with an introductory whole-group session of approximately one hour during those common Fridays, so that the instructor can efficiently communicate his view of the course, and the students can better visualize him/her when receiving electronic communications. Also, social contacts among the students can be facilitated.

6. In place of traditional lectures (now to be only three instead of 10 or 12 per course), the instructor will focus on new forms of student activity, primarily through the use of the Web site and techniques such as fill-in forms for structured communication and reflective activities.

7. The Web system will be a core technology, but complementary technologies, particularly textbooks, are also important. The instructor, not an instructional designer or technician, is the shaper, developer, and manager of his/her own Web site and uses it as a personal tool, not as an instructional product pre-made elsewhere.

The advertisements went out; many working students started enrolling. This was during the 1997-1998 school year. Since then the model has become so commonplace that no one questions it. We have more students attending flexibly (i.e., while remaining at their jobs) than traditionally (i.e., coming to the campus most days). All students are active contributors, in flexible ways. We believe the pedagogical model is the core of the change.

THE CONTRIBUTING STUDENT PEDAGOGY

A pedagogical approach requires an underlying pedagogical model, a general strategy for implementation, and specific ideas for realization in practice. It also involves requirements and implications for the teacher.

Pedagogical Model

Our pedagogical model is based on two key principles that we believe are central to our focus of flexible learning. These two key principles are:

1. Learning situations should be designed for flexibility and adaptability.
2. Learning situations should involve not only acquisition of skills and concepts but also opportunities to participate in and contribute to a learning community.

These principles are similar to those expressed by Jonassen, Peck, and Wilson (1999), who assert that the primary goal of education at all levels should be to engage students in meaningful learning–which they define as active, constructive, intentional, authentic, and cooperative. Interaction with learning materials and with others is also important to Laurillard's interaction-oriented approach (Laurillard, 1993). However, in both these approaches, it is possible that all the activities and interactions that take place are based on predetermined and prestructured learning materials. In our approach to pedagogy, prestructured learning materials are not the main focus. Instead, the activities themselves are central in our pedagogical vision, combined with an appropriate Web-based system. Our model is an approach whereby the student can contribute to the learning material based upon his/her own experiences, experiences from others, material available in the Web-based system, in reality, or in the literature. This approach is similar to the participation aspects of Sfard's two metaphors for learning–acquisition and participation (1998); Kearsley and Shneiderman's (1998) *Engagement Theory*; and *Action Learning* (Simons, 1999). Table 1 shows the key ideas of our pedagogical model, the "contributing student."

The "Before-During-After" Approach

How does this work in practice? The key pedagogical strategy is the "before-during-after" approach. Figure 1 shows the main ideas of the approach.

How are flexible learning and distance education integrated in the before-during-after approach? The strategy that we use begins with the

TABLE 1. Principles of the Contributing Student Pedagogy (from Collis & Moonen, 2001, p. 88)

"The Contributing Student"
Key ideas:
Learners contribute to the learning materials via contributions made available to others in a Web-based system. The others may be others in the same group or others at other times. The others may be at the same or different locations.
Key characteristics:
The Web site is largely empty at the start of the learning experience; the learners and the instructor will fill it via the process of many activities during the course.
Learners learn from realistic materials as well as peer-created materials as much as or more than professionally developed materials.
Learning materials contributed by students are re-used in other learning settings.
Role of instructor:
Designer of activities and of feedback and monitoring strategies for activities. Manager of the activities, feedback, and monitoring processes.
Role of technology:
To facilitate all aspects of the activities.

idea of thinking of a course as a series of cycles of *before*, *during*, and *after* activities. The "during" part of the cycle is some sort of focal activity, such as a lecture, a group meeting, or other form of contact. The contact event does not have to be face-to-face, although that is a familiar model for educational institutions. It is an event that is prepared for, that has an agenda that someone leads or otherwise is responsible for. For participants who happen to be at the same location and can come physically together for the contact session, it is something during which there is some special interaction among course participants, and something that has a follow up. If participants are not at the same location, contacts can be made using technological means, such as audio- or videoconferencing. If participants are not available at the same time, asynchronous contacts focusing on the activities of the contact session can be organized. In terms of pedagogy, we do not make a distinction between a student physically attending a course on campus, a student attending only occasionally (a part-time student), or a student at a dis-

FIGURE 1. Before-During-After Cycle (Collis & Moonen, 2001, p. 92)

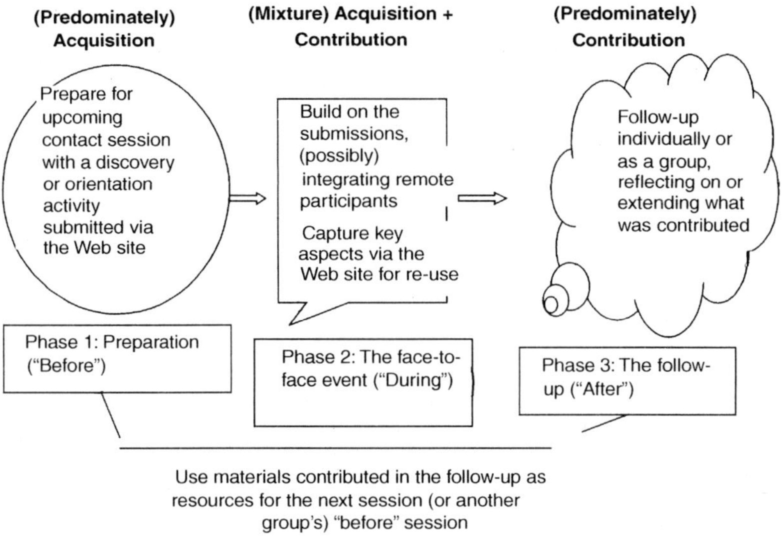

| **(Predominately) Acquisition** | **(Mixture) Acquisition + Contribution** | **(Predominately) Contribution** |

Prepare for upcoming contact session with a discovery or orientation activity submitted via the Web site

Build on the submissions, (possibly) integrating remote participants

Capture key aspects via the Web site for re-use

Follow-up individually or as a group, reflecting on or extending what was contributed

Phase 1: Preparation ("Before")

Phase 2: The face-to-face event ("During")

Phase 3: The follow-up ("After")

Use materials contributed in the follow-up as resources for the next session (or another group's) "before" session

tance. The pedagogical approach takes care of all of them, in an appropriate way (for an elaboration, see Collis & Moonen, 2001, Chapter 5). In order to make such an approach feasible, we assume a Web-based course-management system is available. Such a course-management system provides technological facilities through which users (instructors and students) can retrieve resources, but also can add resources or comments, can communicate with each other, but also whereby the instructor can monitor or assess the contributions of the students.

"Before" Activities

Students should prepare themselves before a contact session so that they attend (physically or asynchronously) the contact session ready to act upon what they have been studying. This is no new idea in education, but in practice students often come to lectures unprepared. To stimulate the preparation, we believe that students need to do some sort of assigned activity (and thus an activity that counts toward their assessment in the course). These activities will usually include some reading, but can also involve other sorts of preparation, such as identifying examples that illustrate the study materials from the Web and submitting them into the course Web environment, or submitting questions or doing practice exercises and comparing their work to a model answer. The course Web environment provides the tool for this submission process, and facilitates the re-use of submitted materials in the contact session. The *before* phase of each *before-during-after* cycle also serves the purpose of stimulating students to stay on tempo and be prepared for active participation in the subsequent contact session. Conversely, it can point the instructor's attention toward students who do not prepare (as shown by no submission), so that personal intervention can occur, or to problems that the students are having, so that the contact session can be tailored appropriately.

"During" Activities

During the contact session, the instructor can make use of materials and comments submitted by the students/participants during the *before* periods. For example, results of a preliminary quiz can alert the instructor to concepts that need more or less attention during the contact session, and examples submitted by the students can be used as demonstration and discussion materials at the contact session. By copying various samples of student/participant *before* submissions into the portion of the course environment that will support the contact session, the materials can easily be used as points of reference for discussions or further activities.

During the contact session, there will usually be some period of instructor-led explanation, but we believe that an important step toward increasing the flexibility as well as the learning quality of the contact session is that students are active during this contact session. Listening to a lecture may involve cognitive activity, but we mean activity that involves interaction and communication with other students and the instructor. For this to occur, a mini-cycle of the before-during-after approach can be used for the structure of the contact session itself. For example:

1. The instructor starts the event with a certain amount of explanation, building upon materials submitted in the *before* phase. In preparation for this explanation, the instructor has notes and demonstration materials, such as PowerPoint slides, already uploaded into the course

Web environment. While this start-off period can have some of the attributes of a traditional lecture, it differs in two important ways:

a. It is relatively short, and all demonstration materials are available via the course Web site so that students who were not present can catch up on what was communicated.
b. It is aimed at launching a subsequent discussion or practice activity during the contact session itself, in which students who are present are engaged during the focal session and students who are not present are engaged either at a later time or from a different location at the same time.
c. If feasible, this start-off period can be captured on video and made available via the course Web site as video on demand, synchronized with any visual aids such as PowerPoint slides that were being shown at the same time as the short presentation.

2. For the *during* phase of the contact session, the students are active, doing something besides listening. The instructor is available to monitor and interact, but is no longer lecturing. The course Web site needs to make the instructions for this activity available for all students, including those not present at the contact session. The course Web site can also serve as the tool via which submissions from this activity are obtained and organized, perhaps directly during the session or afterward, particularly for students who were not present. Students who are not physically present can have the benefit of building upon the submissions of those who were.

3. For the concluding part of the contact session, the instructor brings the students back together and makes culminating comments on what has occurred as students were engaged. The instructor can use this time period to motivate the third part of the before-during-after cycle: the follow-up activities. If key issues emerged during this concluding session, the instructor should add a comment about them to the Web site for students who were not present.

"After" Activities

After the contact session, students remain active. The instructor devises some sort of follow-up activity that builds upon and extends what happened in the contact session. Students have a certain period of time to do this activity, individually or in groups, and submit their results via the course Web site. The instructor gives feedback, but in a limited manner, usually not detailed comments to each student's submission.

Often peer feedback is used, and evaluated, as part of the follow-up process. Misconceptions that show up in the *after* activities can be addressed in the next round of *before* activities or the next focal session.

Figure 2 shows the generic planning setup for a contact session, expressed on the Web site for the course. Of course, each instructor will modify the details of this generic planning, but instructors are encouraged to start with it as a framework.

Activities for the Contributing Student Pedagogy

Activities can take many forms and be carried out both in an individual fashion or by a group. A sample of activities that can be adapted to the "contributing student" approach follows (Van der Veen, De Boer, & Collis, 2000). In each case, the Web environment is used as the workplace for working on, contributing, and subsequently accessing the contributions.

1. Searching for additional information or examples and making these available for others.
2. Working with a case as a basis for problem solving and contributing some additional materials for the case for use by others.
3. Participating in a role-play situation and leaving some record of the results of the role-play for others to consider.
4. Creating a report to then be used as a learning resource by others.
5. Creating a product, such as a multimedia resource or a design, that is also a resource for others.
6. Extending and applying theoretical principles in new settings and adding these results to a course repository of extension materials.
7. Testing one's insight through the development of test questions to be used by others.
8. Participating in a discussion and leaving a record of key aspects of the discussion for use by others.

The "others" in the above list of activities may be other students in the same course or within a student's group in the course. "Others" may also be other students in other cycles of the course or students in other courses or learners who are not in a course context at all but could refer to the materials via a database as they now use a library. The idea of re-use of students' work and of moments of good communication in a course supports flexibility: for those who were not present when a moment of good communication occurred, for example, or to facilitate the

FIGURE 2. Generic Planning for a Contact Session, Present in the Web Site to Support the Contact Session. Planning Is Based on a Contact Session of 75 Minutes for a Hypothetical Session on October 4

Overview for the contact session October 4:

10 minutes: 1. Highlights and comments on submissions from the previous follow-up exercises (main comments are summarized in the file "comments-Oct4.doc" below)

15 minutes: 2. Introduction to the next topic (see PowerPoint file "newtopicOct4.ppt" below)

40 minutes: 3. Contact session activity, based on the introduction (see instructions below)

10 minutes: 4. Discussion of the contact session activity (main points emerging during the activity will be summarized in the site by the next day as the file "comments-contact session Oct4 activity.doc" for students who were not present or for follow-up for everyone)

Contact session October 4 activity:

1. Open the attached worksheet ("worksheet-contact session Oct4.doc") to see the instructions for the contact session activity. Submit your responses via the Roster.

2. For students who are not physically present, do the activity described in the worksheet ("worksheet-contact session Oct4.doc"). Then look at the submissions of your fellow students for the activity; add a comment to your response in which you compare your submission to that of one or more fellow students. Submit your response via the Roster no later than October 10.

Resources for the contact session:

"comments-Oct4.doc"

PowerPoint "newtopicOct4.ppt"

"worksheet-contact sessionOct4.doc"

"comments-contact session Oct4 activity.doc" (to be added on Oct. 5)

development of a substantial database of learning resources that can be re-used and combined in many different combinations.

Implications for the Teacher

As another way of looking at contribution-oriented activities, we can view them in terms of the types of changes they bring for the teacher. These often involve:

*   Less reliance on lectures and more time spent on new forms of learning activities, such as new forms of activities, where the con-

tact between students and the instructor takes place at least some of the time via a Web environment

- More student participation, often via the practice of students entering new resources into the course Web site or being involved in asynchronous discussions via computer conferencing or Web boards
- More group projects or collaborative activities, supported by groupware tools
- New forms of learning activities involving international aspects such as students in two different courses in different countries working together on some common task
- New forms of assessment activities, such as electronic portfolios and journals; also more opportunities for self and peer assessment
- More time spent on student presentation of their work; work is made for and presented to an audience via the Web site, and comments are given on the work by those in the audience (Collis & Moonen, 2001, p. 106).

These changes for the instructor bring about many implications involving more work and new types of tasks. These include:

1. Select and use appropriate tools to make flexible participation possible and support students in the use of these tools.
2. Think of new forms of student activities.
3. Learn how to set up and describe the activities, explaining very clearly what the expectations are both content wise and also related to time, form, and method of submission.
4. Communicate precisely how students will be evaluated on the new forms of activities, particularly for group projects and peer evaluations.
5. Monitor and appropriately intervene when there are problems within groups with group work.
6. Handle much more contact with students, via their submissions into the Web site or e-mail, their comments and discussions, their comments on one another's work.
7. Develop new methods of grading student performance, so that process is also graded; apply these methods in a consistent way and so that students understand your criteria.
8. Monitor the quality of what students submit into the course Web environment for other students to see and study; inappropriate material must be quickly removed and the individual submitting it contacted. *Inappropriate* covers a large number of aspects, from being factually wrong to being potentially offensive to others.

9. Monitor potential copyright problems with what students submit into the course Web site.
10. Keep records relating to aspects of the learning process, such as participation, to use for monitoring and grading.
11. Manage incoming and outgoing activities, e-mail, and contacts from individual students.
12. Become an "expert participant" and co-learner as well as the instructor still responsible for the acquisition aspects of the course (Collis & Moonen, 2001, p. 106).

We are well aware of the time and stress implications for the teacher of having to handle these new responsibilities; in our research and practice we are working on strategies for the teacher in order to lessen the time required while maintaining a quality learning experience.

CONCLUSION

Flexible learning, including flexibility in distance, requires the combination of institutional vision and policy, technology, and pedagogy. We believe that a pedagogy based on the Contributing Student not only can facilitate flexible participation but also change the dynamics of the learning experience for all involved. Thinking of a course as a structure for activities whose results led to contributions of the learners to the learning environment is different from traditional instructional design approaches that begin by a focus on what is going to be prepared ahead of time for the students to read and respond to. A contribution-oriented approach fits well with a "before-during-after" cycle in which occasional contact sessions do still occur, participated in by those who are physically present and who participate via the Web site. The implications for the teacher are a concern, but as teachers gain experience with the formulation of instructions for activities, with ways to lessen the time needed for guidance and feedback, and begin to re-use student work as examples for new groups of students, the time and workload burdens can decrease and the pleasure of interacting with students in new ways can increase. We see this in our own institution as well as in our own courses.

REFERENCES

Carleer, G., & Collis, B. (1998). Extending good teaching with technology. In A. Szucs & A. Wagner (Eds.), *Universities in a digital age: Transformation, innovation and tradition* (pp. 368-371). Budapest: European Distance Education Network.

Collis, B., & Moonen, J. (2001). Flexible learning in a digital world: Experiences and expectations. London: Kogan Page. (see also http://education1.edte.utwente.nl/00FlexibleLearning.nsf/framesform?readform)

Jonassen, D.H., Peck, K. L, & Wilson, B. G. (1999). *Learning with technology–A constructivist perspective*. Upper Saddle River, NJ: Prentice-Hall.

Kearsley, G., & Shneiderman, G. (1998). Engagement theory: A framework for technology-based teaching and learning. *Educational Technology, 38*(5), 20-24.

Laurillard, D. (1993). *Rethinking university teaching: A framework for the effective use of educational technology*. London: Routledge.

Sfard, A. (1998). On two metaphors for learning and the dangers of choosing just one. *Educational Researcher, 27*(2), 4-13.

Simons, P. R. J. (1999). Three ways to learn in a new balance. *Lifelong Learning in Europe, 4*(1), 14-23.

Van der Veen, J., De Boer, W. F., & Collis, B. (2000). *Didactics for Web learning environments: Active learning*. Report for the SURF-TeleTOP Alpha-Beta Project, DINKEL Institute, University of Twente, Enschede, NL.

Index

221

SPECIAL 25%-OFF DISCOUNT!

Order a copy of this book with this form or online at:
http://www.haworthpress.com/store/product.asp?sku=4829
Use Sale Code BOF25 in the online bookshop to receive 25% off!

Distance Education
Issues and Concerns

____ in softbound at $24.71 (regularly $32.95) (ISBN: 0-7890-2031-9)
____ in hardbound at $37.46 (regularly $49.95) (ISBN: 0-7890-2030-0)

COST OF BOOKS _____

Outside USA/ Canada/
Mexico: Add 20% _____

POSTAGE & HANDLING _____
(US: $4.00 for first book & $1.50
for each additional book)
Outside US: $5.00 for first book
& $2.00 for each additional book)

SUBTOTAL _____

in Canada: add 7% GST _____

STATE TAX _____
(NY, OH, & MIN residents please
add appropriate local sales tax

FINAL TOTAL _____
(if paying in Canadian funds, convert
using the current exchange rate,
UNESCO coupons welcome)

❑ **BILL ME LATER:** ($5 service charge will be added)
(Bill-me option is good on US/Canada/
Mexico orders only; not good to jobbers,
wholesalers, or subscription agencies.)

❑ **Signature** _____

❑ **Payment Enclosed: $** _____

❑ **PLEASE CHARGE TO MY CREDIT CARD:**

❑ Visa ❑ MasterCard ❑ AmEx ❑ Discover
❑ Diner's Club ❑ Eurocard ❑ JCB

Account # _____

Exp Date _____

Signature _____
*(Prices in US dollars and subject to
change without notice.)*

PLEASE PRINT ALL INFORMATION OR ATTACH YOUR BUSINESS CARD

Name

Address

City   State/Province   Zip/Postal Code

Country

Tel   Fax

E-Mail

May we use your e-mail address for confirmations and other types of information? ❑Yes ❑No
We appreciate receiving your e-mail address and fax number. Haworth would like to e-mail or
fax special discount offers to you, as a preferred customer. **We will never share, rent, or
exhange your e-mail address or fax number.** We regard such actions as an invasion of
your privacy.

Order From Your Local Bookstore or Directly From
The Haworth Press, Inc.
10 Alice Street, Binghamton, New York 13904-1580 • USA
Call Our toll-free number (1-800-429-6784) / Outside US/Canada: (607) 722-5857
Fax: 1-800-895-0582 / Outside US/Canada: (607) 771-0012
E-Mail your order to us: Orders@haworthpress.com

Please Photocopy this form for your personal use.
www.HaworthPress.com

BOF03